Cool Pubs & Inns

Britain's Best Pubs with Rooms

cool places

Cool Pubs & Inns

Britain's Best Pubs with Rooms

cool places

Llandogo Trow Ale
ABV
4.2%
KINGSTONE BREWERY
Butty
Bach
Premium Ale
WYE VALLEY
BREWERY

Contents

A Great British Invention

There is nothing which has yet been contrived by man, by which so much happiness is produced, as by a good tavern.

Samuel Johnson

It's hard to describe what makes the perfect pub, but if you are in one, you will know. It's a combination of factors, including, of course, good food and lashings of drink. But it's also the fact that you can walk into a pub on your own and immediately feel at home: partly because all pubs are essentially variations on the same theme, and perhaps also because they are supposed by nature to be cosy and welcoming to strangers. There's a feeling that nothing bad can ever happen to you in the best pubs, and that is what keeps us coming back again and again.

Amid scary statistics of closures during recent years, pubs have had to adapt to changing habits. Almost every pub nowadays serves food, whereas a generation ago you would often be lucky to get a packet of crisps. Children no longer have to wait outside with a bottle of pop for company. And almost all pubs now accept that not everyone drinks beer, with the result that many places stock a good choice of decent wines, funky new gins and other spirits, and – whisper it – you can even get a cup of tea or coffee if that's what you desire.

The most forward-looking pubs have, however, gone one step further, cooking food that's a cut above pub grub, while adding rooms that compete with top-notch hotels and B&Bs, and generally leading a return to the kinds of inns where a good meal and a comfortable bed for the night are offered as standard. That is what this book is about: a new wave of pubs with rooms that are still rooted in their local communities but also imbued with fresh life and energy by a new generation of owners, most of whom have contemporary ideas of what a modern pub should be, and for whom hospitality is second nature.

No book can do justice to the diversity of Britain's pubs. However, inspired by the resurgence of modern coaching inns, we've done our best to include as wide a cross-section as possible, while focusing on pubs that you can stay in overnight – and ideally also eat some great food. Some places have rooms and facilities that are more on a par with luxury hotels than common boozers; others are unashamedly restaurants with a few rooms attached. But there are many more (our favourites, if we're honest) that remain firmly and deliberately pubby in nature, serving good food and offering a selection of comfortable bedrooms while remaining convivial places to just drop by for a drink, with lazing dogs, roaring fires and all the other things that make pubs so special.

There are pubs in scenic locations that have long been targeted at walkers, with hearty food, simple rooms and occasionally bunk-bed accommodation; others have their own campsites or rent yurts and shepherds huts; while some pubs have their own self-catering country cottages available. A few have access to their own swimming pools or spas, and others are firmly targeted at family groups and activities.

There are also the oddballs: a pub in a medieval monastery, perhaps, or an abbot's palace; pubs perched in impossibly dramatic and remote locations; or pubs that are perfectly situated for observing Britain's darkest skies, a couple of which even have their own observatory.

It's worth remembering also that many pubs have simply been around in some form for hundreds of years, and are local and reassuring landmarks in towns and villages across the country. Like Britain's many and varied pub names, there is a pub for every mood or occasion, and we need them now more than ever. Long may they prosper!

Martin Dunford, coolplaces.co.uk

The Rise, Fall and Rise of the Pub

The pub – or 'public house' – has been around for quite a while. But like so much that we consider traditional and indispensable, what we now think of as a pub didn't really find its feet until Victorian times. Until then, public houses either catered to people travelling the country, often by horse-drawn stagecoaches, or were literally places that were simply open to the public and where people congregated; almost all of them served alcohol but in every other respect were much like private houses. Gin was a popular drink, whose cheapness led to a drunkenness and general degradation (as popularised by Hogarth) that the government tried and failed to control throughout the 18th century. Eventually, the 1830 Beer Act restricted the supply of spirits and promoted the sale of beer instead by allowing more or less anyone to set up their own brewery and open a public house. The result of this was a proliferation of pubs all over the country, which grew from a few hundred to almost 50,000 licensed premises within a decade – oddly enough about the same number that exist today (down from around 65,000 in 1990).

The decline of Britain's pubs has been going on for decades, and it's become commonplace to see them either boarded-up or being turned into shops or flats – something that has recently been exacerbated by the coronavirus. But the news isn't all bad. As pubs have closed, so craft breweries have opened, and post-lockdown it's clear that the nation's love affair with the pub is by no means over. There are still so many great pubs in Britain, run by people who are devoted to their trade, and they continue to play an important part in their local communities. They are also increasingly reverting to their role as traditional inns – a source of food, drink, a comfortable bed for the night and all-round warmth and hospitality. As such, they remain the perhaps the best way to discover the UK and its multiple moving parts – its produce, people, landscapes and history. This book is published in celebration.

How to use this book

All the pubs we've included in each chapter are places that you can stay overnight, with bedrooms in most cases but occasionally also self-catering accommodation in the form of cottages, apartments or even glamping and camping options. We've given a guide to rates throughout, including details of whether breakfast is included, along with contact details that include not only an address and phone number but also a website url, which is always the best place to go for the most up to date details. Many pubs have dog-friendly policies which sometimes extend to their overnight rooms; again, for the full picture, it's best to get in touch direct. Finally, each chapter ends with a 'Lucky Dip', which is a round-up of some more of our favourite pubs in each region. A few of these may have rooms but mostly they are included for extra variety, and because the book would have seemed incomplete without them.

THE
SWAN

What's in a name?

We could have written a separate book on the endlessly fascinating subject of pub names. Many are very common, popping up all over Britain; others – particularly the newer names – are deliberately eccentric, for example 'The Cat & Custard Pot', while some are more prosaic, simply a statement of location or fact, like The Bridge just outside Edinburgh, or Suffolk's Station Inn – where the station has long since gone but the pub remains. What pub names don't do very much is change, which sometimes leads pubs to become their locations, for example the Peat Inn, in, er, Peat Inn, Scotland.

20 MOST POPULAR PUB NAMES

1 Royal Oak
2 The Crown
3 The White Hart
4 The Rose & Crown
5 The King's Head
6 The White Horse
7 The King's Arms
8 The Queen's Head
9 The Swan
10 The Prince of Wales
11 The Plough
12 The Wheatsheaf
13 The Black Horse
14 The Bell
15 The Fox & Hounds
16 The Coach & Horses
17 The White Lion
18 The Three Horseshoes
19 The George
20 The George & Dragon

The Olive Branch p.157

Cool Pubs & Inns

Gastropubs with rooms, revamped coaching inns, family pubs, country boltholes, ancient seaside hostelries, pubs for walkers and much more. Read on to find some of Britain's best pubs with rooms and food.

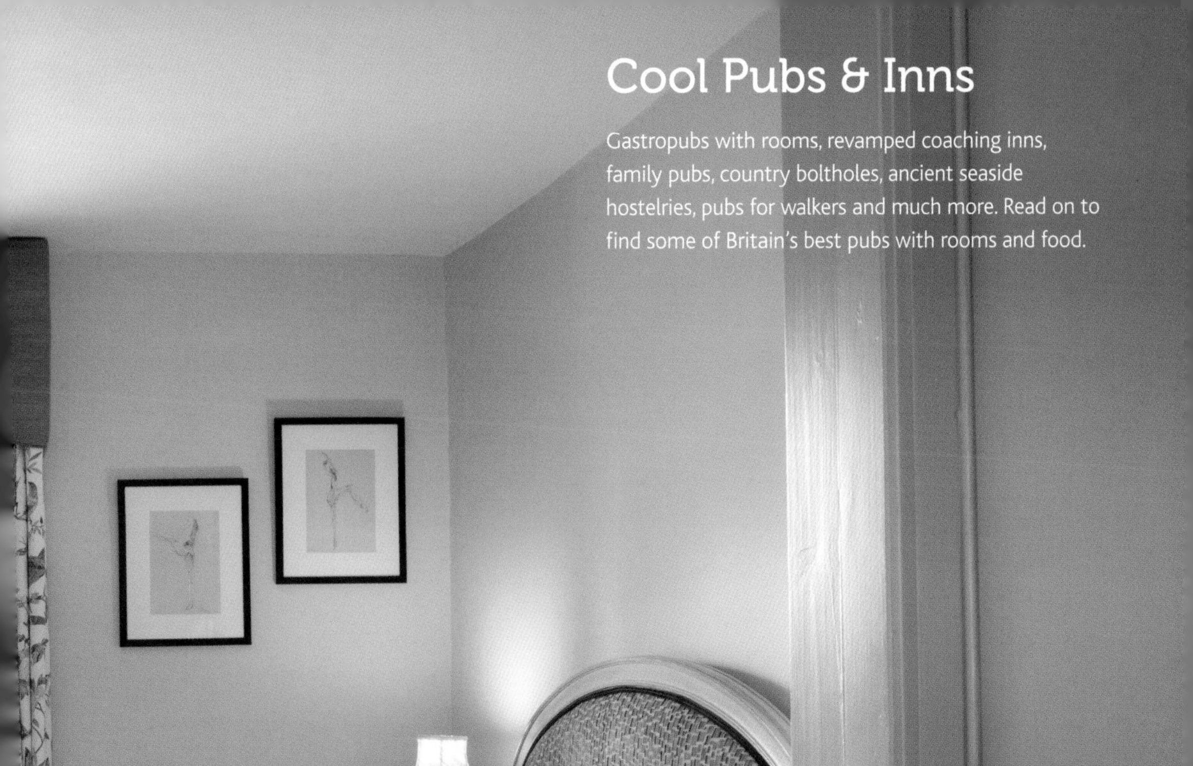

Seaside

The Ship Inn at Elie p.242

Countryside

George and Dragon p.207

Waterside

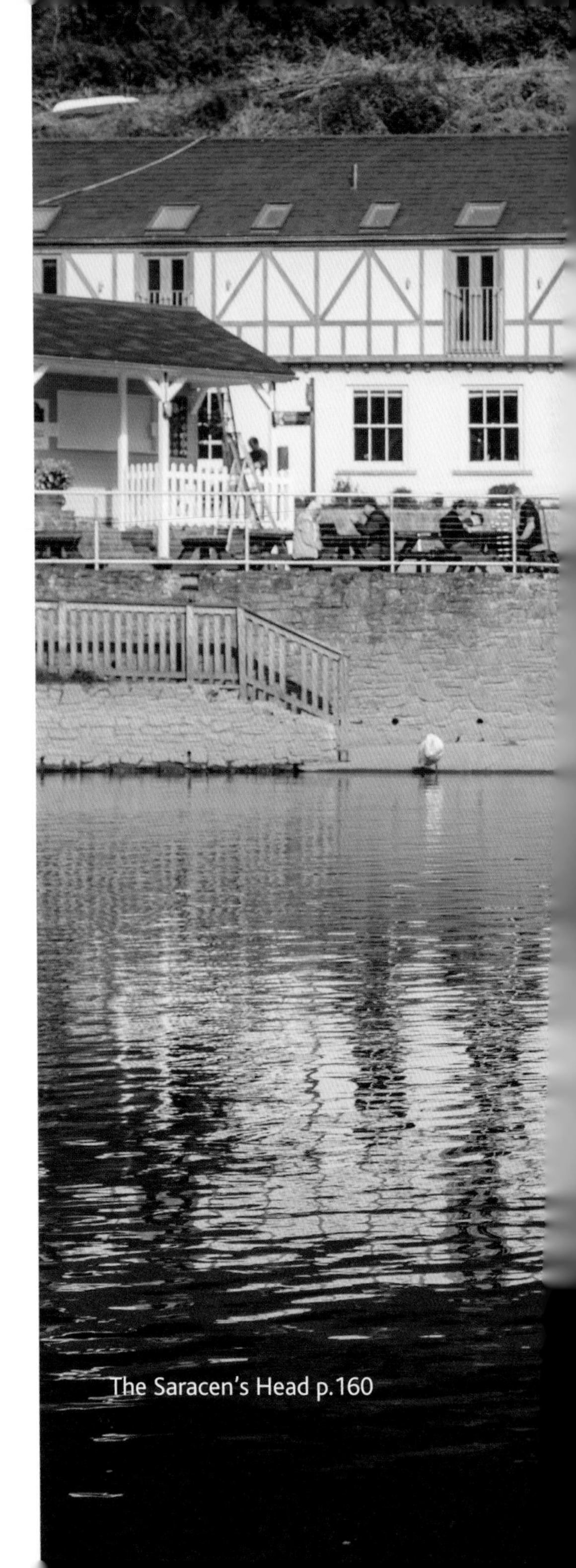

The Saracen's Head p.160

Saracens Head
Inn
The Saracens Head
CENTURY INN
KEEP CLEAR AT
ALL TIMES

Town & City

Broad Street Townhouse p.103

History

Lord Crewe Arms p.172

WYLAM
WYLAM

Outdoors, Walking & Dark Skies

The West Arms p.224

Family & Community

The Boathouse p.120

Food & Luxury

The Angel at Hetton, **NORTH YORKSHIRE** 171
Applecross Inn, **WESTER ROSS** 245
Artist Residence, **OXFORDSHIRE** 58
The Bell at Skenfrith, **MONMOUTHSHIRE** 223
The Bell Inn, **ESSEX** 122
The Bonnie Badger, **EAST LOTHIAN** 248
The Black Swan, **NORTH YORKSHIRE** 180
The Bull, **ANGLESEY** 231
The Carpenters Arms, **NORTH YORKSHIRE** 175
Champany Inn, **WEST LOTHIAN** 247
The Cricketers, **ESSEX** 137
The Crooked Billet, **OXFORDSHIRE** 79
The Double Red Duke, **OXFORDSHIRE** 46
Drunken Duck Inn, **CUMBRIA** 198
The Duck Inn, **NORFOLK** 143
The Ebrington Arms, **GLOUCESTERSHIRE** 84
The Fauconberg, **NORTH YORKSHIRE** 187
The Flitch of Bacon, **ESSEX** 144
The Fox & Hounds, **NORTH YORKSHIRE** 193
The Gin Trap Inn, **NORFOLK** 138
The Gunton Arms, **NORFOLK** 134
Harbourmaster, **CEREDIGION** 226
The Ingham Swan, **NORFOLK** 136
The KIngham Plough, **OXFORDSHIRE** 50
The Kinmel Arms, **CONWY** 231
The Meikleour Arms, **PERTHSHIRE** 255
The Olive Branch, **RUTLAND** 157
The Peacock at Rowsley, **DERBYSHIRE** 149
The Peat Inn, **FIFE** 240
Pentonbridge Inn, **CUMBRIA** 240
Pipe & Glass Inn, **EAST YORKSHIRE** 178
The Plough, **CUMBRIA** 200
The Richmond Arms, **WEST SUSSEX** 63
The Salutation Inn, **DEVON** 103
The Sportsman, **KENT** 76
The Star Inn, **NORTH YORKSHIRE** 170
The Station Hotel, **SUFFOLK** 144
The Swan, **OXFORDSHIRE** 74
The Unruly Pig, **SUFFOLK** 142
Wild Boar Inn, **CUMBRIA** 196

Pentonbridge Inn p.240

Ales & Brews

Twice Brewed Inn p.188

TWICE
BREWED
BREW HOUSE
HADRIANS WALL

Coaching Inns

The Allanton Inn, **SCOTTISH BORDERS** 255
The Bear Hotel, **POWYS** 226
The Bell at Sax, **SUFFOLK** 119
The Bildeston Crown, **SUFFOLK** 130
The Brigands Inn, **POWYS** 227
The Brown Horse Inn, **CUMBRIA** 203
The Bull, **GLOUCESTERSHIRE** 96
The Cavendish Arms, **CUMBRIA** 199
The George Townhouse, **WARWICKSHIRE** 150
The Guinness Arms, **SUFFOLK** 136
Kilchrenan Inn, **ARGYLL & BUTE** 255
The Lamb Inn, **DEVON** 94
The Lion Inn, **GLOUCESTERSHIRE** 85
The New Inn, **HEREFORDSHIRE** 160
The Old Inn, **ROSS-SHIRE** 246
The Old Stocks Inn, **GLOUCESTERSHIRE** 90
The Red Lion, **NORTH YORKSHIRE** 177
The Rose & Crown, **NORTH YORKSHIRE** 183
The Royal Oak, **CUMBRIA** 209
The Sun Inn, **ESSEX** 126
The Talbot Inn, **SOMERSET** 92
The White Lion, **WEST YORKSHIRE** 212

The Sun Inn p.126

Cottages & Glamping

The Haughmond p.158

Pools & Spas

Cary Arms and Spa p.104

Music

The Vicarage p.213

London and the Southeast

Who doesn't dream of getting out of London from time to time and holing up at a country pub for a night or even two? Kent, Sussex and the Home Counties pack quite a punch when it comes to pubs you can stay in, with some terrific food, and, frequently, five-star rooms. Also, don't forget the pub if you're visiting London, where a number of cosy hostelries make a great alternative to the capital's notoriously overpriced hotels.

The Double Red Duke, p.46

The Fox at Willian

A brilliantly updated country pub, close to London, serving great food – and it's dog-friendly too!

Situated in the pretty Hertfordshire village of Willian, The Fox is a revamped pub that does everything a country inn should do: it has a set of very comfy guest rooms, decorated in crisp contemporary style; it serves excellent food that's very moderately priced; and it's not a bad place to pop into for a pint either. It's a pub that's at the heart of its community and it even runs the village shop next door. But with its position just five minutes off the A1, it also happens to be a very handy place for tired folk from The Big Smoke to recharge their batteries at the weekend.

The Fox's style is the same as its brethren in the Anglian Country Inns group (for example the long-established The White Horse and its sister The Kings Head in North Norfolk, as well as nearby The Farmhouse at Redcoats near Hitchin) – a contemporary village pub with a stripped-down bar, good food and a set of comfortable, boutique-style rooms.

The pub has eight guest rooms in all, each of them turned out in contemporary style with crisp, retro designs. There are five 'Garden Rooms' accessible from outside the pub, and each with patio seating in front, and three rooms in the main building, one of which has a free-standing bath in the room. All the rooms have king-size beds, good wifi, Freeview TVs, digital radios, coffee- and tea-making facilities, air-conditioning and modern bathrooms with aromatherapy toiletries and rainfall showers. Dogs are allowed in the garden rooms, where they get treats, bowls and suchlike. They're also allowed in the bar, where you can eat from either the simple bar menu or the slightly fancier restaurant menu. Both are relaxed places to eat, with stripped floors, Lloyd Loom chairs and lots of light. The restaurant is a slightly more elegant alternative, with no beer-swilling folk at the next table, but the quality of the food is really high throughout, with The Fox a destination place to eat for locals hereabouts – there's an emphasis on locally sourced ingredients (the furthest anything travels is the fish and seafood from North Norfolk) and lots of things are homemade.

There are plenty of walks you can do in the surrounding area, a couple of which take in a decent pub or two along the way, plus you're just a short drive away from Hitchin, Cambridge and historical attractions like Hatfield House, one of Elizabeth I's favourite palaces. Failing that, you could just potter about the village: there's another pub, plus there's a diary of events at The Fox throughout the year and an annual beer festival. Whatever you decide to do, this is the perfect, easy, last-minute escape for the jaded city-dweller.

CONTACT Willian, Letchworth Garden City, Hertfordshire SG6 2AE • 01462 480 233 • foxatwillian.co.uk

HOW MUCH? The smallest rooms start at £130 a night, including breakfast, and rise to £165 for the most expensive.

ROOMS 8 double rooms – 3 upstairs in the main building and 5 'garden rooms'. One of the garden rooms serves as a family room, with a double bed and sofa bed.

The Bull

This old hostelry lies on a crossroads at the centre of the lovely village of Ditchling, which straggles picturesquely at the foot of Ditchling Beacon, one of the highest points on the South Downs. The pub itself, a 16th-century coaching inn, is just the sort of place you want to retire to after a long tramp across the hills, with plenty of candlelit nooks, sagging beams and crackling log fires, plus a beer garden for sunny days; and it has its own eco-friendly brewery next door so you can be sure of a good pint of ale. The pub also has 6 very smart bedrooms and is a terrific place to stay, right in the middle of the South Downs National Park. It's a short 1.5 mile walk up to Ditchling Beacon, linking with the South Downs Way long-distance footpath, and yet the bright lights of Brighton are just a 15-minute drive away. The rooms are contemporary and individually designed, with super-comfy king-sized beds, Smart TVs, Roberts radios, minibars and crisp, modern bathrooms, plus there is a separate family suite with 2 bedrooms, 2 bathrooms and a huge Smart TV.

CONTACT 2 High St, Ditchling, East Sussex BN6 8TA • 01273 843 147 • thebullditchling.com

HOW MUCH? Double rooms from £135 a night, not including breakfast.

The Pointer

Situated in a pretty hilltop village that has not one but 2 village greens, and also inspired Tolkien when writing 'The Hobbit', The Pointer is a proper country pub with rooms – a venue for country walks, dogs and muddy boots, and the prospect of a pint and a good meal at the end of it. Revamped a few years ago and now part of the Oakman Inns group, it serves a Mediterranean-inspired menu along with grilled steaks and Sunday roasts, much of which is sourced from the butchers next door. It's all beautifully presented and the service is excellent, with an emphasis on high-quality, fresh ingredients. As for the rooms, there are 8 in all, divided between the pub and a house across the road, and all stylishly decorated in a rustic yet contemporary fashion, with exposed beams, soothing greys and creams on the walls, big comfy beds and good wifi, Freeview TVs and Nespresso coffee-makers, tea, biscuits and fresh milk and mineral water. There are roomy bathrooms, with robes, nice toiletries and powerful rainfall showers, and some bedrooms have free-standing baths. You even get a copy of 'The Hobbit' to read!

CONTACT 27 Church St, Brill, Buckinghamshire HP18 9RT • 01844 238 339 • thepointerbrill.co.uk

HOW MUCH? Double rooms £89–£199 a night, not including breakfast.

The White Horse

Just off a B-road, seemingly in the middle of nowhere, The White Horse in Chilgrove is a fantastic little country pub with rooms. There's prime walking territory right outside the front door – laminated maps available on the bar will guide you on a 4.5-mile hike over the hills, through the woods and back to the cosy pub. But much of the action is centred around shooting parties on the nearby Goodwood Estate, so if you find yourself in the bar at the end of the day, expect to see men wearing military green trousers tucked into inordinately long socks, and flat caps galore. Even if shooting isn't your bag, it's worth coming here for the great hospitality, and dogs are naturally welcome and get a bed, bowl and blanket of their own. Bedrooms are modern and comfortable with faux-fur touches and funky décor, and some even come with hot tubs under a gazebo in their own private garden. All but 2 have direct access to the communal lawn, and the restaurant serves pub classics like fish and chips or game favourites such as local partridge and pheasant.

CONTACT 1 High St, Chilgrove, West Sussex PO18 9HX • 01243 519 444 • thewhitehorse.co.uk
HOW MUCH? Double rooms with breakfast from £140 a night.

The Lion at Wendlebury

This 18th-century Oxfordshire pub is an inviting and characterful place, with a cosy bar, stone-walled dining room and a beer garden, ideal for a pint on warm days. Food-wise, ingredients are locally sourced from the Cherwell Valley and surrounding countryside – think pressed chicken, tarragon and apricot terrine, or roast guinea fowl with chorizo – while Wendlebury is a picturesque spot, with the inn at its centre. Blenheim Palace and Oxford are close by, and shopaholics will be pleased to know that the pub is just 2 miles from Bicester Village. Just as well, then, that the pub is home to 13 chic rooms, each of which is dog-friendly and has an en-suite bathroom with a high-pressure walk-in shower. Features include Feather & Black beds, velvet blackout curtains and Nespresso machines, and some rooms feature full-height doors leading on to Juliet balconies; others have dual-aspect windows, and several are suitable for families. Perfect for a spot of retail therapy, then back to The Lion for a tasty meal and a cosy place to lay your head.

CONTACT Wendlebury, Oxfordshire OX25 2PW 01869 388 228 • thelionwendlebury.co.uk
HOW MUCH? Double rooms with breakfast from £100 a night.

The Double Red Duke

Despite being within an hour or so of London, this Thames Valley coaching inn, in the appealing and ancient Oxfordshire village of Clanfield, with its two village greens, babbling brooks and Norman church, is about as close to the idyll of rural England as you can get. The village of Bampton, where much of the TV series 'Downton Abbey' was filmed, is close by, as is the village of Kelmscott, whose manor William Morris described as "heaven on earth" when he moved there in 1871. But the best bit is that you can stay here too, at this 17th-century stone Cotswold coaching inn, formerly known as The Plough and recently revamped by the owners of the Swan at Ascott-under-Wychwood. Newly opened in 2021, it has 19 lovely bedrooms, cosy public spaces with roaring log fires and excellent food provided by an ex-Hawksmoor chef, some of it cooked over an open fire. The rooms are a highly contemporary mix of antiques and modern features, while the property also benefits from a terrace for outdoor summer dining and beautiful mature gardens perfect for a wander.

CONTACT Bourton Rd, Clanfield, Bampton, Oxfordshire OX18 2RB • 01367 810222 • countrycreatures.com
HOW MUCH? Double rooms from £200 a night, including breakfast.

Fox & Anchor

A Victorian pub on the edge of Smithfield Market that has reinvented itself as a gastropub, with 6 luxury rooms upstairs. It's not just a few rooms above a boozer, though; the rooms are superb, and very well equipped, with Hypnos mattresses, flatscreen TVs with Sky, Nespresso machines and fresh milk and well-stocked minibars. Some rooms have claw-footed roll-top baths and copper hand basins, others waterfall showers, and they all come with Bramley toiletries. Each one is locally themed, with St Bart's and the Market Suite on the first floor, Charterhouse and St Paul's on the second and Smithfield and Barbican at the top. There's a butchery theme too – look out for the lengths of butcher's chain mail used as alternative lamp shades – and the Market Suite has a private decked terrace. Don't forget to nip downstairs to the wood-panelled mahogany bar to enjoy a pint and some of the traditional meaty dishes on the menu, including the excellent and enormous 'City Boy Breakfast'. (Note that meals are not included in the accommodation cost).

CONTACT 115 Charterhouse St, London EC1M 6AA • 020 7250 1300 • foxandanchor.com
HOW MUCH? Double rooms from £159 a night, not including breakfast.

The Wife of Bath

Named after one of the best-known of Chaucer's 'Canterbury Tales', this pub with rooms is featured in the stories as a place of rest for weary pilgrims en route to Canterbury. The theme continues with 6 stylish bedrooms – 4 above the restaurant, 2 in a cottage annexe – each named after a character from Chaucer's famous work. Exposed timber beams blend with contemporary furniture and colourful works of art and muted tones on the walls, making for a relaxing Kentish haven. En-suite bathrooms have complimentary toiletries and flatscreen TVs, and guests also have access to a communal honesty pantry. Food-wise, it's terrific, with anything from Spain-inspired dishes to pan-fried halibut or venison Wellington. For breakfast, choose from a hamper delivered to your door or a cooked breakfast in the restaurant. There's much to do in the local area: check out the nearby nature reserve or explore the Kent Downs Area of Outstanding Natural Beauty on the Wye Downs circular walk, which takes about 3 hours and offers some spectacular views alkong the way.

CONTACT 4 Upper Bridge St, Wye, Kent TN25 5AF • 01233 812 232 • thewifeofbath.com

HOW MUCH? Double rooms with breakfast from £125 a night.

The Olde Bell

Tucked down a cul-de-sac between Marlow and Henley, the village of Hurley is the Thames-side bolthole of many a stockbroker's daydream, all weathered Tudor piles and weeping willows. At its heart, this 12th-century coaching inn was originally refurbished in 2010 by design maven Ilse Crawford, and its rooms, which are spread across 5 buildings – the main inn, plus assorted barns and a malthouse – have recently received a fresh lick of paint. They have king-sized beds, Ercol rocking chairs, freestanding baths, good wifi, flatscreen TVs and tea and coffee. The beams sag and the floorboards are wonky but it all adds to the homely atmosphere. Downstairs a crackling fire warms a proper pub bar and beyond it a handsome restaurant looks out through leaded windows onto clipped lawns, a kitchen garden and a tennis court. Apart from the raucous parakeets in the trees, it would be hard to imagine a more English scene, which you can also enjoy on the local 'Willow Walk', which loops for 5 miles along a lovely stretch of the Thames through ivy-draped woodland.

CONTACT High St, Hurley, Berkshire SL6 5LX • 01628 825 881 • theoldebell.co.uk

HOW MUCH? Double rooms £115–£150 a night, not including breakfast.

The Duke William

A quintessential Kentish pub with superb food and stylish rooms.

What could be better than hunkering down in a cosy pub and enjoying a lazy meal, before retiring to a comfy room upstairs? That's exactly what you get at The Duke William. Located in the heart of the Kentish countryside, just 20 minutes' drive east of Canterbury and close to the quaint village of Wingham, it's a perfect weekend getaway.

The Duke William was the first property taken on by the Kent pubs group run by Mark Sargeant, the former head chef at Claridges, back in 2015. It has four super-comfortable rooms that are named after some of his culinary heroes – the likes of Ramsay and Floyd – and decorated in calming shades of grey, with flashes of colour on cushions and quirky prints. Each has an en-suite shower room and a king-size bed, plus a helpful welcome pack with information on local walks (Route 86 is a good option) and attractions – Wingham Wildlife Park makes for a great day out. Stay in Stein and make the most of the sun terrace and spectacular views out to rolling fields. Whichever room you opt for, enjoy the breakfast included in the pub's rates – choose from the excellent Full English or lighter options, such as cereal or seasonal fruit. All rooms have DAB radios, flatscreen TVs and good wifi.

The pub is a lovely spot for a drink or two – sup on an Aspall, or, if beer's your thing, try a Racing Tiger, an offering from local brewery Angels & Demons. Sit in front of the roaring fire (board games and puzzles optional) or head out to the well-kept sun-terrace and garden, complete with children's play area. Peckish? Snack on Scotch eggs with caper mayo, sausage rolls with Branston pickle or mussel popcorn for the slightly more adventurous. If you fancy something more substantial, the main menu features dishes such as Cumberland sausage toad in the hole with onion gravy, or pork belly with peas, broads beans and black pudding. You can choose to eat in the light and airy conservatory, the restaurant area or the pub itself. What's more, there's an array of themed food evenings throughout the week, ranging from Steak Monday to Fish and Chip Friday along with fêtes and summer barbecues.

The Duke William is one of three Kent places under the Mark Sargeant umbrella, with Rocksalt in Folkestone and The Wife of Bath in Wye also well worth a look. Bear in mind that Wingham is only twenty minutes' drive from Canterbury, so the pub is a perfect base for seeing the cathedral city, and handy also for any number of rural walks if you want to strike out across the Kentish countryside!

CONTACT The Street, Ickham, Kent CT3 1QP • 01227 721 308 • thedukewilliamickham.com

HOW MUCH? Double rooms from £120 a night, including breakfast.

ROOMS 4 en-suite double rooms.

The Kingham Plough

Great food and rooms in a terrific village pub in the Oxfordshire Cotswolds.

This 17th-century Oxfordshire pub with rooms has undergone quite a makeover in the last ten years or so. Not much more than a decade ago you couldn't get so much as a cheese roll in what was a typical village boozer; then Kingham's Plough became a gastronomic temple that drew people from far and wide. More recently, it has reverted to being a bit more of a pub – albeit one that serves really good food and has half a dozen very comfortable rooms upstairs for those who want to stay over. Our kind of place in fact – welcoming and relaxed while making a big effort to make your stay extra special.

Katie and Matt Beamish took over the place in early 2019 and are keen to retain the foodie heritage of The Plough but also want to put their own stamp on the place. It remains a gastropub at heart, however, and they continue to source local, seasonal ingredients for both pub classics and more adventurous British dishes, which you can enjoy from an all-day bar menu or lunch and evening à la carte menus. The food is splendid, and overnight rates include an excellent breakfast, lots of it homemade, from the cereals to the baked beans, and relatively unusual options like kedgeree as well as an excellent Full English.

As for the rooms, there are six in all – some above the pub and others in a two-storey annexe next door – each individually decorated and very comfy. All but one have super-king-size beds, with high-quality linen and duvets, tea- and coffee-making facilities and minibars with fresh milk, good wifi and large Smart TVs and DVD players. Bathrooms have baths with showers (two have roll-top standalone baths), complete with locally made Bramley toiletries. It's not deliberately a family sort of place but parents with small children will be pleased to know that two pairs of rooms share a landing so you can effectively have two adjoining rooms, and baby monitors reach the bar. Two dog-friendly rooms are also available, and include a dog bed, water bowl, treats and a towel for muddy paws, and the overall vibe is one of comfort and relaxation with a quirky twist – lots of grainy wood, flagstone floors and pubby nooks and corners, open fires in winter and a sun terrace for summer. Finally, Kingham is lovely, a typical Cotswolds village, and the pub sits rather idyllically on the village green. There are lots of walks in the surrounding countryside, but, to be honest, you might have everything you need right here – Kingham even has a mainline station just a 15-minute walk away, so you don't even have to bring the car.

CONTACT The Green, Kingham, Chipping Norton, Oxfordshire OX7 6YD • 01608 658 327 • thekinghamplough.co.uk

HOW MUCH? Double rooms from £145 a night, including breakfast.

ROOMS 6 en-suite double bedrooms, all but one with super-king-size beds (the other is a king-size), 2 of which can be used as twins.

PLEASE MIND YOUR HEAD

The Greyhound Inn

A proper village pub with comfy rooms and top-quality food on the edge of the Berkshire Downs.

The Greyhound is the type of place that welcomes you with open arms. Set in Letcombe Regis, a pretty village in south Oxfordshire, owners Martyn and Catriona took over this Grade-II-listed Georgian property in 2014 and have lovingly refurbished it, making it into a proper pub that serves top-notch food, with eight tastefully decorated bedrooms above, in case you're looking for a weekend retreat in the countryside.

Recently and quite rightly awarded CAMRA's White Horse Region 'Country Pub of the Year' award (for the second year running), and Muddy Stilettos 'Best Destination Pub' (voted by the public), the inn is a relaxed place for an ale, craft beer or cider, while the rooms upstairs provide a comfy space to unwind. Each has an en-suite bathroom, is individually decorated, and comes complete with a pocket-sprung mattress, flatscreen TV and Bramley bath products – plus homemade biscuits, a thoughtful extra. For guests who are after something special for their loved one, flowers or a bottle of fizz can be arranged for their bedroom. Don't want to leave Fido at home? Bring him with you: a couple of the rooms are dog-friendly. And if you're after a family-sized suite, that's no problem either – just opt for 'Lambourn' or 'Oxford'.

Much importance is placed on food at The Greyhound – the regularly changing menu features an array of locally sourced produce, with imaginative dishes, such as twice-baked Cheddar soufflé (a popular mainstay), rabbit boudin with warm lentil and tarragon salad, chestnut and bacon velouté or pork loin with pork nuggets, English prawns, orange-braised chicory, black pudding and hazelnuts. But, if pub classics are more your thing, go for the beer-battered haddock with chips, homemade sauce and mushy peas, or the burger with bacon jam, smoked Cheddar and fries.

The area is the ideal spot for walkers – the ancient Ridgeway National Trail (described as Britain's oldest road) is close by, as is the Thames Path. The friendly staff are more than happy to help with routes: they have a number mapped out of varying lengths and difficulties for guests. For those after something less strenuous, the historic market town of Wantage is just two miles from the inn, and the Uffington White Horse (a 100-metre-long prehistoric hill figure formed from deep trenches filled with crushed white chalk) is 15 minutes away by car. Then it's back to the pub for a pint in the bright, airy bar followed by dinner in one of the cosy dining rooms.

CONTACT Main St, Letcombe Regis, Wantage, Oxfordshire OX12 9JL • 01235 771 969 • thegreyhoundletcombe.co.uk
HOW MUCH? Double rooms £95–£115 a night, including breakfast. Family suite £145.
ROOMS 8 individually decorated rooms – all en-suite with a bath, a shower or both.

THE GREYHOUND

The Richard Onslow

Guildford resident Lewis Carroll was apparently inspired to create the character of the grinning Cheshire Cat by a gurning gargoyle on Cranleigh's church. And if you like historic boozers that have been transformed into upmarket pubs with rooms, then Cranleigh's Richard Onslow might put a smile on your dial too. All the period charm of this old timber-framed building has been preserved, but the current owners – the Peach Group – have positioned the Onslow several notches above your basic inn. The 10 rooms here are predominantly en-suite doubles, some with king-size beds, others with twins, but families are also accommodated and there is a box room if you just need somewhere to crash for the night. All newly decorated, a big effort has been made to retain original features such as fireplaces, wooden beams and head-bangingly low doorways. But the rooms also boast power showers and flatscreen Freeview TVs. Located on Cranleigh High Street, the pub is also right in the middle of England's biggest village!

CONTACT 113–117 High St, Cranleigh, Surrey GU6 8A • 01483 274 922 • therichardonslow.co.uk
HOW MUCH? Double rooms start at £75 a night, not including breakfast.

The Royal Oak

This lovely Georgian country inn is snuggled in beautiful West Sussex countryside just within the South Downs National Park. To the north are the rolling chalk Downs; to the south, Chichester; and beyond that the pretty estuaries and inlets of Chichester harbour and West Wittering's fabulous beach. It's a great location, and happily everything else about The Royal Oak is pretty good too, with 5 en-suite rooms in the pub, a family room in a converted barn, and a couple of 2-bedroom serviced cottages down the lane. Rooms come with smart bathrooms with robes and Temple Spa toiletries, and cheering touches such as fresh milk in the fridge and complimentary newspapers for lazy mornings. There's lots to see and do locally and it's tempting to get out and about – to see the Downs, the beach, Chichester harbour – after which you can relax in the inn's fire-lit restaurant, which serves really great food, with the likes of local venison, fish and seafood from the south coast, Southdown lamb, even local ice-cream and cheese - all washed down with the pub's own beer, brewed in nearby Arundel.

CONTACT Pook Lane, East Lavant, West Sussex PO18 0AX • 01243 527 434 • royaloakeastlavant.co.uk
HOW MUCH? Double rooms from £160 a night, not including breakfast; family room £200, cottages £250.

The Mulberry Inn

Located close to the village of Chiddingfold, close to the Surrey-Sussex border, the Mulberry used to be owned by celebrity DJ and former 'Top Gear' presenter Chris Evans. Sold to new owners a couple of years ago, it remains a terrific village pub in every respect – a good place to srink, stay or eat, with a uniquely Lebanese-tinged menu that has proved massively popular with locals and draws diners from much further afield. Tuck into superb babaganoush and mezze, chicken skewers and kofta, and wash it all down with the house gin or ales from the local Hogs Back Brewery. They also serve a good variety of non-Lebanese dishes including an excellent and very popular roast on Sundays, and have a beer garden that is a lovely place to drink and dine during summer. You can also retire to one of the pub's 3 crisp and comfortable double rooms, which all have comfy double beds, flatscreen TVs, tea- and coffee-making facilities and en-suite bathrooms with toiletries. Dogs are welcome too – which is just as well, as there are any number of country walks possible in the vicinity.

CONTACT Petworth Rd, Chiddingfold, Surrey GU8 4SS • 01428 644 460 • themulberryinn.co.uk

HOW MUCH? Double rooms £90–£110 a night, not including breakfast.

The Merry Harriers

Fresh air, country views, bracing walks, B&B rooms and shepherds' huts are the offerings at this country-style inn, which has been serving thirsty customers since the 16th century. The pub has 10 en-suite rooms, either in the pub itself or in a converted barn in the garden, and 5 shepherds' huts. The pub rooms are beamed and characterful, those in the garden more contemporary, but all are very comfy and equipped with flatscreen TVs, wifi, en-suite bathrooms and toiletries, while each hut is set up with bedding, towels and toiletries, bathroom, underfloor heating and a kettle and coffee machine. Basically, whether you're sleeping indoors or glamping, this is a place to relax with someone else doing the cooking, which means you can enjoy not only the pub's excellent breakfasts but also its lunches and dinners too – pub grub mainly, but beautifully cooked and presented and made using ingredients sourced from within a 15-mile radius. You can also join a walk with the pub's resident llamas or just enjoy the countryside of the Surrey Hills Area of Outstanding Natural Beauty.

CONTACT Hambledon Rd, Hambledon, Surrey GU8 4DR • 01428 682 883 • merryharriers.com

HOW MUCH? Double rooms £100–£160 a night, including breakfast. Huts from £195 per night.

The Bell Inn

First and foremost, The Bell in Ticehurst is a great local village pub – cosy and comfortable, with plenty of beams and battered sofas, bare boards and faded rugs, open fires and candlelight, and an invitingly long, well-stocked bar. But what The Bell is perhaps best known for, in its own words, is its "hint of quirk" – bowler hat light fittings, coat hooks fashioned from cutlery, a tower of books forming a twisted column by the bar, a Banksy hanging in the hall, and, best of all, shiny tubas in place of urinals in the gents' (sadly the ladies' are nowhere near as much fun). Upstairs the 7 stylish bedrooms are equally eccentric, with rustic handmade beds with comfy mattresses, antique mirrors and weird bedside lamps; one has its own roof terrace; another – the 'Love Nest' – a copper bath in the room. They also have 4 garden lodge apartments, with mezzanine floors, huge baths and their own terraces, wood-burners and firepits. The food celebrates local produce, with small and large plates to share – anything from a decent burger to sea bream teriyaki – and good English wines.

CONTACT High St, Ticehurst, East Sussex TN5 7AS • 01580 200 300 • thebellinticehurst.com
HOW MUCH? Double rooms from £150 a night, not including breakfast. Lodges from £240 a night.

The Jack Russell Inn

This pub has long seen weary travellers staying in its cosy bedrooms, as it sits on what was once a busy trade route from London. Today, it's very much an inn for country pursuits, set within the village of Faccombe and surrounded by a large estate of the same name. This is prime shooting territory, so it's not uncommon to see the bar overrun with men dressed in green wearing trademark red socks. It's prime pheasant and partridge country, too, as you'll discover if you go for a walk on the nearby footpaths – the unmistakeable sound of game birds clucking from the bushes as you walk by is the main soundtrack around here. The pub itself is a lovely little hideaway, however, whether you're into shooting or not. The food in the restaurant is very game-focused but also includes favourites like pork belly and steaks, and the property boasts some decent eco-credentials too. You can feel good about staying here as the hotel's electricity comes from a wind turbine, heating is powered by a biomass boiler and the water comes from a borehole on the Faccombe estate.

CONTACT Netherton Hilll, Faccombe, Hampshire SP11 0DS • 01264 737 315 • thejackrussellinn.com
HOW MUCH? Double rooms £110–£170 a night, including breakfast.

The Plough Inn

Though The Plough – set in rural north Kent near the little creekside town of Faversham – is a great place to savour a pint of well-kept real ale, it's the food that makes it special. Nothing fussy or forced, just good, tasty dishes made from local produce and the freshest seasonal ingredients, and it's all the better for the fact that you can stay overnight in one of the pub's sumptuous garden suites, housed in a purpose-built barn. These are on 2 floors, with bedrooms downstairs and a spacious upstairs sitting room with countryside views. A double sofa bed means they can easily accommodate a family with young children, and they all come equipped with luxury toiletries, a breakfast hamper and a proper coffee machine with fresh milk, wifi and a Smart TV. Meanwhile, in the pub, the menu includes a selection of classics and regularly changing blackboard specials that could be anything from steamed mussels in local cider to roasted shoulder of saltmarsh lamb. On summer days you can enjoy this in the pub itself, at tables on the green, or in the grassy back garden (complete with clucking chickens).

CONTACT Stalisfield Rd, Faversham, Kent ME13 0HY • 01795 890 256 • theploughinnstalisfield.co.uk
HOW MUCH? Double rooms with breakfast from £130 a night.

The Griffin Inn

This pub has perhaps the loveliest pub garden in Sussex, but even without this it would be a gorgeous spot, deep in the countryside in the pretty village of Fletching, a family-friendly place with bags of charm – beams, panelled walls and cheerily blazing log fires in winter. There's a daily-changing bar menu on the blackboard and a separate menu in the more formal restaurant, both making the most of local ingredients: fish from Rye Bay, venison and game from local farmers, and vegetables from Fletching's market garden. The pub also has 13 very comfortable guest rooms that you can stay over in – 4 fairly traditional rooms in the beamed upper floor of the main building, 4 brighter, more contemporary rooms in a converted woodshed, all with 4-posters, and 5 beautifully decorated, quirky rooms in the house next door, one of which is named after local resident and pub regular, Colin Thubron. All the guest rooms have en-suite bathrooms with toiletries, and they're all set up with big comfy beds, good wifi, flatscreen TVs and DVD players.

CONTACT High St, Fletching, East Sussex TN22 3SS • 01825 722 890 • thegriffininn.co.uk
HOW MUCH? Double rooms £110–£150 a night, including breakfast.

Artist Residence Oxfordshire

A contemporary country inn with boutique rooms in the midst of the Oxfordshire countryside.

Nestled in the Oxfordshire countryside, just a few miles west of Oxford on the eastern fringes of the Cotswolds, Artist Residence Oxfordshire is the ultimate country inn – with five bedrooms tucked away in the eaves and excellent food and drink served downstairs in its pub, The Mason Arms.

The rooms really set this place apart, equipped with large, comfy beds, powerful showers and the sort of vintage-tinged but contemporary décor we've come to expect from the quirky Artist Residence group (which has sister properties in London, Brighton and Penzance). Rooms all have free wifi, flatscreen Freeview TVs, digital radios, Nespresso coffee machines, and mini-fridges stocked with local goodies – and there are Bramley toiletries in the bathrooms, some of which have standalone roll-top baths. The rooms range in size, from the compact 'Rabbit Hole' through the more spacious 'Farmhouse Loft' rooms (which are dog-friendly) to the gorgeous 'Farmhouse Suite', which has a lovely copper bath tub in the room itself, a separate bathroom with shower and an adjoining seating area. They also have three newer rooms (all dog-friendly) located in the outbuildings: the spacious 'Stable Suite', a luxurious take on the bohemian countryside retreat; 'Stable', with its private terrace; and 'Barn Suite', which comes complete with a four-poster bed. If you fancy something a bit different, there's even a homely Shepherd's Hut to hunker down in, overlooking the herb garden.

The location, too, couldn't be better – close to Oxford, Blenheim Palace and the Cotswolds, and with country walks and cycle rides galore on your doorstep – and handily the inn lays on free bikes for you to explore. Back in the tavern, enjoy an open fire, local ales, armchairs to lounge about in, and homemade bar snacks. The full menu served in the dining room hits all the right buttons – local, seasonal produce, beautifully cooked and presented. It's been included in the Michelin 'Eating Out in Pubs' guide, has been awarded 2 AA Rosettes for culinary excellence, as well as being rated as a five-star inn.

All in all, we love the confident, distinctive way the whole package is put together – very contemporary but with a traditional approach to comfort, service and food. It will certainly have you coming back for more.

CONTACT Station Rd, South Leigh, Witney, Oxfordshire OX29 6XN • 01993 656 220 • artistresidence.co.uk
HOW MUCH? Double rooms from £165 a night, Loft suites from £285. Shepherds' Hut from £165.
ROOMS 8 rooms and suites and a shepherds' hut.

CASINO

The Crown Inn

With great food, local ales and comfortable boutique rooms, this Sussex village pub is hard to beat.

Occupying an almost impossibly desirable position overlooking Dial Post's village green, The Crown Inn is a properly cosy country pub. Originally a 16th-century coaching inn, it was taken over 15 years ago by Penny and James Middleton Burn, who have launched it into the 21st century while relinquishing none of its innate pubby charm. It has a lovely beamed bar with stone floor and antique rugs, mismatched furniture, and a wood-burner squeezed into an ancient brick hearth. Penny and James have also developed a big and deserved reputation for the quality of their food, and also added four comfy and beautifully appointed rooms upstairs in case you want to stay over. And it's dog friendly! As village boozers go, it's hard to beat.

The Crown's food is as unpretentious as it is high quality, offering a daily-changing menu consisting of both pub classics and seasonal favourites. James is the chef, and he not only pretty much exclusively uses local farmers and other producers but also regularly forages for wild ingredients nearby. Penny oversees the pub, which has both a cosy bar and a light, bright garden room, plus a beer garden at the back and tables overlooking the village green at the front. It is patronised as much by local drinkers as diners, but it is also a terrific place to stay, with four comfortable and quirky guest rooms, each individually designed to a high spec.

All the guest rooms have fast wifi, Smart TVs, mini-fridges and Nespresso machines, complimentary water, homemade biscuits and fresh fruit as well as high-quality vintage beds and bedding. En-suite bathrooms come with spacious walk-in showers or a bath with a shower, plus toiletries, and there's a family suite with two double beds that can comfortably accommodate four people. Also included in the room rates is a delicious breakfast of homemade muesli, fresh fruit, and yoghurt, with some additional hot options available too.

Finally, the location is ideal for a short break from London, just off the A24 Worthing Road and reachable in a little over an hour by car. You are close to some of the loveliest scenery of the South Downs National Park, and just a 20-minute drive from the coast, plus you have the wonderful Knepp Castle Estate to visit on your doorstep, whose re-wilding project set the template for many others across the UK. In short, this is a perfect venue for a West Sussex break.

CONTACT Worthing Rd, Dial Post, Horsham, West Sussex RH13 8NH • 01403 710 902 • crown-inn-dialpost.co.uk

HOW MUCH? Double rooms with breakfast £120–£155 a night.

ROOMS 4 en-suite guest bedrooms.

The Ram Inn

Huddled beneath the ridge of the South Downs, Firle is one of Sussex's prettiest villages, and its sole pub – the rambling, centuries-old Ram Inn – is just as appealing. It's primarily a dining pub nowadays, serving up excellent, locally sourced meals, but despite the focus on food The Ram never loses sight of the fact that it's also the village local, and you'll still see plenty of muddy boots, ambling dogs and locals chatting over a pint. It's perhaps nicest of all as a place just to stop for a drink on a summer's afternoon, with plenty of tables and benches at the front of the pub, plus a lovely walled garden shaded by apple trees at the back, which is usually packed with families. Inside there are several public areas and a tiny bar serving local Harveys ales, and 5 individually decorated upstairs rooms, furnished with a carefully mismatched mixture of antiques and contemporary items, flatscreen TVs, good wifi and tea and coffee. Unsurprisingly, given the pub's location, there are great walks all around, with the South Downs Way running along the top of the blowy ridge above the village.

CONTACT Firle, Lewes, East Sussex BN8 6NS • 01273 858 222 • raminn.co.uk
HOW MUCH? Double rooms with breakfast £130–£175 a night.

The Crab & Lobster

Really special places to stay are few and far between on the Manhood Peninsula, south of Chichester, but the lovely Crab & Lobster is one of them – a pretty, 17th-century pub tucked away on the quieter, eastern side, backing on to the banks of peaceful Pagham Harbour Nature Reserve (you can join the short circular Sidlesham Nature Trail, which skirts part of the bay, at Sidlesham Quay, just up the lane from the pub). Upstairs, the pub has 4 tranquil, luxurious rooms, decked out in pastel shades, with fresh flowers and REN toiletries. An extra £20 gets you one of the deluxe rooms at the back, which overlook the nature reserve and come kitted out with binoculars. Part of the fun of staying here for a night or 2 is having the opportunity to see the bay's extraordinary transformation, as high tide brings the sea slapping up against the Quay, before it ebbs away to reveal an entirely different landscape of mudflats and saltmarsh stretching off into the distance. Downstairs there's a flagstoned bar and excellent restaurant – look out for Selsey crab on the menu.

CONTACT Mill Lane, Sidlesham, Chichester, West Sussex PO20 7NB • 01243 641 233 • crab-lobster.co.uk
HOW MUCH? Double rooms £125–£145 a night, not including breakfast.

The Richmond Arms

It's worth a trip to The Richmond Arms in the pretty village of West Ashling for the bar snacks alone: smoky sardines with chilli, gremolata-coated haloumi fries, tiny fried chiperone squid, or just Serrano ham cut to order. Better still, stay for a meal, and settle down at one of the scrubbed wooden tables to enjoy tempting mains like sticky slow-cooked brisket with dripping fries or crispy sea trout fillet with lime, washed down with a glass of homemade loganberry schnapps and finished off with a scoop of homemade ice-cream. You wouldn't suspect such culinary pizzazz from the pub's rather plain exterior, but inside it's smart and stylish, with slate-grey paintwork, bare brick and quirkily decorated ducks adorning the walls – the last of these a nod to the village's picturesque duck pond down the lane. Upstairs there are 2 luxurious bedrooms with king-size beds, tea and coffee and mineral water, flatscreen TVs and contemporary bathrooms with large bathtubs and luxury toiletries; one is large enough for a young family. At the back of the pub, a snazzy pizza wagon serves up crispy, artisan-style pizzas on weekends.

CONTACT Mill Rd, West Ashling, West Sussex PO18 8EA • 01243 572 046 • therichmondarms.co.uk
HOW MUCH? Double rooms £125–£135 a night, including breakfast.

The Five Bells Inn

You'd be hard pushed to find a nicer country pub than The Five Bells, a 16th-century inn idyllically located just footsteps from the Pilgrims Way in the tiny North Downs village of Brabourne. The pretty garden, strewn with coloured lights, its tables set with checked cloths and fresh flowers, evokes the easy panache and joie de vivre of a French village hotel, while inside the comfortable, well-worn space is filled with quirky bits and bobs and offbeat rustic accoutrements, warmed by fragrant log fires. This isn't style over substance, however; it's a refreshingly modern place but with a profoundly traditional heart. Come for a quiet pint in the early evening, or join the local crowds on weekend afternoons when convivial hours are spent eating, supping and enjoying occasional live music. The food is great, taking in burgers, hot dogs and lots of yummy pub grub items done with a contemporary twist. The pub also serves flavoursome local ales, chilled local cider and fruity Kentish wines – all of which provide a cue for the 4 sumptuous, individually designed suites, named after local hops and grapes.

CONTACT The Street, East Brabourne, Kent TN25 5LP • 01303 813 334 • fivebellsbrabourne.co.uk
HOW MUCH? Double rooms from £125 a night, including breakfast.

The Bull Inn

A terrific country pub that's a great base for exploring the eastern Cotswolds.

Midway between Woodstock and Chipping Norton, Charlbury is an excellent base for exploring the eastern Cotswolds. It also has a terrific place to stay in the 16th-century Bull Inn – Charlie and Willow Crossley's self-styled 'home away from home', which is bang in the centre of this small market town and manages to be both sharp and stylish and comfortable at the same time. It's the sort of place in which it's impossible not to relax, with all the bells and whistles a good gastropub should have – delicious, locally sourced, unpretentious food, decent ales and an all-round cosy atmosphere – together with a very comfortable set of boutique rooms.

The pub has been around for a while but it has been updated with sensitivity and care. There are 8 en-suite guest rooms in all, 4 in the pub and 4 in a converted barn. Each room has a distinctive and individual colour palette and all come with extremely comfortable super-king-size beds with high-quality linen and big squashy pillows, upholstered headboards and bold, ample curtains. Everything is right up to date and chosen with care and huge attention to detail – essential in what is a seriously ancient building. Some rooms have bathrooms with either a bath or a shower, some have both, and a couple have free-standing baths in the room itself; every room comes with good wifi, flatscreen Freeview TVs, tea- and coffee-making facilities, complimentary mineral water, bathrobes and Bramley toiletries. Dogs are allowed in half the rooms and small children can be easily accommodated with a fold-down bed or travel cot for a small additional charge.

The pub serves an excellent breakfast, and at lunch and dinner the menu features the sort of high-end yet well-priced gastropub food you might expect to find in these parts – simple and delicious, with great steaks and burgers, pork belly, fish and chips, lovely sharing platters and homemade bar snacks, and a choice of three roasts on a Sunday. You can enjoy this either in the bar or restaurant area.

There's loads to see and do nearby: for the energetic, Wychwood Forest offers a wonderful 8-mile-long circular walk, and the Glyme Valley Way passes nearby; for culture-vultures, Winston Churchill's birthplace Blenheim Palace is a short drive away, as are the popular outlet shops at Bicester Village and the remains of a Roman Villa at North Leigh. But really the pleasures of this part of the world are aimless ones – country walks, cosy pubs and farm shops stacked with local produce. Days out from The Bull, finished off with dinner back at the pub, are heaven, and it's easy to forget that you're just a 90-minute drive from London. Not only that: Charlbury is just over an hour away on the main line from Paddington, so you can just leave the car keys at home.

CONTACT Sheep St, Charlbury, Oxfordshire OX7 3RR • 01608 810 689 • bullinn-charlbury.com

HOW MUCH? Double rooms with breakfast £109–£129 a night.

ROOMS 8 en-suite guest bedrooms.

The Orange

Located in a snazzy part of central London, with Sloane Square and the King's Road both a 5-minute walk away, this classy spot is part of the Cubitt House group, and home to a gastropub with 4 chic rooms upstairs. After a busy day seeing the sights of London, you can pull up a pew back at the pub and sup on a craft beer or a glass of vino and peruse the modern European menu, which features dishes such as pan-roasted chicken with forestière potatoes and rosemary jus or whiskey cured beef with charcoal mayonnaise and salsify, alongside more casual options like wood-fired pizzas. Guests can choose to eat in the ground floor area or upstairs in the atmospheric dining space, complete with lovely views over Orange Square. Then it's up to one of the spacious and contemporary rooms, which are each furnished with king-size beds, en-suite bathrooms with robes and toiletries, good wifi, DAB alarm radios and flatscreen TVs. After a good night's sleep you'll be ready to enjoy an excellent breakfast before before hitting the town the next day.

CONTACT 37–39 Pimlico Rd, London SW1W 8NE • 0207 881 9844 • theorange.co.uk

HOW MUCH? Double rooms from around £200 a night, not including breakfast.

The New Inn

Sitting on the edge of Regent's Park in swanky St John's Wood, The New Inn is a north London pub that not only serves inventive cocktails and really good pub food but also has 5 coolly contemporary and quite recently refurbished double rooms upstairs. Three of these have super-king-size beds, 2 king-size, and one a regular double, and all have large en-suite bathrooms, TVs with Sky, good wifi and tea- and coffee-making facilities. Location-wise, it's a nice part of the city to stay in, with a well-heeled villagey feel, yet also extremely well-placed for the West End, with St John's Wood tube station just a 10-minute walk away and giving easy access to Bond Street and the capital's shopping areas. You're also close to Primrose Hill and Camden, not far from the delights of Regents Park and London Zoo, and it's easy to take the tube to Westminster and the Houses of Parliament, Big Ben and the meandering Thames. The pub is a nice place to return to each evening, with a seasonal dinner menu and an easy stagger to your room at the end of the night.

CONTACT 2 Allitesen Rd, London NW8 6LA • 0207 586 6981 • thenewinnlondon.co.uk

HOW MUCH? Double rooms £150–£220 a night, not including breakfast.

The Old Ship

If you're looking for somewhere to stay in London's cooler eastern regions, and preferably somewhere with a bit of character, this might just be the place. The Old Ship, just off Hackney's main drag, is not only a very convivial place to drink and eat but has a handful of comfy and well-equipped upstairs rooms as well. First the pub, which is a proper boozer, but one which has kept up with the best 21st-century trends, with a good range of craft ales and excellent pub food, including good rotisserie chicken and burgers and a decent Full English in the morning (though this costs extra). There are 10 crisply furnished rooms, all with decent wifi, flatscreen Freeview TVs, hairdryers, tea and coffee and up-to-date en-suite bathrooms with toiletries. Downstairs, food is served all day and night, and the pub offers a laundry service and is open 24 hours so it's just like a proper hotel. Not only that, you're a two-minute walk from Hackney Central station, and close to loads of quick routes into central London.

CONTACT 2 Sylvester Path, London E8 1EN • 0208 986 2732 • oldshiphackney.com
HOW MUCH? Double rooms £98–£118 a night, not including breakfast.

The Grazing Goat

Part of Cubitt House, a collection of independent London watering-holes and hotels, this West End gastropub not only serves quality food but also houses guests overnight in 8 stylish rooms set over 3 floors. Think country house décor with plenty of modern amenities, including flatscreen TVs, en-suite batrooms with robes and toiletries and tea- and coffee-making facilities. Positioned a stone's throw from Edgware Road and Oxford Street and a few minutes from Hyde Park, it doesn't get much better in terms of location: you're also a 5-minute walk from Marble Arch tube station, and can explore the shops of the West End, stroll to the Serpentine or check out one of the nearby bars or pubs. Then it's back to the Grazing Goat, where you can feast on daily changing pies, a dry-aged burger with fries or opt for something a bit fancier like pan-fried hake with celeriac, hispi cabbage and lobster sauce, or pork loin and belly with bacon rösti. They serve wonderful breakfasts, too, and a great selection of roasts on Sunday – just like a proper pub in fact!

CONTACT 6 New Quebec St, London W1H 7RQ • 0207 724 7243 • thegrazinggoat.co.uk
HOW MUCH? Double rooms from around £200 a night, not including breakfast.

The One Tun

Just a skip away from Farringdon tube station lies The One Tun, a cosy spot dishing up pan-Asian food, with 8 rather lovely bedrooms upstairs. The sizeable menu is filled with tasty delights, like chicken siu mai, duck and watermelon salad, miso salmon and Thai green curry. To drink? Alongside a varied draft beer selection, there's a host of innovative cocktails. We love the Mexican Bracer, a blend of mezcal, Malibu, strawberries, pineapple juice and agave syrup. Fed and watered, you can head upstairs to one of the stylish guest rooms, each decked out with funky wallpaper and shades of mauve and grey and featuring king-size or super-king-size beds, Smart TVs with Netflix, coffee- and tea-making facilities including Nespresso machines and air-conditioning; bathrooms are en-suite and come with toiletries, robes and slippers, . Choose from a standard or large double or a twin room. The pub is in a fab position, close to public transport, the City and the West End, and in the heart of Clerkenwell, home to innumerable restaurants and pubs.

CONTACT 125 Saffron Hill, London EC1N 8QS • 0207 405 1521 • onetun.co.uk
HOW MUCH? Double rooms £165–£185 a night, not including breakfast.

The Tiger Inn

Situated on a picture-perfect village green lined by flint-walled cottages, The Tiger Inn's setting is about as idyllic it gets, and – at just half a mile from Birling Gap and the Seven Sisters – it's a popular lunchtime stop for walkers tramping the South Downs Way. It's a thoroughly cosy old place, located in a delightful Sussex village, with 5 country-style bedrooms upstairs – 4 doubles and 1 twin – all with en-suite bathrooms with toiletries, flatscreen TVs and wifi. They serve really good pub food all day – pies, fish and chips, whitebait, good burgers – but it's a good place just to stop for a pint, either enjoyed in the pub's lovely 15th-century interior or at the tables outside. The same owners also rent 8 self-catering cottages, which are set in a delightful walled garden nearby, and there is also the opportunity to stay in the B&B rooms at the spectacular Belle Tout lighthouse, high on the chalk cliffs of nearby Beachy Head, which has been recently restored and still enjoys a magnificent position. Tell us if you know of any other pub that has its own lighthouse!

CONTACT The Green, East Dean, East Sussex BN20 0BY • 01323 423 878 • beachyhead.org.uk/the-tiger-inn
HOW MUCH? Double rooms with breakfast £120–£160 a night. Belle Tout rooms from £175 a night.

The Standard Inn

CAMRA's 'Best Pub in Southeast England' for 2 years running, this old-fashioned inn is a successful revamp of what was a tired but popular old pub, and it says something for the team here that they've retained the affection of local drinkers while catapulting the place into the 21st century. The pub has 5 creaky rooms that are comfortable without being tremendously special, with Freeview TVs, tea- and coffee-making facilities and mineral water, decent wifi and comfy beds. They're simply furnished with antiques and bric-a-brac that are not only perfectly in tune with the building but also with Rye itself, which is stuffed full of places selling this sort of stuff. They don't take bookings for food, even for residents, but it's no hardship to have a pint while you wait. The seasonally changing menu has 3 ever-present pub classics and 4 main courses, and is focused around local saltmarsh lamb and beef, fish and seafood from Rye Harbour, plus a veggie dish. Breakfast is served in the bar and is like the rest of the food – simple, delicious and made from local ingredients.

CONTACT The Mint, Rye, East Sussex TN31 7EN • 01797 225 231 • thestandardinnrye.co.uk
HOW MUCH? Double rooms £130–£150 a night, including breakfast.

The White Hart

Just half a mile from the A1 yet situated in a very pleasant village, this old coaching inn was done up not long ago by a couple of local pub entrepreneurs who cut their teeth at the Tilbury restaurant in nearby Datchworth. It's been a roaring success, partly for the quality of its food, which consists of well-cooked pub classics and more adventurous dishes and a restaurant-quality wine list; excellent local lamb, beef and fish are delivered daily and cooked on the grill. You can enjoy this in the front bar or the flagstoned restaurant at the back, and there's a warm welcome and good service from staff, who clearly identify with the mission of the owners. The pub also has 13 guest rooms, 9 in the main building and 4 in a converted stable block outside. The 3 so-called 'boutique' rooms are the nicest, with larger TVs and big bathrooms with walk-in showers and spa baths. But all the rooms, including those outside, have been nicely refurbished in an up-to-date but not overly contemporary style, and all have TVs, tea- and coffee-making facilities, biccies, water and wifi (2 rooms have 4-poster beds if that's your thing).

CONTACT 2 Prospect Place, Welwyn, Hertfordshire AL6 9EN • 01438 715 353 • whitehartwelwyn.co.uk
HOW MUCH? Double rooms £95–£115 a night, including breakfast.

The Swan Inn

We love a pub with bags of personality, and The Swan at Swinbrook is a paragon example. In the 1920s–1930s, scenic Swinbrook was home to the Mitfords, the madly talented debutante sisters who came to fame as writers and revolutionaries. The youngest, Debo, who became the Duchess of Devonshire, bought the wisteria-clad village pub, filled it with her family photographs and asked Archie and Nicola Orr-Ewing to manage it. Now, some years after her death, it's owned by the Chatsworth Estate, leased by the Orr-Ewings and is still filled with Mitford memorabilia. Set beside the River Windrush, it emanates charm. The front is a 16th-century tavern with creaking parlour rooms. At the back is a sunny extension and an idyllic garden strolled by bantams. Meals are an unfussy joy – the likes of homemade soup with sourdough bread, and fish cakes with beetroot salad – and the accommodation is similarly understated. The rooms are in 2 separate annexes away from the pub bustle; 5 in a riverside cottage, 6 in the old stable block. Clad in creams and taupe, all are devised with sophisticated simplicity.

CONTACT Swinbrook, Near Burford, Oxfordshire OX18 4DY • 01993 823 339 • theswanswinbrook.co.uk
HOW MUCH? Double rooms from £130 a night, including breakfast.

The Chequers

This long-established Marlow pub, bang in the heart of town and just footsteps from the river, has been a popular place for a pint and a bite for a while. But it now has a set of rather stylish rooms that are a perfect complement to the funky modern pub downstairs, which offers a reasonably priced menu of pub classics – a high-quality burger, fish and chips, decent salads, and a great selection of steaks from their 'Butcher's Block': British, American and Argentine beef, all priced by weight so you can have as much or as little as you like. You can eat in the front bar or in the slightly posher dining room at the back, plus there's the adjoining Churchill Tap, which is more of a traditional pub, serving a huge list of craft ales. All the rooms are spacious and creatively furnished with retro furniture and bespoke headboards on bright feature walls, and all except one boast comfy king-size beds. They have spacious bathrooms with high-pressure showers and Temple Spa toiletries, Freeview TVs and good wifi, Nespresso machines, complimentary water and homemade biscuits.

CONTACT 53 High St, Marlow, Buckinghamshire SL7 1BA • 01628 482 053 • thechequersmarlow.co.uk
HOW MUCH? Double rooms from £145 a night, including breakfast.

The Coach

Once The Coach was just an old-fashioned Clerkenwell pub, a favourite watering-hole for journos from the nearby 'Guardian', and like most pubs, the food it served was basic. But the welcome was always as warm as the beer and the pub didn't need to try much harder to attract its thirsty clientele. Nowadays gastropubs are two-a-penny, but very few are a match for The Coach, which serves great food and has 4 very spacious and stylish rooms upstairs for those wanting to stay the night. And why wouldn't you? It's in a brilliant location, on the fringes of Clerkenwell and Holborn, the Modern European food is as good as anything served in this part of London – quite a claim in an area where places to eat are thick on the ground – and the bedrooms are much more than just rooms above a pub. Each one is different but they all boast classic 20th-century furnishings, flatscreen TVs with Freeview, air-conditioning and good wi-fi, king-size comfy beds with good-quality linen and en-suite bathrooms divided from the main part of the room by glass screens.

CONTACT 26–28 Ray St, London EC1R 3DJ • 0203 954 1595 • thecoachclerkenwell.co.uk
HOW MUCH? Double rooms from £165 a night, including breakfast.

The Pilot

Those of a certain age might recognise the row of workers' cottages butting up next to this North Greenwich pub. They featured in Blur's video for 'Park Life' back in 1994, and look much the same now as they did then, although the area around has changed beyond recognition. The Pilot has changed too, but in a good way, from what was a tremendous neighbourhood pub in an area where you'd least expect it to an even better pub that serves good food and has some cosy boutique rooms upstairs for those looking for an alternative to the charms of the nearby Holiday Inn. Occupying a lovely Georgian building, owned and run by Fullers, it's a homely sort of place, with lots of nooks and crannies and a terrace and secluded garden out the back, and it serves a menu of tasty bar snacks, sandwiches and pub classics. There are 10 contemporary rooms, equipped with comfy cast-iron beds, high-quality bed linens, Freeview TVs and en-suite bathrooms, wifi and tea- and coffee-making facilities; the cheaper ones are quite compact but they have everything you need.

CONTACT 68 River Way, London SE10 0BE • 0208 858 5910 • pilotgreenwich.co.uk
HOW MUCH? Double rooms £99–£149 a night, including breakfast.

The Percy Arms

This Kentish North Downs pub is the perfect village stopover – with a South African theme!

Beautifully positioned beneath the beauty spots of Chantries and St Marthas – two eye-candy vantage points along the North Downs Way – in the Surrey hamlet of Chilworth, The Percy Arms looks like the quintessential English village pub. Inside, however, things are a little bit different. With energetic and innovative South African owners at the helm, the pub has become a classy grill and restaurant as well as a traditional boozer. The bar is still there, and it still serves a good range of ales and lagers, and there's a cracking beer garden from where you can admire the views of the Surrey Hills. But the overall theme is Africa, with authentic artefacts and the odd animal-skin floor-covering all serving to create an unusually comfy hunting-lodge vibe.

The food will also tickle your tastebuds here. As anyone that's visited South Africa will tell you, Saffas know their beef cuts like no one else, and while there's a good selection of other meals on the menu – including some great fish and veggie dishes – carnivores should really sink their canines into one of the steaks. The wine list, too, is in part a stroll through some of South Africa's best vineyards: wine is taken seriously here, and there are regular tasting evenings. With a belly full of biltong and bobotie, washed down with a few glasses of Pinotage, you might just be getting into the African vibe.

If so, you'll be pleased to learn that The Percy also has five very comfortable bedrooms upstairs, each named after one of the 'Big Five' game animals in Zulu and other African dialects, so you can, if you wish, spend the night here too. There are two rooms, massive Ndlov (elephant) and Ingwe (leopard) – both with gigantic super-king-size beds and roll-top slipper baths – plus two double rooms – Tau (lion) and Nyati (water buffalo) – with king-size beds. The last room, Tshukudu (rhino), is a twin that can be converted into a double. Both Tshukudu and Ndlov can accommodate families of four, and Ingwe has wonderful views of the Surrey Hills walking spot, St Marthas, while all guest rooms feature en-suite bathrooms, flatscreen TVs, wifi, goosedown duvets, Egyptian cotton linen and tea and coffee.

CONTACT 75 Dorking Rd, Chilworth, Surrey GU4 8NP • 01483 561 765 • thepercyarms.net

HOW MUCH? Double rooms £105–£125 a night, including breakfast.

ROOMS 5 en-suite bedrooms.

ENTRANCE

The Swan

This honey-stone country inn is now a chic rural haven that prides itself on its foodie vibe.

A chic rural haven in a particularly pretty, unsung village near Chipping Norton, Oxfordshire, the Swan at Ascott-under-Wychwood prides itself on its foodie vibe. In spring 2019, this 16th-century honey-stone inn was given a major and much-applauded reboot under the talented management team of Sam and Georgie Pearman (the couple behind the Chequers in nearby Churchill and the Double Red Duke near Oxford).

It's a relaxing venue with an old-school bar with beams and handsome stone fireplace, a marginally more formal dining area with eye-catching art on the walls, a wine room, a room for private parties and an expansive courtyard garden. The owners are very focused on the outdoors, and can arrange walks and bike tours of the Cotswolds countryside, shooting parties and the odd gourmet event. Meals are a treat of modern dining. The menu, mainly based on artisanal produce, offers everything from conventional pies and generous salad bowls to sharing plates (there's an excellent tarte flambée) and adventurous mains such as pork belly with celeriac and toffee apple. Breakfast is a glorious feast, with options such as almond pancakes and French toast with apple sauce.

Upstairs are six super-comfy bedrooms, and two more in a garden annexe. Some rooms have feature baths, all have sumptuous soft furnishings; each has been boldly devised by a different designer. They all have good wifi and Smart TVs, tea- and coffee-making facilities and biscuits, and lovely en-suite bathrooms with Three Acres toiletries. Most rooms are doubles or twins with either baths or showers. The pub also has a family room with its own entrance area and sitting room and two upstairs bedrooms with a family bathroom in between. This room, and a couple of others, also accept dogs.

Finally, the village is a typically Cotswolds ensemble of honey-coloured stone cottages, one of a trio of 'Wychwood' villages midway between Burford and Kingham in a particularly rural part of Oxfordshire. You can actually reach the village by train to nearby Shipton station, and there are any number of loop walks you can do from the village – so it's maybe time to leave the car behind for a truly relaxing weekend away.

CONTACT Ascott-under-Wychwood, Near Chipping Norton, Oxfordshire OX7 6AY • 01993 832 332 • countrycreatures.com/the-swan

HOW MUCH? Double rooms from £119 per night; family rooms from £179; prices include breakfast.

ROOMS 8 en-suite guest rooms, including one family room.

THE
SWAN

Lucky Dip

The Sportsman

It describes itself very simply as a 'pub by the sea', but The Sportsman is not just any seaside boozer – in fact, its unassuming setting belies its reputation for delicious food, which makes use of nearby produce, including lamb from the surrounding salt marshes, local oysters and good fresh fish (try the seared ray or slip sole). The only drawback is that you need to book months in advance to get a table at the weekend, but it's worth it – not just for Stephen Harris's Michelin-starred food but also for the genuinely relaxed ambience and service and an undeniably unique setting. No rooms.

CONTACT Faversham Rd, Seasalter, Kent CT5 4BP • 01227 273 370 • thesportsmanseasalter.co.uk

The Bounty

An air of happy anarchy prevails in this quirky Thameside pub, not least because the only access is on foot or by boat. A sign over the door declares 'Welcome to the People's Republic of Cockmarsh' – while a chalkboard adds 'Muddy boots, dirty hounds and children welcome' – and you're likely to find large numbers of all 3 inside the barn-like pub, which has a festival vibe on summer weekends, decked out with more flags, slogans and colourful memorabilia than a 1960s student digs. If you're not arriving by boat, just stroll along the Thames Path from Cookham or Marlow, or park your car in Bourne End and nip over the footbridge. No rooms.

CONTACT Cockmarsh, Bourne End, Buckinghamshire SL8 5RG • 01628 520 056

Royal Standard of England

Wonky of beam and weathered of pew, this country pub claims to be England's oldest freehouse, and certainly looks the part. Tucked up a lane near the village of Forty Green, it's a wonderful warren of a place, with drinking nooks behind stained-glass screens and a dining room festooned with candelabras, tapestries and suits of armour. A mixed crowd of locals, tourists, walkers and families share a jovial atmosphere and ales from local breweries. The food is a blend of locally-sourced pub stalwarts and local game, while to the side of the pub there's a pleasant short walk through woods and a wildflower meadow wheeled over by red kites. No rooms.

CONTACT Brindle Lane, Forty Green, Buckinghamshire HP9 1XT • 01494 673 382 • theoldestpub.com

The Perch

Nestled on the Thames Path in the tiny village of Binsey, this 17th-century pub is one of the oldest places to drink in Oxford. A regular haunt of Lewis Carroll, rumour has it he based the 'Treacle Well' at the Mad Hatter's Tea Party on the nearby churchyard. The pub was also one of Inspector Morse's favourite watering-holes and a popular venue for jazz in the 1960s. Aside from that, and its frankly glorious riverside setting, The Perch has one more draw: fantastic food, including superb fish and triple-cooked chips, Dorset crab on toast, potted rabbit and roasts on Sunday. They do a great burger and excellent steaks too, and host an annual beer and cider festival in September. No rooms.

CONTACT Binsey Lane, Binsey, Oxford, Oxfordshire OX2 0NG • 01865 728 891 • the-perch.co.uk

The Buddle Inn

Tucked away in the deep south of Niton, this is a popular, secluded Isle of Wight pub whose gorgeous gardens have a terrace with spectacular Channel views. Parts of the inn date back to 1550 and it serves decent pub meals and an excellent range of local ales, including island beers and guest ales from the mainland. An old haunt that still retains its rustic charm, the pub's blackboard displays deliciously fresh daily specials. No rooms.

CONTACT St Catherines Rd, Niton, Isle of Wight PO38 2NE • 01983 730 243 • characterinns.co.uk/the-buddle-inn

The Spotted Dog

This 15th-century freehouse, converted from a number of clapboard cottages, is the kind of village inn that dreams are made of. It's close enough to Tunbridge Wells and attractions like Hever Castle to be a brilliant stop-off on any tour of the Kentish Weald, but even if it weren't it would be worth beating a path to get here. It's particulary cosy in winter, when the low beamed rooms are warmed by crackling log fires. It serves local real ales and tremendous food – big on meat and fish dishes, hearty, filling and using good local ingredients. In summer, you can enjoy meals in the garden, which has wide views across the surrounding Weald. Sitting out here on a summer Sunday, pint in hand and muddy dog at your feet, it can feel that life doesn't get much better. No rooms.

CONTACT Smarts Hill, Penshurst, Kent TN11 8EP • 01892 870 253 • spotteddogpub.com

(Top) The Sportsman; (middle) The Perch; (bottom) The Spotted Dog.

The Fox Goes Free

This splendid countryside pub, tucked away in the South Downs National Park midway between Chichester and Midhurst, is a real winner. It serves its own beer for starters – the eponymous 'Fox Goes Free' – and has one of the loveliest pub gardens in Sussex, with tables set out under apple trees and a low stone wall at the end of the garden allowing uninterrupted views over Levin Down. Inside, it has bags of character, with well-worn stone floors, beams and inglenook fireplaces that roar into life in winter. The food is excellent, with everything made in-house, from the lip-smackingly good crunchy chips to the ice-cream. No rooms.

CONTACT Charlton, Near Goodwood, West Sussex PO18 0HU • 01243 811 461 • thefoxgoesfree.com

The Foresters Arms

Part of the excellent Little Pub group, the Foresters – known locally as the 'Donkey pub' for the donkeys that often cluster outside – is a welcome stopping-off point for weary walkers. Dogs are welcome, there's a lovely garden for when the weather is clement, and when it's not they crank up the wood-burner indoors. The food served isn't anything out of the ordinary – fish and chips, burgers, homemade pies and steaks – but it's moderately priced and well prepared, and perfect fuel for tramping the woods and meadows of the New Forest. No rooms.

CONTACT Abbots Well Rd, Fordingbridge, Hampshire SP6 2JA • 01425 652 294 • the.littlepubgroup.co.uk/the-foresters-arms

The Old Neptune

Slap bang on the beach, The Old Neptune features in almost every photo of Whitstable. Originally serving the men of the boatyards, a storm in 1897 washed the wooden beer house away and the pub was rebuilt using timber reclaimed from the original structure. Now this old haunt is a bustling local, with tables outside that are over-run on sunny days by locals, hikers and cyclists. Inside it's atmospheric in a spit-and-sawdust way, and surprisingly small, but there's decent ale, simple pub grub and live music on Friday, Saturday and Sunday nights. No rooms.

CONTACT Marine Terrace, Whitstable, Kent CT5 1EJ • 01227 272 262 • thepubonthebeach.co.uk

The Loch and The Tyne

Chef Adam Handling's take on the traditional pub in Old Windsor not only serves food that is a notch above usual pub grub but also has 2 luxurious guest rooms available – furnished with comfy king-size beds, free-standing bath tubs in the room and swanky en-suite bathrooms.

CONTACT 10 Crimp Hill, Old Windsor, Berkshire SL4 2QY • 01753 851 470 • lochandtyne.com

The Ginger Fox

The country outpost of a Brighton-based pub group, and like its sister premises, emphasizing local and seasonal food and drink, with Harveys beer and Ridgeview wine behind the bar, and local meat and fish on the menu. The pub itself is a picture-perfect thatch (topped by a thatched fox), with a lovely large garden. No rooms.

CONTACT Muddleswood Rd, Hassocks, East Sussex BN6 9EA • 01273 857888 • thegingerfox.com

The Crooked Billet

Run since 1990 by musician Paul Clerehugh, this trad-looking pub near Henley has developed a great following for its food, and foodies and celebs love it: Kate Winslet had her first wedding reception here, and the 'Observer' once voted it the 'UK's best Sunday lunch'. Much of the daily-changing menu comes from Clerehugh's smallholding and neighbouring farms, including beef, lamb, buffalo milk and honey ice-cream, and the pub hosts regular live music. No rooms.

CONTACT Newlands Lane, Stoke Row, Henley-on-Thames, Oxfordshire RG9 5PU • 01491 681 048 • thecrookedbillet.co.uk

The Running Horses

This 16th-century Surrey village local was once a popular coaching inn on the main road to Brighton and is still a comfy place to stay, though a much quieter one since they built the M23! They have just 5 rooms, all en-suite, and downstairs the pub serves a simple and short menu of rustic food that changes regularly but always includes a selection of steaks. It's a great base for scaling the heights of nearby Box Hill, the highest point on the North Downs, on foot or by bike.

CONTACT Old London Rd, Mickleham, Near Dorking, Surrey RH5 6DU • 01372 372 279 • therunninghorses.co.uk

The Stag on the River

This historic riverside village pub just outside Godalming has 7 lovely bedrooms and serves terrific food, culminating in a a superb breakfast. Very easy to reach too, just off the A3.

CONTACT Eashing, Near Godalming, Surrey GU7 2QG • 01483 421 568 • stagontherivereashing.co.uk

(Top) The Ginger Fox; (middle) The Stag on the River; (bottom) The Running Horses.

The Southwest

England's West Country is for many its most beguiling region, as well as its most diverse, varying in terrain from the flat lands of Salisbury Plain and the Somerset Levels to the rugged moors and cliffs of Devon and Cornwall. As a holiday region, it's blessed with legions of B&Bs and hotels, but you might just find staying in a pub a better alternative, at any number of superbly located seaside and country inns.

Lord Poulett Arms p.91

The Crown & Anchor

This Wiltshire village hostelry ticks all the boxes – with terrific food and some comfy upstairs rooms.

Situated in a pretty Wiltshire village, on the edge of the North Wessex Downs Area of Outstanding Natural Beauty, local pubs don't get much better than Ham's Crown & Anchor. Newly reopened a couple of years ago, it ticks all the boxes a proper 21st-century pub should – welcoming dogs, walkers and cyclists and serving local ales and excellent food. It even has some cosy rooms upstairs to collapse into at the end of the evening.

The pub has been completely refurbished following a brief period as a restaurant and is all the better for it – quite as inviting as a pub should be, with flagstone floors scattered with antique carpets, a curved wooden bar, a fireplace with a wood-burner and oak-panelled walls. Artworks range from old photographs to contemporary pieces by local artists,and are surrounded by the sort of informal mismatched furniture that urges you to take the weight off your feet, order a pint and pick up a newspaper. And on hot summer days the terrace at the back of the pub beckons.

The pub offers a good selection of local ales, including its own locally brewed bitter, and the short, moderately priced menu is a perfect blend of local, seasonal and above all British dishes, but with a modern twist – bar snacks like spicy lamb Scotch eggs, Brixham crab and shrimp ravioli, lovely local partridge and venison along with classics such as fish and chips and pithivier pie. There are eight individually furnished, very comfortable en-suite bedrooms, each named after a nearby farm and equipped with Hypnos mattresses and good-quality linen, Freeview TVs, tea- and coffee-making facilities, fresh milk and water and good wifi. The newly refurbished bathrooms are simple and elegant, with reclaimed wooden doors and decent showers (only one has a bath), and are provided with 100 Acre toiletries in eco-friendly sizes. Dogs are allowed in all rooms and get treats, a blanket and a dog bowl.

Finally, there's the location, which is the West Country, but only just, midway between Newbury and Marlborough and well placed for visiting Wiltshire's many highlights, from Avebury, Stonehenge and Salisbury to the gorgeous Vale of Pewsey and the real Downton Abbey, Highclere Castle. It's also in a perfect position for enjoying country walks, with three long-distance footpaths nearby and a great cycle route too. City folk take note – this is the ideal Friday night escape: you can be here in around an hour and a half from London, and, once here, you won't want to go back home. We guarantee it!

CONTACT Ham, Wiltshire SN8 3RB • 01488 503 040 • crownandanchorham.co.uk

HOW MUCH? Double rooms with breakfast £110–£130 a night.

ROOMS 8 very comfortable double bedrooms with en-suite bathrooms .

CROWN & ANCHOR
FREE HOUSE
RESTAURANT
ROOMS
GARDEN TERRACE

The Wheatsheaf Inn

Oh, where to start with this one? Except to say, if you're heading for the Cotswolds and are looking for somewhere offering top-notch food and some seriously stylish rooms, look no further – this 17th-century inn is a gem. The 14 individually styled and contemporary bedrooms offer king-size beds with Egyptian cotton duvets, B&O TVs with Sky, wifi and handmade toiletries. Power showers come as standard, but the top-line 'Excellent' rooms have baths as well – indeed one has a 2-person tub. Children are welcomed with open arms (there's a playhouse and fun kids' menu as well as rows of child-size Hunter wellies) and the pub 'welcomes dogs as much as people'. They're not kidding – dogs get a welcome bag complete with branded bandana and natural shampoo products! The area is full of glorious walks – a 4-hour round trip is particularly popular - and walking maps are provided. The large new garden, complete with pizza oven and bar, was opened a couple of years ago and is packed in summer, as is the restaurant, which is a destination in its own right.

CONTACT Northleach, Cheltenham, Gloucestershire GL54 3EZ • 01451 860 244 • cotswoldswheatsheaf.com
HOW MUCH? Double rooms from £135 a night, including breakfast.

The Ebrington Arms

It would be a challenge to find a pub more bucolic than the Ebrington Arms. Dating from the 1640s, this idyllic-looking inn backs on to rolling pastures at the edge of the tucked-away village of Ebrington, near handsome Chipping Campden in the north Cotswolds. Complete with inglenook fireplace, exposed beams and settles crafted from old beer barrels, it emanates warmth and is very much a village hub. It's also an epicurean, field-to-fork place to eat with a largely organic menu that offers such seasonal joys as stuffed courgettes with heritage tomatoes, and guinea fowl with white asparagus (you can practically see many of the ingredients arriving from the outlying fields!). The owners even make their own Yubberton ales, which sit alongside the carefully selected choice of beers. To one side of the property is a pretty walled garden and dining terrace. Upstairs are 5 rustic-chic bedrooms, mainly decorated in soothing cream and taupe. Room 2 (the smallest) has a cast-iron bed; the others have handcrafted oak beds made for each space. For the best views, go for Room 4.

CONTACT Ebrington, Gloucestershire GL55 6NH • 01386 593 223 • theebringtonarms.co.uk
HOW MUCH? Doubles from £169 a night, £199 at weekends, including breakfast.

The Lion Inn

Who wouldn't love a pub that combines the old and the new with characterful flourishes? The Lion does so with aplomb. This 15th-century coaching inn is in the heart of the timeless market town of Winchcombe, which lies in wonderful walking country, criss-crossed by long-distance footpaths. Step inside the pub and you're in a bright venue with rugs on flagstone floors, exposed stone walls and limed beams. To one side is an expansive dining area, to the other a cosy snug with a fireplace and armchairs. Behind this is the bar serving not only ales and wines but also seriously good cocktails. Food is a big draw here; the menu offers modern British cuisine (the likes of venison haunch with celeriac, and beetroot and lentil burgers) mainly based on local produce – Winchcombe residents are even encouraged to bring in homegrown veg for the kitchen in return for a drink. Decorated in soothing colours, the 8 bedrooms are rustic-stylish with retro touches, such as old-school phones; there are 4 upstairs above the pub and 4 set around the lovely courtyard garden.

CONTACT 37 North St, Winchcombe, Gloucestershire GL54 5PS • 01242 603 300 • thelionwinchcombe.co.uk
HOW MUCH? Double rooms £130–£160 a night, including breakfast.

The New Inn

A foodie burger pub with gorgeous accommodation and hip flourishes might sound an improbable mix. But at this 16th-century inn the combination has proved a winning one, thanks mostly to a duo known as Baz & Fred – aka Harry Henriques and Fred Hicks, who first launched The Stump pizza pub near Cirencester, and then, in 2020, revamped The New Inn. Décor in the public spaces is down-to-earth yet stylish, with open fires, retro church chairs and settles. There's a dedicated bar area if you just want a pint, as well as a series of restaurant rooms complete with a Negroni bar. Poster art on the walls adds funky touches. The menu presents affordable, handmade burgers as well as small plates and a couple of other main dishes like chicken and chips or grilled fish. The pub gives on to a courtyard where interconnecting buildings house 14 generously large bedrooms. Swathed in soothing greens and browns, they offer understated luxury with sink-into beds and eye-catching features such as, in one room, a mirror created from an antique door.

CONTACT Coln St Aldwyns, Gloucestershire GL7 5AN • 01285 708 080 • thenewinncoln.co.uk
HOW MUCH? Double rooms from £115 per night; garden suite from £179, all including breakfast.

The Gurnard's Head

Comfortable rooms above a perfectly placed dining pub overlooking the ocean.

A short walk inland from one of the most wild and rugged sections of the South West Coast Path, The Gurnard's Head is the sort of place where you can kick off your muddy boots by the roaring fire and sip a glass of world-class wine while the dog snoozes at your feet.

A glance at the art hanging on the granite walls hints also that – despite rustic appearances – this is the sort of place with an eye for the finer things in life, and sure enough the menu in the downstairs pub advertises all kinds of delicious seasonal, locally sourced and often innovative dishes. You can look forward to starting your meal with local mackerel or St Austell mussels before moving on to the likes of gurnard katsu curry or a magnificent lemon sole with samphire and capers, or maybe a wood pigeon, pig's head or pollock. They serve Cornish ales and local ciders on tap, and they are keen enough on vino to offer up to 20 wines by the carafe, so you can mix and match a little. They also have an interesting selection of Cognacs, Armagnacs and Calvados, including cider brandy from the West Country.

You can consider all this while you seek out your upstairs room, which will be furnished with a Vispring bed draped with Welsh wool blankets, a Roberts radio, fresh flowers, local art and shelves stacked with novels to distract you from the moorland views. Room sizes vary quite a bit, from small doubles with showers to large doubles with baths, but they're all priced accordingly, and some have sea views.

The briny air, hearty food and comfort levels at the Gurnard's Head tend to encourage such a deep sleep that you might not stir until the cows pass to be milked in the morning. But you need not stress: breakfast is a lazy affair (home-baked breads, kippers, Full English, local apple juice) and you won't be in a hurry to leave. Dogs and children are welcome – dog treats and cots are provided at no extra cost. B&B, Dinner B&B, and weekend escape packages are available – and the same people run the excellent Old Coastguard on the south side of Cornwall near Penzance.

CONTACT Near Zennor, St Ives, Cornwall TR26 3DE • 01736 796 928 • gurnardshead.co.uk
HOW MUCH? Double rooms from £140–£205 a night, including breakfast.
ROOMS 7 double en-suite rooms of various sizes, some with sea views.

GURNARDS
HEAD

The Old Coastguard

The last word in relaxation and good food, Cornish-style.

The folk behind this hotel cut their teeth on the excellent Gurnard's Head near Zennor and the two places have plenty in common, not least a glorious scenic location, great food and a determinedly laid-back vibe that is infectious. Situated in the picturesque seaside village of Mousehole, near Penzance, The Old Coastguard is not only back in business after a devastating fire a couple of years ago, it remains a supremely relaxing place to stay, with fourteen comfy guest rooms, all of which have some sort of view over the sea.

Downstairs, too, the laid-back atmosphere of the hotel is evident throughout: rows of sofas look seaward, children and dogs get a hearty welcome, and there's often live music in the restaurant alongside Sunday lunch. As with its sister hotel, the emphasis throughout is on comfort, good food and relaxation, with big comfy beds in spacious rooms equipped with Roberts radios and posh toiletries, high-quality tea and coffee, and lots of books to browse. Some rooms have balconies, and most have baths, but all are that little bit different. Whichever you choose you'll be so cosy you may not want to leave, but luckily there is plenty to tempt you downstairs, not least the hotel's outdoor terrace and lovely gardens, which stretch all the way down to the sea, plus a wood-panelled bar and of course what is a very high-quality restaurant. You can eat at stripped-down tables on the 'Upper Deck' or in the bar, or in the sun room or outside terrace overlooking the sea. What will you eat? It changes all the time, but naturally fish and seafood play a starring role: think Fowey mussels, skate wing with fennel and cockles or red mullet with cabbage and bacon, or pheasant sausage with puy lentils followed by duck breast with pickled pears. They also serve a selection of roasts on Sundays.

As for Mousehole itself, it's an archetypal Cornish harbour village, albeit with a contemporary patina of cafés, restaurants and galleries. Beyond, you can take to the coastal path – St Michael's Mount and the Lizard Peninsula are on your doorstep – take in a performance at the nearby Minack theatre, or just go to the beach – in which case you'll be delighted to be fairly close to wonderful Sennen Cove, which is a grand place for both lounging and more high-adrenaline activities like surfing.

CONTACT The Parade, Mousehole, Penzance, Cornwall TR19 6PR • 01736 731 222 • oldcoastguardhotel.co.uk
HOW MUCH? Double rooms £157.50–£265 a night, including breakfast.
ROOMS 14 en-suite guest rooms, all with sea views.

The Five Alls

If you want to stay somewhere a little bit off the radar on your trip to the Cotswolds, The Five Alls is the perfect place, set in the tiny village of Filkins and well-placed for the offbeat, undiscovered countryside hereabouts. In the same small group as The Bull in Fairford and The Plough in Kelmscott, the 9 rooms here – 4 in the original building and 5 in outhouses – are cosy, well-decorated and comfortable, with quirky local artwork, throws from nearby Cotswold Woollen Weavers, flatscreen TVs, high-quality mattresses and duck-feather duvets; one of them is large enough for a family and the bathrooms are smart and have Ren toiletries. Nothing is too much trouble for the staff who are welcoming and helpful to all. The main draw of The Five Alls, however, is the food – good gastropub fare served in the pub's 3 cosy dining rooms and including not only a great breakfast but a good roast on Sundays, too. As for the location, you're a short drive from Burford and the edge of the Cotswolds, but take time also to explore the nearby church and the pretty village before you leave.

CONTACT Filkins, Lechlade, Gloucestershire GL7 3JQ • 01367 860 875 • thefiveallsfilkins.co.uk
HOW MUCH? Double rooms £72–£92 a night, not including breakfast.

The Old Stocks Inn

Located in the popular tourist honeypot of Stow-on-the-Wold, this 17th-century coaching inn was refurbished a few years ago and now has 16 stylish bedrooms that blend old and new, with original features mixing seamlessly with contemporary design. Needless to say, there is a variety of rooms in all sorts of shapes and sizes, and they have been quirkily titled to help you decide: 'Amazing Great Rooms' are for pushing the boat out, with capacious bedrooms complete with a complimentary minibar and bags of character; 'Cosy House Rooms' are slightly smaller, tucked away at the top of the hotel – think original beams, soothing colours and views down to the Square or the attractive walled garden; or there is the super-cool 'Bunker' family option – which has a double bed and a triple bunk bed and games console and is the perfect place to keep kids occupied. There is also a 6-person self-catering cottage, Parson's Barn, just footsteps from the pub. As for food, it's more of a restaurant than a pub, if we're honest, dishing up decent local and seasonal British cuisine.

CONTACT The Square, Stow-on-the-Wold, Gloucestershire GL54 1AF • 01451 830 666 • oldstocksinn.com
HOW MUCH? 'Cosy House Rooms' from £129 a night.

The Plough Inn

Under the same ownership as The Five Alls in Filkins, this pub has a similarly enticing formula: good food in cosy surroundings, with a group of guest rooms upstairs (7 doubles, 1 single) that have been refurbished to a standard that is chic but also eminently comfortable, with luxurious king-size beds with high-quality linen, walk-in showers or baths and great views over the surrounding countryside and the village. Downstairs, it is – at least in part – still a proper pub, where people come just to have a pint, but it also serves food that is both hearty and refined and can be enjoyed in the pub or in the pleasant garden. Kelmscott itself is a great place to stay, within easy reach of London and Bristol but with a fabulous get-away-from-it-all feel. There are lots of lovely walks nearby, not least on the Thames Path just a few minutes away. You're also a hop, skip and a jump from William Morris's country house at Kelmscott Manor, and Blenheim Palace and the Cotswold Wildlife Park are just a short drive away. All in all, it's a great place for a romantic weekend escape!

CONTACT Kelmscott, Lechlade, Gloucestershire GL7 3HG • 01367 253 543 • theploughinnkelmscott.com
HOW MUCH? Double rooms from £95 a night, not including breakfast.

Lord Poulett Arms

Contender for one of Somerset's prettiest villages, Hinton St George is also home to one of the county's most enduring hostelries, the 17th-century Lord Poulett Arms, owned by the same people as the excellent Talbot in Mells. A beautifully proportioned building, it has 6 bedrooms of contrasting styles and sizes – 2 with private bathrooms across the hall (the others are all properly en-suite), one with a slipper bar in the bedroom, while the largest has a double bed and 2 bunks so is great for families. Throughout, creamy-white and bare brick walls are offset with splashes of colour from throws, patterned rugs and bedside lamps, while Siberian goose-down bedding offers the promise of a marvellous night's sleep. There's a time-worn bar brimming with villagey atmosphere thanks to a merry band of locals, while the restaurant features a choice of innovative dishes and pub standards made with ingredients harvested in the kitchen garden. The real revelation, however, is the outdoor space, comprising a French parterre with pétanque piste and pelota wall, beyond which is a heavily scented orchard.

CONTACT High St, Hinton St George, Somerset TA17 8SE • 01460 73149 • lordpoulettarms.com
HOW MUCH? Double rooms £95–£115 a night, including breakfast.

The Talbot Inn

A photogenic building set around a sunny cobbled courtyard, this venerable inn retains over 500 years of history. The current owners took charge in 2013 and have since created a haven of style and comfort, with in-room facilities to rival the very best boutique hotels. There are 8 differently sized rooms – all but one located above the pub – the largest boasting a magnificent 4-poster bed alongside a freestanding tub and a separate sitting area. All rooms come with thoughtful extra flourishes, like hot-water bottles, an array of magazines and pure wool Welsh blankets. Enticing guests downstairs is a sequence of 4 separate areas – dining room, sitting room, snug and bar, the latter with an inglenook fireplace to warm your bones. The barn across the yard offers further possibilities: perhaps a game of scrabble, or just a space to chill. Sunday night film screenings, meanwhile, give the perfect excuse to extend that weekend stay. A gut-busting breakfast will set you up nicely for a day's exploration of this almost unprecedentedly historic village, which 'Conde Nast Traveller' reckoned to be one of the country's 'Top 20 Villages' as recently as 2020.

CONTACT Mells, Somerset BA11 3PN • 01373 812 254 • talbotinn.com

HOW MUCH? Doubles £110–£170 a night, including breakfast.

The Sheppey

Secreted away at the heart of the Somerset Levels, you wouldn't give this unprepossessing roadside pub a second glance. But step inside and the Sheppey is fun and funky, from the cool-as-a-cucumber bar to the retro furnishings and Hockney prints. Actually a converted dairy farm, the accommodation comes in the guise of 3 rooms above the pub and 2 adjoining cottages a short walk across the fields. The modest-sized rooms are artfully decorated with paisley-style wallpaper and music- and film-themed pictures and posters; the best has reclaimed vintage telephone doors and a copper bath, while another offers unencumbered views of Glastonbury Tor; bathrooms come with freestanding tubs and jumbo-sized rain showers. The two cottages offer more solitude, each with an upstairs bedroom and a well-equipped kitchen and a living space with good-sized sofas, book-packed shelves and a wood-burner. While here it'd be remiss not to sample the pub's awesome food – perhaps a bowl of Sheppey fish stew out on the waterside terrace – and if you're staying on a Friday, expect to hear some top-drawer live music.

CONTACT Lower Godney, Glastonbury, Somerset BA5 1RZ • 01458 831 594 • thesheppey.co.uk

HOW MUCH? Doubles £100–£140 a night. Cottage £120–£140. Rates include continental breakfast.

The Litton

On the eastern fringes of the Mendips, this sprawling complex of stone buildings from the 15th-century has been brilliantly revived by owner Sally Billington after laying dormant for years. Originally the site of a mill, The Litton harbours 12 polished rooms, roughly split between the pub itself and a neighbouring cottage. Bearing ethereal names like Litune and Watery Combe, they variously feature stripped-back walls and oak beams alongside a vaulted ceiling here or an exposed fireplace there. All but 2 come with garden or river view, while those in the cottage share a private patio. Families are catered for with 2 linked rooms; one room has facilities (including a wet room) for disabled guests; and dogs are welcome – towels, snacks and a drop of Pawsecco are among the treats. There's a long, light-filled restaurant, a log-warmed bar, a waterside terrace with firepit, and landscaped garden furnished with upcycled beer barrels and a re-purposed horsebox bar. And if you don't fancy an extended yomp around the Mendips, Sally has devised a less strenuous local walk before you roll back to the bar.

CONTACT Litton, Near Wells, Somerset BA3 4PW • 01761 241 554 • thelitton.co.uk

HOW MUCH? Doubles £140–£180 a night, including breakfast.

The Royal Oak

A hop and a skip from Tetbury's engaging centre, this handsome 18th-century tavern is a winner for homespun charm, community spirit and eco-friendliness. The heartbeat of the enterprise is a long saloon with an art deco upright piano, reconditioned jukebox and upcycled furnishings. Locals pop in for a pint, and to enjoy well-priced meals and live music events. Food – Thai fish burgers, roasted coconut and lime salmon and always a choice of vegan dishes – is also served in the upstairs dining room, a wonderfully atmospheric space complete with exposed beams and wrought-iron chandeliers. During the summer an Airstream trailer offers world street food on the garden terrace. There's a separate annexe for the stylish accommodation - a former barn with a skittles alley that has been beautifully revamped to contain 6 bedrooms over 2 floors. These have retro-chic furnishings and are decorated in quiet cream, blues and browns. The largest and most sumptuous of the lot is the Oak Lodge suite, with leather armchairs and the capacity to comfortably sleep 4 people.

CONTACT 1 Cirencester Road, Tetbury, Gloucestershire GL8 8EY • 01666 500 021 • theroyaloaktetbury.co.uk

HOW MUCH? Double rooms £90–£135 a night, including breakfast.

The Lamb Inn

A proper village pub with rooms and great food in the green heart of Devon.

There are some pubs that get just about everything right, and The Lamb Inn, just outside Crediton, bang in the middle of the green heart of Devon, comes pretty close. It's a proper village pub, for a start, with plenty of locals popping by just for a drink, but it serves excellent food too and has a handful of rooms upstairs to tempt you into staying overnight. No surprise, then, that it has featured in the Daily Mail's '20 Best British Country Pubs', has won 'Best Devon Pub' and was voted the i-newspaper's 'Best UK Summer Pub' a couple of years ago. Clearly this is no ordinary village boozer, although we're pleased to say that it still has the feel of one.

The Lamb is actually a 16th-century coaching inn at heart, but its eight guest rooms are by no means stuck in the past. They're crisply refurbished in a contemporary style, with luxurious king-size beds, flatscreen TVs with Freeview, good wifi, tea- and fresh coffee-making facilities and complimentary water, and recently updated bathrooms, some of which have giant baths in which to luxuriate. There's good wifi and a scattering of newspapers in the bar downstairs to make you feel at home, and overall the feel is both cosy and comfortable, but with the sort of service and facilities you would expect from a decent hotel.

The pub itself is furnished in a traditional style, with a roaring fire in winter and a pleasant beer garden to enjoy in summer. The food is excellent – with a short and fairly traditional menu with innovative touches and really good cooking; there's plenty for vegetarians and the Sunday roasts are superb. Like all good pubs, The Lamb is also dog-friendly, with dogs welcome throughout the pub and in all guest rooms.

Finally, The Lamb is an easy place to reach – just outside the small Devon market town of Crediton, not far from the M5 and just off the main north–south Exeter to Barnstaple route. Dartmoor is a short drive away, as is Exeter and the coast beyond. All in all, this is a terrific place for a a short but indulgent countryside break.

CONTACT The Square, Sandford, Crediton, Devon EX17 4LW • 01363 773 676 • lambinnsandford.co.uk
HOW MUCH? Double rooms £94–£124 a night, including breakfast.
ROOMS Guest rooms from £59–£149 a night, not including breakfast.

It's all about me
DEVON LIFE

The Bull

Reopened in March 2017, this revamped coaching inn sits invitingly on the market square of the Cotswolds town of Fairford. It's actually made up of what used to be 2 separate pubs, The Bull and The George, and has a spacious interior decorated with bold colours and styles that drag the building into the 21st century while still managing to retain a sense of timelessness with an eclectic assortment of antiques, lighting and well-chosen textiles. There is a large and comfortable bar with open fires, local ales and plenty of places to loll about, and a welcoming restaurant fashioned out of the inn's old stables that serves a menu of hearty Mediterranean and modern British dishes along with stone-baked pizzas. It has 21 rooms, individually furnished to reflect their various shapes and sizes, and decorated mainly in off-whites and greys with splashes of colour here and there. They have feather and down duvets and good-quality linen, flatscreen Freeview TVs, wifi and tea- and coffee-making facilities, and en-suite bathrooms with walk-in showers; toiletries are by local outfit Wold Garden.

CONTACT Market Place, Fairford, Gloucestershire GL7 4AA • 01285 712 535 • thebullhotelfairford.co.uk
HOW MUCH? Small double rooms from around £75 a night, including breakfast; £120 for a junior suite.

The Noel Arms

This old Cotswolds stone inn is steeped in history – it is even said that Charles II stayed here during the Civil War – and is situated in one of the most picturesque villages in the Cotswolds. But it has been considerably updated over the years and now shares ownership with its sister property across the road, Cotswold House, which makes it one of the few pubs in this book where you can enjoy the benefits of a steam room or a massage. Not only that, its 28 rooms are comfortably furnished and well equipped; bathrooms are serviceable and come with White Company toiletries, while all of them are dog-friendly and a couple come with 4-posters. You can eat in the bar or the more formal restaurant downstairs, and the food is high quality and locally sourced, although what the Noel Arms is really known for is its Indian food, with chef Indunil Sanchi named Best Curry Chef at the Great British Pub awards on 3 occasions; his monthly Curry Nights are hugely popular, in particular because of his Black Lamb curry signature dish.

CONTACT High St, Chipping Campden, Gloucestershire GL55 6AT• 0844 815 9833 • bespokehotels.com/noelarmshotel
HOW MUCH? Doubles with breakfast £130 a night.

The Crown Inn

For a great pub in a truly glorious setting, look no further. Dating from 1633, the Crown's venerable main building was originally a cider house; in the course of time it became the quintessential Cotswold inn - with a welcoming fireplace, exposed honey-stone walls and ancient, undulating beams. Its outlook on to the Golden Valley of the River Frome is serene. The location is very rural yet easily accessible – pretty Frampton Mansell is just 12 miles from Cirencester. From its hearty menu (homemade burgers, spicy veg mains, Sunday roasts) to its bar stocked with an impressive range of Gloucestershire ales, the Crown is a no-nonsense, traditional inn with lots of local flavour, and most nights of the week a local crowd, too (Bonfire Night here is near-legendary). It exudes a sense of cordiality. In a separate, purpose-built annexe away from all the pub activity and noise, there are 12 peaceful, streamlined bedrooms offering homey comfort at pleasingly competitive rates – it would be a difficult call to find better value in the Cotswolds.

CONTACT Frampton Mansell, Gloucestershire GL6 8JG • 01285 760 601 • thecrowninn-cotswolds.co.uk
HOW MUCH? Doubles from £95 a night, including breakfast. Family room from £150 a night.

The Cat & Custard Pot

If you're after local flavour and quietly traditional style, The Cat & Custard Pot will absolutely appeal. Back in 2014, four families in the Shipton Moyne area acquired this characterful pub primarily to preserve it for the community. They've been careful to keep its old-school spirit, with a cosy log burner, armchairs and rugs on wooden floors, tankards and horse brasses. In the bar and the dining area, it offers good, honest food at down-to-earth prices: homemade pies and fish and chips, seasonal delights like slow-cooked ox cheek with celeriac, and vegetarian Wellington with wild mushrooms. There's also a terrace where traditional-style pizzas are served, and a back room has a large TV showing sporting fixtures, especially equestrian events – the pub is in the heart of horse country. It offers good walking, too, and is close to the cafés and antique shops of Tetbury. There's an almost tangible sense of cordiality; The Cat is much loved by local residents and a growing band of repeat visitors. Simply clad in creams and browns, its 8 bedrooms, set above the bar and in a neighbouring cottage, offer sink-into beds and homely comfort.

CONTACT The Street, Shipton Moyne, Gloucestershire GL8 8PN • 01666 880 249 • catandcustard.co.uk
HOW MUCH? Small double from £90 a night; bigger doubles £120–£140; prices include breakfast.

The Swan at Wedmore

A quintessential Somerset pub located in a beautiful Somerset village.

Anyone seeking a quintessential Somerset pub in a quintessential Somerset village need look no further than the lovely Swan at Wedmore – and with the gregarious Annie overseeing operations, and Tom Blake, formerly of River Cottage, heading up the kitchen, this handsome former coaching inn is currently in great hands.

The pub's seven rooms consist of one small, two medium and three large rooms as well as a restful second-floor loft room. Size aside, the main difference between the small and medium rooms and the larger ones is that the former have a bathtub only, and wall pegs for clothes instead of wardrobes. Rooms are decorated in elegant greys with splashes of bright colours courtesy of scatter cushions and throws, pictures and posters, and hummingbird print wallpaper. Furnishings are mostly French vintage style: mirrored dressers, bedside tables, armchairs and window shutters – all very chic. Fresh milk is provided, along with scrummy biscuits, cafetiéres and Teapigs teabags, and handmade Lovegrove bath and body products are provided in the bathrooms.

Downstairs, locals and visitors happily rub along together in the spacious bar – part lounge, part snug – beyond which is a slightly more formal dining area, the only part of the pub in which dogs (who are otherwise made very welcome) are not allowed. The food is local and seasonal and much of its is homemade – bread and cakes, home-cured ham and bacon – on a nice, simple menu focused around local lamb, fish and veggie dishes, and a selection of roasts on Sundays. The pub also serves sandwiches and bar snacks all day in case you're peckish. You can eat in the bar or restaurant, or, in summer, both drinkers and diners move out to the stone terrace or the immaculate lawned garden.

Finally, Wedmore itself is a pleasant village on the edge of the Somerset Levels, that offers wonderful sanctuary, along with some of Britain's finest birdwatching. The peaks and gorges of the Mendip Hills are also just a few miles to the north.

CONTACT Cheddar Road, Wedmore, Somerset BS28 4EQ • 01934 710 337 • theswanwedmore.com

HOW MUCH? Double rooms £75–£165 a night, including breakfast. Dogs £10 a night.

ROOMS 7 guest bedrooms – one small, 2 medium, 3 large, plus a loft room.

THE SWAN
WINES & SPIRITS
PARKING

The Horse & Groom Inn

A proper country coaching inn, recently refurbished and situated in an attractive Wiltshire village.

Dating back to the 16th century, this grade II-listed coaching inn reopened a couple of years ago after a major refurbishment, and is a lovely old pub that has had some new life breathed into it by its new owners, the West Country's Butcombe Brewery. Situated on the edge of the Cotswolds, not far from the small but historic town of Malmesbury, Wiltshire, it makes for a tremendous place to stay while soaking up the delights of what is an extremely historic area.

Downstairs, the pub is all beams, bare brick walls and big fireplaces, combined with leather banquettes and mismatched, scrubbed tables that create a contemporary vibe. Upstairs, it has five beautifully updated bedrooms, divided between spacious 'Signature Plus' rooms and cosier 'Snug' rooms on the top floor. They're all nicely decorated with either free-standing baths or showers, and luxury Bramley toiletries – the Snug rooms have roll-top baths while the Signature rooms have showers. Smart TVs, tea- and coffee-making facilities, and – where there's room – a desk. There is also good wifi throughout,

As for the food, it's worth a trip even if you're not staying. It's very seasonal, and pubby too, with a good selection of steaks, delicious local venison in season, a decent burger and fish and chips, as well as more adventurous dishes like ox-cheek bourguignon, duck rillettes and squash risotto – all naturally washed down with some of Butcombe's excellent beers.

Finally, Charlton is a nice village with an ancient church, while Malmesbury is a particularly charming town of independent shops, pubs and cafés – a lovely place for a stroll in the summer sunshine. It has a good Friday market, the river Avon winds a lazy course through the centre, and its partially ruined abbey is a commanding sight near the high street. You're also right on the edge of the southern Cotswolds, for which The Horse & Groom is a viable alternative base.

CONTACT The Street, Charlton, Malmesbury, Wiltshire SN16 9DL • 01666 823 904 • butcombe.com/the-horse-and-groom-wiltshire

HOW MUCH? Double rooms £115–£140 a night, including breakfast.

ROOMS 5 guest bedrooms, divided between spacious 'Signature Plus' rooms and cosier 'Snug' rooms.

THE HORSE
AND GROOM INN

The White Hart

The small Devon town of Moretonhampstead, right on the edge of Dartmoor, is the perfect location for a countryside break. The White Hart is a historic old coaching inn with a diverse selection of rooms, many of which have been recently updated, with flatscreen Freeview TVs tea-and coffee-making facilities and en-suite bathrooms. It's dog friendly too, with dogs staying free in their 20 cosy bedrooms and made very comfortable in their public areas as well, especially the cosy bar, where there's a roaring fire for them to lie in front of after long day's traversing the moor, along with a selection of local ales for their thirsty owners. As for food, the menu is perfectly pitched at weary walkers: short, sweet and very local, with Dartmoor beef, lamb and venison and local fish alongside pub standards. Moretonhampstead itself is a pleasant town and very much the gateway to Dartmoor, with countless footpaths to explore: try the recently opened 'Wray Valley Trail', which follows an old railway line for around 6.5 miles to Newton Abbot, via the impossibly picturesque Dartmoor village of Lustleigh.

CONTACT The Square, Moretonhampstead, Devon TQ13 8NQ • 01647 440 500 • whitehartdartmoor.co.uk
HOW MUCH? Double rooms from £120 a night, including breakfast.

The Cricket Inn

Tucked away in the pretty little coastal village of Beesands, just 7 miles from Kingsbridge and 12 miles from Dartmouth, The Cricket Inn is a beautiful seaside spot by any standards – a quaint fishing inn that has been reinvented as a light and spacious gastropub with a handful of comfortable rooms upstairs to collapse into after a pleasant evening. It feels wonderfully remote, with 7 rooms in all, 5 of which have jaw-achingly beautiful views of nearby Start Bay, which you can enjoy without even getting out of bed. There's a seaside-cum-nautical theme throughout, and all the rooms – variously named after cricket grounds and cricketers – come with en-suite baths (some have spacious walk-in showers too), complimentary toiletries, flatscreen TVs, tea and coffee and room treats, free wifi and extremely comfortable king-size beds. In the morning its mighty Devonshire breakfast is a fabulous herald of what's to come later on: local crab, lobster and scallops, fish and chips, and local lamb and beef from the green rolling pastures that surround the inn, cooked on a charcoal grill.

CONTACT Beesands, Kingsbridge, Devon TQ7 2EN • 01548 580 215 • thecricketinn.com
HOW MUCH? Double rooms from £120 a night, including breakfast.

The Broad Street Townhouse

Part of the West Country-based Butcombe Brewery group, this is a boutique hotel with pub attached, right in the heart of Bath. The hotel is a slick Victorian townhouse with a selection of bedrooms on one of the city centre's most interesting streets, home to a typically Bath-esque mixture of indy shops and places to eat and drink. It has 11 cool and sassy bedrooms, each making the most of the building's 19th-century origins while elevating them to the 21st century, with a neutral palette and splashes of colour on the beds, windows and walls. Bathrooms are right-up-to-date, with faux old-fashioned tiles and spacious walk-in showers – just what every West Country hipster needs. There are Dyson fans, Roberts radios, espresso makers and mini fridges crammed with Butcombe ales, soft drinks and fresh milk for tea and coffee. A continental breakfast is laid out every morning in the downstairs café, which is also open all day for drinks and snacks. Next door, The Pig & Fiddle has been revamped as a thoroughly modern boozer, serving excellent food and bar snacks, live TV sport, and naturally a range of Butcombe ales.

CONTACT 32 Broad St, Bath, Somerset BA1 5LP • 01225 485 760 • butcombe.com/broad-street-townhouse-bath
HOW MUCH? Double rooms from £120 a night, including breakfast.

The Salutation Inn

This classy revamp of a 17th-century pub is a terrific place to stay and to eat, with 4 bright, spacious rooms and 2 suites, all turned out in crisp tones, featuring very comfortable handmade beds and en-suite bathrooms with upscale toiletries. Topsham itself is a lovely place to stay, an old heritage port, handy both for Exeter and the coast at Exmouth, and it's perhaps no surprise that The Salutation won 'Food & Travel' magazine's 'Best UK B&B' award a few years ago. There's no pub bar any more, but the Glass House café in the historic inn's courtyard makes a cheery port of call any time from breakfast through to afternoon tea, while the restaurant gives the chance to sample some of the best local fish and seafood you'll find, from a menu that features Lyme Bay scallops, Teignmouth lobsters and pan-roasted pollock, alongside local wood pigeon and beef. There are also lighter options served at lunchtime, when you can enjoy anything from a Caesar Salad to moules mariniéres or a steak baguette. Finally if you like what you've had, you can buy it at The Salutation's very own fresh fish counter.

CONTACT 68 Fore St, Topsham, Exeter, Devon EX3 0HL • 01392 873 060 • salutationtopsham.co.uk
HOW MUCH? Double rooms £120–£145 a night, suites £190–£210, not including breakfast.

Cary Arms & Spa

Perhaps the perfect Devon seaside inn, updated as a sumptuous boutique hotel for the 21st century.

Despite the name, this is, if we're honest, more of a hotel and restaurant than a pub. But its location, tucked away on scenic Babbacombe Bay, makes it impossible to leave out. That and the fact that this is a seaside inn to die for, brilliantly combining traditional Devon delights with good food and a unique array of accommodation options: ten boutique rooms and suites, four restored fisherman's cottages, six quirky huts and two beach suites on the beach. The hotel was famously visited by Queen Victoria and Prince Albert, who were apparently rowed ashore here for a cream tea, and it remains at heart a coastal inn but with an up-to-date feel that is more New England than the English Riviera.

The rooms and suites all have fabulous sea views and their own terraces, along with king-size beds with good-quality linen, Smart TVs, tea-and coffee-making facilities, complimentary bottled water and a decanter of sloe gin, and White Company toiletries and waffle bathrobes in the en-suite bathrooms – two of the ground floor rooms welcome dogs, as do the three of the four cottages, which are a great alternative for couples seeking a bit more privacy, or for families. Dogs are also welcome in two of the beach huts and one of the beach suites, right at the water's edge.

You may be reluctant to leave your little capsule of comfort down by the sea, and you could quite happily spend a few days here and not emerge, pottering around on the beach, having a pint or two in the beamed bar while you watch the sunset, or eating in the hotel's excellent restaurant, which serves good simple gastropub food centred on local beef and lamb, and of course the freshest fish and seafood; it's moderately priced and it also offers a great-value set lunch menu. They have a comfy lounge and billiard room, and a spa with a gym, steam room, sauna, hydrotherapy pool and the usual treatments. There's also a decked sun terrace with an outdoor fire and boxes of blankets for winter days.

It is worth leaving occasionally, however, if only to experience the 1920s funicular railway that takes you up to Babbacombe proper – best known for its model village, which remains one of the Torquay area's best-known attractions. Beyond here you can explore the nearby bays of Oddicombe and Petitor Downs, which are connected by footpath. The Petitor cliffs are the source of Torquay's extraordinary marble pavements, while the waters off Oddicombe are a haven for divers who come here to explore the reedy shallows and various nearby wrecks.

CONTACT Babbacombe Beach, Devon TQ1 3LX • 01803 327 110 • caryarms.co.uk
HOW MUCH? Rooms and suites from £269 a night; beach huts and suites from £389 a night; cottages from £495 a night; £990 for 3 nights or £2475 for 7 nights. Dogs cost £20 a night, for which they get their own bed and bowl.
ROOMS 10 guest rooms and suites in the main building, plus 4 2–3 bedroom holiday cottages and 8 2-person beach huts and beach suites by the water's edge.

Lucky Dip

Cove House Inn

A cosy pub with thick stone walls, wooden floors and a wood-burner, offering views of Chesil Beach and the sea. It has outside tables overlooking the beach and it's a great spot for a drink on a warm summer's evening. Good-value pub staples are served and there's also a daily specials board, which is strong on local fish dishes, such as Portland crab linguine. No rooms.

CONTACT 91 Chiswell, Portland, Dorset DT5 1AW • 01305 820 895 • thecovehouseinn.co.uk

The Square & Compass

A Dorset institution, built as a pair of cottages in the 18th century and with a bar that is simply a hatch in the wall and an interior that's just a couple of rooms, warmed in winter by log fires and a mass of people and dogs. The pub puts on frequent live music, crams in its own museum of local fossils and marine life and hosts a number of annual festivals, including a stone-carving festival and an autumn competition for the biggest local pumpkin. The garden, too, is a fascinating hotchpotch of stone stools and carved chairs overlooking superb countryside, while the pub's ales, ciders and famous homemade pies and pasties really hit the spot. No rooms.

CONTACT Weston Rd, Worth Matravers, Dorset BH19 3LF • 01929 439 229 • squareandcompasspub.co.uk

The Smuggler's Inn

Nestled in a pretty valley by the sea, this thatched 13th-century pub has a lovely garden with a stream running through and a children's play area, while inside it couldn't be cosier, with wooden beams and real fires. Run by local brewery Hall & Woodhouse, it has a good range of Badger local ales and serves freshly made, unpretentious pub grub, such as steak and Tanglefoot ale steak pie. No rooms.

CONTACT Osmington Mills, Weymouth, Dorset DT3 6HF • 01305 833125 • smugglersinnosmingtonmills.co.uk

Scott Arms

The pretty village of Kingston is frequently used as a film backdrop, and when it is the Scott Arms is often the centrepiece. You'll be hard pushed to find a better view than the one from the pub's garden – a dazzling panorama of Corfe Castle – and inside it's as cosy as can be and serves a menu that champions local, seasonal ingredients. The pub's not based in Kingston for nothing – the garden hosts a Jamaican barbecue between June and September, and they have live music most weekends. There is a couple of rooms to let upstairs too.

CONTACT West St, Kingston, Corfe Castle, Dorset BH20 5LH • 01929 480 270 • thescottarms.com

Haunch of Venison

Salisbury's most celebrated watering hole dates back to the 12th century, but what could have been a tacky medieval theme pub is instead a no-nonsense boozer where locals sup a pint in shoebox-sized rooms of wood panelling and old beams. There's a great choice of real ales, including local beers from the Hop Back Brewery down the road; and, if you want to eat, there's a larger, lighter restaurant upstairs, where you can feast on the likes of slow-braised pig cheeks and local venison. There are 2 kinds of spirits too, most interestingly a ghostly lady and a phantom card cheat, whose mummified hand was found interred in a wall when they knocked through to the restaurant. No rooms.

CONTACT 1 Minster St, Salisbury, Wiltshire SP1 1TB • 01722 411 313 • haunchpub.co.uk

Bankes Arms

This ivy-clad Purbeck stone pub is a perfect winter bolthole just off the South West Coast Path – though it truly comes into its own in the summer when you can chill out in its huge grassy front garden, which has dazzling views over the coast. The pub has its own microbrewery and serves a range of home-brewed ales and ciders, as well as generous portions of pub grub. And if you can't face the journey home, it has 10 comfortable rooms to let upstairs.

CONTACT Manor Rd, Studland, Dorset BH9 3AU • 01929 450 225 • bankesarms.com

The Compasses Inn

Oozing history and character, one of Wiltshire's finest country pubs also serves sensational food – mainly gutsy British dishes using local ingredients, with the odd Asian or international influence, as well as a handful of pub classics. Factor in good real ales and a genuinely welcoming host and you have a gem of a pub. Expect to lose an afternoon – or better still, stay the night in one of 4 pleasant rooms upstairs.

CONTACT Lower Chickgrove, Tisbury, Wiltshire SP3 6NB • 01722 714 318 • thecompassesinn.co.uk

(Top) The Square & Compass; (middle) Bankes Arms; (bottom) The Smuggler's Inn.

The Rising Sun

On a summer's day the terrace at The Rising Sun is packed with punters jostling for a pew with a view over the beach and the mouth of the River Fal. Welcoming dogs and children into the mix, there's hardly a reason to pass by without popping in for a pint or a plate of decent food, which is local and seasonal with a traditional pub-grub edge – scallops, scampi, sausage and mash, or local catch with homemade chips. And you don't need a summer's day to enjoy the offerings of this traditional pub, which manages to stay cosy all winter, and has 8 comfy rooms upstairs in case you want to stay over.

CONTACT The Square, St Mawes, Cornwall TR2 5DJ • 01326 270 233 • risingsunstmawes.co.uk

The Pigs Nose Inn

Think of Camden Town circa 1985 transported to the middle of nowhere and you'll get some idea of this popular pub and music venue. Set on the most southerly point of Devon, this former smugglers' inn is now cluttered with junk and fading muso-memorabilia, and is usually full of regulars. There's often live music going on in the adjacent parish hall, and in the summer it's frequented by the campers who use the fields around the village to wild camp. There's a pool room, games and toys for children and the whole place is laid-back, shambolic... and great. Food is basic but tasty pub fare. Play 'spot the once-famous ageing punks' in the high season. No rooms.

CONTACT East Prawle, KIngsbridge, Devon TQ7 2BY • 01548 511 209 • pigsnoseinn.co.uk

The Maltsters Arms

Located on a creek off the River Dart, just a few miles from Totnes, this pub offers a warm welcome, great beer and good food – indeed it was once owned by infamous TV chef, Keith Floyd. Above all it's a great place to enjoy a meal al fresco, but you need to allow yourself plenty of time if you want a table with a waterside view. It's a lovely spot, too, to wake up in, and they have 6 contemporary rooms so you can!

CONTACT Tuckenhay, Near Totnes, Devon TQ9 7EQ 3RR • 01803 732 350 • the-maltsters.co.uk

The Shave Cross Inn

You'd be hard pushed to find a prettier beer garden than that of The Shave Cross Inn, a quaint 700-year-old pub in the heart of West Dorset, which has flagstone floors and roaring open fireplaces. Outside there's a thatched well, pond, and, if that's not enough, Britain's oldest skittle alley, which now serves as the local cinema! It also has 4 spacious guest bedrooms, and glamping pods in its paddock.

CONTACT Shave Cross, Bridport, Dorset DT6 6HW • 01308 868 358 • shavecrossinn.co.uk

The Greyhound Inn

With a garden backing on to Corfe Castle, this 15th-century pub is the social hub of the village, with live music most weekends and good pub food, including Blandford sausages, local game casserole with dumplings and Poole Bay mussels. The pub hosts various foodie festivals, including a Cider and Sausage Festival, a Seafood Festival and a Beer and Cider Festival. No rooms.

CONTACT The Square, Corfe Castle, Dorset BH20 5EZ • 01929 480 205 • greyhoundcorfe.co.uk

The Rock Inn

Excellent real ales and historic character are good reasons to visit this 17th-century inn. But it's the menu that makes it an institution for locals and in-the-know visitors. Expect local crab, Exmoor steak, Fowey river mussels, half a pint of prawns with lemon garlic aioli or tapas-style browsing boards alongside upmarket pub classics. No rooms.

CONTACT Rock Hill, Georgeham, Devon EX33 1JW • 01271 890 322 • therockinn.biz

The Godolphin

Located in the historic market town of Marazion, The Godolphin sits by the water's edge facing St Michael's Mount. and boasting several drinking and dining spaces decked out in chic style, with coastal hues and local art; there's an upper deck with sofas and a log-burner, and a chilled-out lower deck with a beach bar.The food is good and they also have 10 stylish rooms in case you want to stay.

CONTACT West End, Marazion, Cornwall TR17 0EN • 01736 888 510 • thegodolphin.com

The Wheatsheaf

If you're looking for the perfect West Country pub then you might like to try this farmhouse-turned-alehouse in the idyllic village of Combe Hay, just outside Bath. It's a gastropub, farm shop and also a place to stay. It's extremely dog friendly, serves excellent fresh, local, seasonal and sustainable food, and has 3 lovely rooms, a spacious suite and a handful of bell tents for glampers.

CONTACT Combe Hay, Bath, Somerset BA2 7EG • 01225 833 504 • wheatsheafcombehay.com

(Top) The Wheatsheaf; (middle) The Godolphin; (bottom) The Shave Cross Inn.

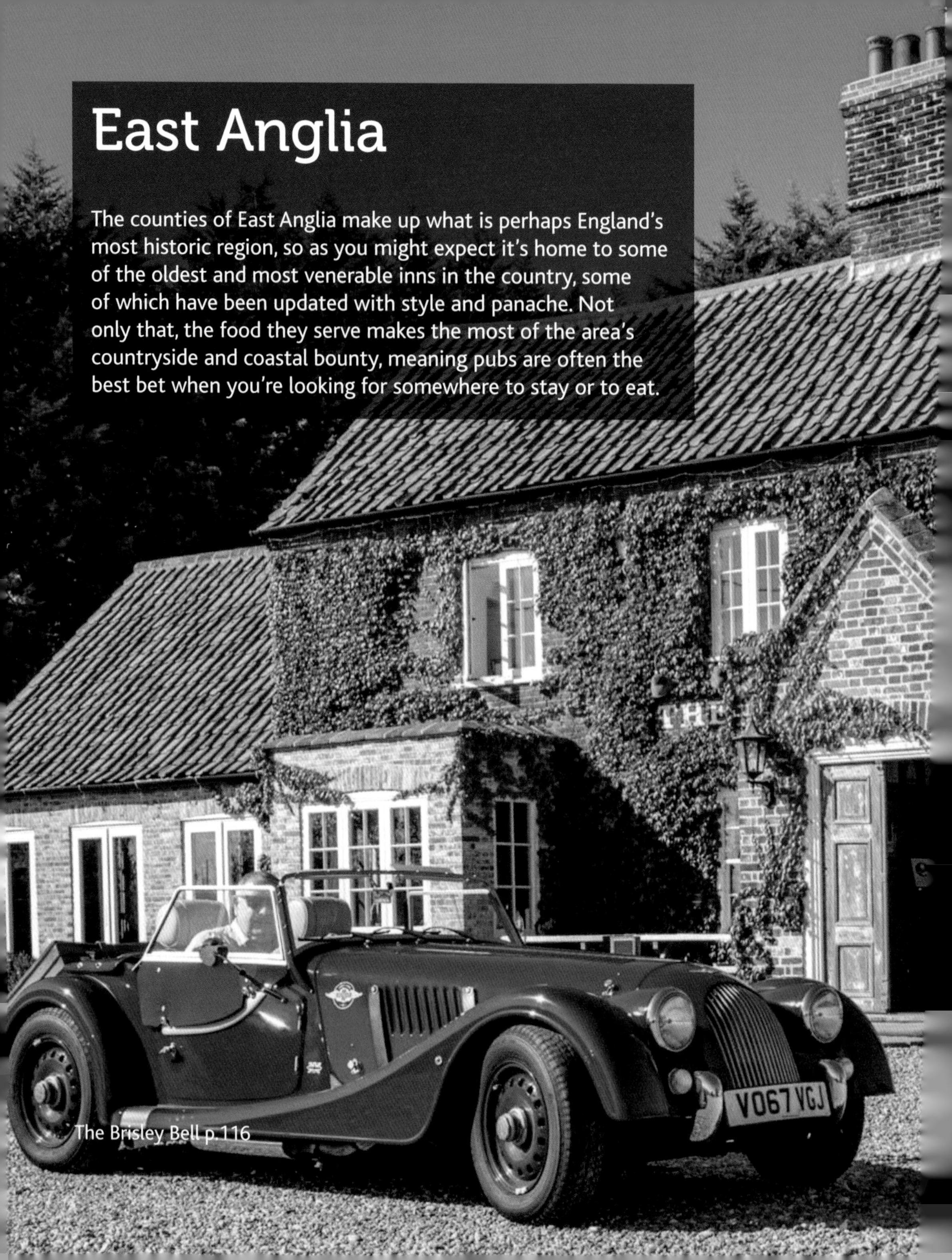

East Anglia

The counties of East Anglia make up what is perhaps England's most historic region, so as you might expect it's home to some of the oldest and most venerable inns in the country, some of which have been updated with style and panache. Not only that, the food they serve makes the most of the area's countryside and coastal bounty, meaning pubs are often the best bet when you're looking for somewhere to stay or to eat.

The Brisley Bell p.116

Sibton White Horse

A charming Suffolk country inn which has a set of cosy rooms and serves food that is a definite cut above.

It was always Neil and Gill Mason's dream to run a country pub, and around 15 years ago they finally managed it with the Sibton White Horse, which is a traditional country pub par excellence, with an atmosphere that couldn't be more inviting or a welcome warmer. Not only have they made it into a destination for food without alienating the regular drinkers, who still prop up the bar while everyone else tucks in, but they also have five cosy rooms in a separate block next door so you can linger a little longer after enjoying your dinner. These have been recently furnished in a contemporary country style and have decent-sized bathrooms, tea- and coffee-making facilities, biscuits, mineral water, Freeview TVs with DVD players and free wifi.

Outside, there's a small summer caravan site, and the pub also plays host to the odd beer and music festival. It also features an outdoor barbecue during the summer months, in the lovely pub garden, where you can also admire the borders, pots and palms along with the well-tended kitchen plot, whose herbs, salad, fruit and veg all finds it way onto the restaurant menu. Neil and Gill are very proud that the pub has been awarded two AA rosettes, and the menu makes the most of the great produce that Suffolk provides, with classic pub grub at lunchtime and a more refined dinner menu that changes about a quarter of its dishes every week - locally sourced dishes like Blythburgh pork belly, Binham Blue cheese soufflé and fresh fish and seafood from the nearby Suffolk coast. They also serve a generous – and delicious - breakfast. You can eat in the front bar of the pub or the raised restaurant area behind, and service is just what you expect from a small family-run place like this – so friendly and relaxed you won't want to leave.

The Sibton White Horse also makes an excellent base for visiting the nearby Suffolk Coast – Dunwich and the popular Minsmere RSPB reserve are close by, Walberswick and Southwold not much further, and there are lots of opportunities for country walks, not only to the coast but also to picturesque neighbouring Suffolk villages like Peasenhall and Yoxford, including three circular routes of between two and five miles (Neil and Gill can supply details and plenty of other suggestions).

All in all, it's a very pleasant weekend retreat in the heart of the Suffolk countryside – perfect for walking enthusiasts, twitchers or just exhausted couples keen to escape the pace of city life for a few days and eat some delicious food.

CONTACT Halesworth Rd, Sibton, Suffolk IP17 2JJ • 01728 660 337 • sibtonwhitehorseinn.co.uk

HOW MUCH? Double rooms £80–£100 a night depending on time of year; 2-night minimum stay during Easter–October. DB&B only on summer weekends, from £155 a night for 2 people.

ROOMS 5 guest rooms in a separate block next door to the pub, consisting of 4 doubles plus a twin with wet room that's accessible for disabled visitors.

SIBTON
WHITE HORSE

The Wiveton Bell

A great gastropub with beautiful rooms in a glorious rural location.

This middle-of-nowhere pub is our sort of place. Situated in a tiny hamlet just a mile from the North Norfolk coast at Blakeney, it's a popular establishment that makes the most of its fabulous location all year round; indeed the lights of The Wiveton Bell are a beacon of welcome on a dark winter's night,while in summer both the pub and garden are a magnet for walkers, birdwatchers and everyone else enjoying this beautiful part of the country.

Perhaps the best thing about the Wiveton Bell is that it has six irresistible rooms to tumble into once you've exhausted the joys of its beamed bar and restaurant. Each of these make a lovely place to wake up. There are four rooms at the back and two at the front, each with big sprung beds with high-quality linen, stylish shower rooms with REN aromatherapy toiletries, flatscreen TVs with Freeview, DVD players (and a library of discs) and lots to read. As an added bonus, you also get your own private entrance and outdoor seating area. Rates include all sorts of room treats (including a small bottle of Prosecco for you to feel properly pampered on arrival), tea and coffee, mineral water and juice, and a continental breakfast hamper, with fresh milk, warm croissants and local yoghurts, delivered to your room each morning along with a choice of newspaper. The owners Bernie and Sandy also have a two-bedroom cottage for rent in nearby Blakeney, which is similarly equipped with king-sized beds, flatscreen TVs and satellite, if you prefer self-catering.

The other good thing about The Wiveton Bell is that the owners are keen to maintain it as a proper pub – somewhere locals and visitors stop by with their dogs for a pint, and indeed they keep a few tables in the front bar reserved for drinkers, however packed the pub and restaurant get. As such, it's a thoroughly relaxing place to stay, encouraging an indolence you'll find hard to shake off, in a part of Norfolk you'll find hard to leave. Luckily they don't make you leave at the crack of dawn but encourage you to linger and enjoy the peace while you can – walking (there are lots of footpaths nearby), cycling, and, of course, eating – in the front bar, bright conservatory or outside in the extensive garden in summer. The food served is locally sourced, seasonal and delicious, and they have 2 AA rosettes and a recent Michelin Bib Gourmand to prove it.

CONTACT Blakeney Rd, Wiveton Near Blakeney, Norfolk NR25 7TL • 01263 740 101 • wivetonbell.co.uk
HOW MUCH? Double rooms from around £150 a night, including continental breakfast – 2-night minimum stay.
ROOMS 6 luxury rooms overlooking the village green.

The Wiveton Bell

The Brisley Bell

A proper village pub in the heart of Norfolk, with very comfortable rooms and seriously good food.

Rescued from permanent closure by partners Marcus Seaman and Amelia Nicholson in 2015, The Brisley Bell is a proper village pub, but one that just happens to serve tremendously good food and also has some very comfortable guest rooms. Marcus and Amelia were regulars at The Bell in their late teens/early 20s; when it closed in 2013, they were so bereft that they bought the place, with a view to making it into their perfect pub. Who hasn't dreamed of doing that? They added two new dining rooms and an outside terrace, created a garden and rebuilt the flint barns next door to serve as guest rooms. But essentially they left it as a pub, with the result that it is as welcoming and comfortable a country inn as as you'll find anywhere.

There are six rooms in all, each of them named after slang Norfolk place names (eg 'Windum', meaning 'Wymondham'). They're all pretty spacious and well proportioned, and have decent wifi, Smart TVs, tea- and coffee-making facilities, complimentary mineral water and homemade shortbread and sloe gin, Roberts radios and underfloor heating. The bathrooms are slick and contemporary: two have baths, two have showers, and two have free-standing baths in the rooms. Each room is fairly similar in style but each one has a slice of individual character endowed by former antique dealer Amelia's well-chosen bits of classic furniture. Two of the rooms are dog-friendly, one has disabled access, and, although they don't have any rooms specifically for families, they are spacious enough to fit in a cot or z-bed.

Breakfast is a buffet plus a decent Full English and is served in the Green Room at the front of the pub. You can eat lunch and dinner here too, as well as in the front bar of the pub or the book-lined Garden Room at the back, which looks out over a covered patio and garden. The moderately priced, meat-led menu changes daily, and French chef Hervé specialises in high-quality country cooking that makes the most of meat from local estates and fish and seafood from the north coast, with the odd nod to the French-Caribbean.

As for location, you're just a few miles from the market town of Dereham so you couldn't be much closer to the centre of Norfolk. Brisley makes a good base for the nearby Brecks, or even the north coast; you're also only half an hour from Norwich. The pub itself overlooks Brisley's large village green, so there's a real sense of being in the country. At times like this, as you amble into the bar for a pint or settle down at your table for dinner, you'll feel glad you chose to stay at The Brisley Bell.

CONTACT The Green, Brisley, Norfolk NR20 5DW • 01362 705 024 • thebrisleybell.co.uk

HOW MUCH? Double rooms £142–£199 a night, including breakfast.

ROOMS 6 double rooms in 2 converted outhouses.

The Angel Inn

The Angel at Larling was Norfolk Pub of the Year a few years ago, and quite right too, for they get all the essentials right at this 17th-century coaching inn, which is not big, not clever, just a great family-run country pub with rooms run by passionate folk who couldn't make you feel more at home. They rent 4 comfy upstairs guest rooms while serving hearty and wholesome pub grub in the bar and dining room, and managing to maintain the feel of a proper village local at the same time; they also host their own annual beer festival. As a village, Larling was somewhat messed up by the dualling of the A11, but the pub survived and is nowadays one of the most welcoming places for miles around. It's been in the Stammers family on and off since 1913, first as tenants and more recently as owners. There are 5 rooms of various shapes and sizes: comfortable rather than posh, with en-suite bathrooms, TVs and wifi and hearty breakfasts that are as excellent as their lunches and dinners. They also run a summer campsite in the field opposite and rent 2 lovely flint self-catering cottages in the village.

CONTACT Larling, Near Norwich, Norfolk NR16 2QU • 01953 717 963 • angel-larling.co.uk
HOW MUCH? Double rooms with breakfast from £80 a night. Camping £15–£20 a pitch (includes 4 people).

The Recruiting Sergeant

This long-standing Broads gastropub not only serves excellent food but has 5 boutique hotel rooms on the 2 floors above to stagger off to at the end of the night. The beamed rooms are as classic and contemporary as the food, with comfy king-size beds, wifi throughout, flatscreen Smart TVs and tea- and coffee-making facilities in each one. Those on the top floor are a bit smaller but are still a decent size, and the beams and eaves add a bit of character. Prices are very reasonable and get cheaper the longer you stay – no great hardship in what is one of the better places to eat in the area. Not only that, at the other end of the village the same owners' resurgent Rising Sun enjoys a perfect spot by the river on Coltishall Common and has a number of brand-new refurbished and very comfortable double rooms with the same facilities but overlooking the water – always a bonus in The Broads. You can stay in one pub and eat in the other, or vice-versa, and at either venue you're in an excellent position to explore some of the best features of the northern reaches of the National Park.

CONTACT Norwich Rd, Horstead, Norfolk NR12 7EE • 01603 737 077 • recruitingsergeant.co.uk
HOW MUCH? Doubles £105–£150 a night, including breakfast. Doubles at The Rising Sun £75–£125 a night.

The Bell at Sax'

The small Suffolk town of Saxmundham often gets overlooked in favour of the more obvious tourist honeypots of the nearby coast, which is a shame because it has a terrific place to stay (and eat) in the funkily re-named Bell at Sax' – the latest reinvention of the town's venerable old coaching inn, The Bell. Owned by local chef Jonny Nicholson, it strives to be a consummate inn, with good food and company, a set of comfy rooms upstairs and an atmosphere that is welcoming and unpretentious. The hotel's lobby certainly fits the bill, with lovely original flagstones and a snug old-fashioned reception that is not remotely posh yet exudes a quirky, contemporary vibe that is a good complement to the excellent but understated service. The 10 double rooms upstairs are spacious and comfortable without having been prissied up like every other boutique hotel you've ever seen, and the bar has a night-time buzz created by locals as much as by the hotel's guests. Finally, the restaurant is relaxed and cosy, with a straightforward and very well-priced menu that offers everything from fish and chips and a good burger to locally sourced crab and sea bass.

CONTACT 31 High St, Saxmundham, Suffolk IP17 1AF • 01728 602 331 • thebellatsax.co.uk
HOW MUCH? Double rooms from £120 a night, including breakfast.

The Rose & Crown

Run by the people behind the excellent Bank House in King's Lynn, this ancient inn has been around since the 14th century, and. in some ways, is still a traditional village boozer. But it's also a place to stay, with 16 pretty en-suite guest rooms and a cracking bar downstairs. The inn does what inns do – hidden corners, low ceilings and beams – but the rooms are all bright and Norfolk seasidey, and come with good-quality beds and linen, wifi, TV, fluffy towels for everyone and Molton Brown toiletries. Children and dogs? No problem – pooches pay a modest extra charge, as do kids under 12 to share their parents' room. The walled garden is a sunny spot for drinkers, while the restaurant is first rate, with proper attention given to local, seasonal ingredients and fast and efficient service – oysters and mussels, burgers and steaks, and a good old Sunday lunch that draws punters in from miles around. The pub is also very handy for some alluring nearby attractions: the nearby Snettisham RSPB reserve, Sandringham and pretty villages like Docking and Bircham that are lovely links in a country walk or cycle ride.

CONTACT Old Church Rd, Snettisham, Norfolk PE31 7LX • 01485 541 382 • roseandcrownsnettisham.co.uk
HOW MUCH? Double rooms from £160 a night, including breakfast.

The Boathouse

Restaurant and bar with boutique rooms and garden lodges in a lovely tranquil waterside location.

Mike and Belinda Minors run the excellent 'Waterside' restaurant a few miles up the road, so they know a thing or two about feeding hungry punters in beautiful Broadside locations. Thus it made perfect sense for them to take over the iconic Eel's Foot pub a a few years ago, which enjoyed a fabulous location right on the banks of Ormesby Broad but was badly in need of a shot of TLC. They went much further than this, however, and have transformed this old Broadside pub into a spectacular pub and restaurant, with a wedding venue and boutique B&B thrown in, which also has some well-appointed lodges in the garden for good measure.

The pub is very nice indeed, with two large rooms and comfy chairs by the fire if all you want is a drink. But it's the rooms upstairs that we like best of all, because waking up here is the best way to enjoy the Boathouse's perfect position by the broad. There are six rooms in all, funkily furnished, cosy and well priced, and four have views or partial views over the water. There are two suites, one of which is very spacious with a downstairs sitting room and upstairs bedroom, and all are decorated to a very high standard, with free wifi throughout, tea- and coffee-making facilities in each room and beautifully decked-out bathrooms.

Downstairs the restaurant is large but has a few cosy nooks, while the wedding venue is a self-contained unit off to the side, with its own waterside decking and gazebo and eating area – which is great if you're getting married here, but even better if you're not and don't want to be knee-deep in wedding guests in the bar or fighting to book a table for dinner. Finally, there are the lodges in the grounds, one of which is used for happy brides and grooms while the rest are comfy two-bedroom affairs, equipped with a sitting room and kitchenette and verandahs from which to watch the sun setting over the water in the evening.

It's the sort of location that makes you want to stick around, but it's worth remembering that from here you're well placed to explore the rest of the Broads National Park and also the nearby coast, which has some of Norfolk's best beaches, particularly those a short drive to the north at Winterton, Waxham and Horsey, where you also have the bonus of seeing one of the country's largest grey seal colonies. Consider also taking a boat out on the water from the same owners' 'Waterside' restaurant, just a couple of miles up the road on Rollesby Broad. Not too many pubs have boat hire and their own wedding venue!

CONTACT Eels Foot Rd, Ormesby St Michael, Norfolk NR29 3LP • 01493 730 342 • theboathouseormesbybroad.co.uk

HOW MUCH? Double rooms £95–£135 a night, not including breakfast. Lodges sleep 6–8 and cost £168–£234 a night (£776–£1148 a week).

ROOMS 4 double rooms, 2 suites, plus self-catering lodges in the grounds.

The Bell Inn

A terrific Essex village pub with boutique rooms and great food.

Gastropubs are two a penny these days but The Bell Inn was one of the very first, a cosy country inn situated in the sleepy village of Horndon-on-the-Hill, high above the Thames estuary on the way to Southend-on-Sea. It was way ahead of its time when owner John Vereker re-launched it as one of the UK's first gastropubs in the 1970s, and it remains a terrific place to eat to this day. Ably assisted by the third generation of the Vereker family, John has also added 26 guest rooms, making it into the perfect venue for an easy-to-reach and affordable foodie escape if you're based in London or the southeast.

The rooms are very comfortable and well equipped and range from characterful beamed affairs above the pub to more contemporary rooms in High House, a few doors up the street, which are generously sized and have large bathrooms with walk-in showers and separate baths. There are also a number of rooms in Hill House, in between the two. All the rooms have good wifi, 'eco-friendly' water, tea- and coffee-making facilities with homemade biscuits – and fresh milk if you want it; some of them have Smart TVs and a few are dog-friendly. High House also has a book-lined guest lounge for guests, with sofas and a television.

Service is friendly and confident throughout, and The Bell Inn remains a proper local, with plenty of people dropping by just for a drink. Some stay and snack on their excellent triple-cooked chips at the bar, but plenty more sit down to enjoy their daily changing menu, which is based around what's seasonal and what's local (including herbs and vegetables from the hotel's kitchen garden), either in the busy front bar or the quieter restaurant area at the back. The prices are extremely keen considering the quality of the food, and it's always busy, which is one of the reasons why they have a second restaurant, The Ostlers, down the street (open Friday and Saturday evenings and Sunday lunchtimes), which serves a slightly cheaper brasserie menu and a generous buffet breakfast every morning to hotel guests.

The pub is just half an hour by train from London Fenchurch Street to nearby Laindon station. From here you can walk in the surrounding Langdon Hills and Langdon Country Park, or follow a footpath down to the Thames to indulge in a spot of mudlarking along the 'Sea Wall' path. Or you could just enjoy the food and hospitality and potter about the village, which has a main street of timbered and clapboard houses that has been a dead end since they built the A13.

CONTACT High Rd, Horndon-on-the-Hill, Stanford-le-Hope, Essex SS17 8LD • 01375 642 463 • bell-inn.co.uk
HOW MUCH? Double rooms in High House £100–£145 a night; double rooms above the pub £80–£120 a night; doubles in Hill House from £90 a night. Rates include a continental buffet breakfast.
ROOMS 26 guest rooms – Small Doubles, Doubles, De-Luxe Doubles & Suites, plus 2-level 'Stable' Rooms.

THE BELL
FREE HOUSE
THE BELL
ENGLAND
expects every man
will do his duty

The Black Lion

A picture-perfect village pub located in a picture-perfect Suffolk village.

Picture for a moment a good-looking pub in a beautiful Suffolk village. Chances are you are imagining somewhere quite like the Black Lion in Long Melford, which occupies a picturesque location overlooking the village green, next to a medieval church. There can't be too many better places to wake up if you're after a weekend in the country, so it's good to know that The Black Lion not only serves good food but also has a comfy set of rooms upstairs to flop into after dinner.

One of the newer properties in the East Anglia-based Chestnut group, The Black Lion is a small Georgian coaching inn that's been updated beautifully: wooden floors throughout, artfully mismatched furniture and a comfy lounge with armchairs and newspapers all combine to suggest a comfortable house in the country at which you are one of the most important guests. There are 10 rooms in all, most of which overlook the village green. Apart from a couple of cheaper 'Snug' rooms, all the guest rooms are spacious and they all come with king-size beds, good wifi, flatscreen Freeview TVs, tea- and coffee-making facilities (with Nespresso machines), homemade biscuits and mineral water. All rooms have en-suite bathrooms with tubs and Noble Isle toiletries (one room also has a standalone shower), and there's a suite with an additional room with bunk beds if you're looking for somewhere big enough for a family.

Downstairs, the pub remains a nice place for an early evening pint and has seating that spills out on to the green during summer, while the next door dining room serves a menu that is deliberately British and seasonal, with a focus on East Anglian produce. It's moderately priced and hearty rather than posh, divided between pub classics and slightly more refined options. They also serve lunchtime sandwiches, while rates include a made-to-order breakfast that includes a choice of a Full English, fruit and yoghurt, eggs various ways or just a breakfast sandwich.

Finally there are the joys of staying not only in this part of Suffolk but also in Long Melford, which has quite a lot of attractions of its own, ranging from the National Trust property of Melford Hall right across the street to more family-orientated Kentwell Hall around the corner. You could also spend some time wandering the village's long main street, peeking into antique shops, but perhaps the nicest thing is the walk to nearby Lavenham, where there is plenty more to see and do and which is an easy-ish 8-mile round-trip partly along a disused railway line. Lazy weekenders ahoy!

CONTACT The Green, Long Melford, Suffolk CO10 9DN • 01787 312 356 • theblacklionlongmelford.com

HOW MUCH? Double rooms £90–£130, including breakfast.

ROOMS 10 guest rooms, made up of 5 Luxury rooms, 3 Snug rooms, a family room and a suite.

The Sun Inn

A proper pub with rooms in the heart of Constable Country, serving excellent food.

If you're the sort of person who likes a proper pub, preferably located on a proper village high street and serving good local ales alongside hearty, locally sourced food, then there's a strong chance that The Sun Inn will be your sort of place. Situated in the picturesque village of Dedham right on the Essex-Suffolk border, the other nice thing about The Sun is that it is independently owned and run, and has a set of cosy rooms upstairs, which means that you don't have to go home at the end of the evening, and can wake up refreshed and ready not only to enjoy The Sun's excellent breakfast but also to explore the countryside around. There is great walking in Dedham Vale, and Dedham is at the heart of 'Constable Country', with lots of sights and places pertaining to the landscape artist, including an easy walk nearby taking you across the meadows to Flatford Mill, the site of perhaps the artist's most famous painting, The Haywain. They also have bikes for the use of guests and can arrange boat trips on the river.

The rooms at the Sun Inn are all on the first floor, a mixture of contemporary and traditional and very comfortable. Most of them have been recently refurbished and have high-quality pocket-sprung beds, digital radios and TVs, wifi throughout and posh toiletries in the bathrooms; they also come with decent tea- and coffee-making facilities, filtered water, and flapjacks and cookies on arrival. Dogs are accepted by prior arrangement. Each room is different: some are very spacious with large en-suite bathrooms, and all but one have king-size or super-king-size beds.

Downstairs, the food is also a central part of the offering, with lunch and dinner served every day, and cream teas in between when booked in advance. The menu changes monthly and they add a roast on Sundays, and you can enjoy your food in the pleasant beer garden outside on sunny days. But the Sun is also very much the pub, with plenty of locals regularly dropping by for a pint or two. In short, we can't think of too many nicer – or easier – places for weary Londoners to stay than Dedham, and The Sun Inn very much does what it says on the tin: good food, comfortable rooms, and a warm welcome. What more could you ask for?

CONTACT High St, Dedham, Essex CO7 6DF • 01206 323 351 • thesuninndedham.com

HOW MUCH? Double rooms £145 a night, including breakfast.

ROOMS 7 nicely furnished double rooms, all with en-suite facilities, 4 at the front of the pub and 3 at the back.

THE SUN INN

The King's Head

Set back from the main drag, surrounded by meadows, The King's Head is the sort of solid Georgian building that shouts at you to pull over and take the weight off your feet in its cosy bar. It's a great example of a contemporary country pub, serving excellent food and local ales and with 4 upstairs bedrooms. These are all furnished in the same cosy but up-to-date style that's in keeping with the building and its period, with large comfy beds and en-suite bathrooms with powerful showers and a bath in one of the rooms. The pub is a welcoming mix of contemporary style and old-fashioned: rustic, funky, family- and dog-friendly, with a snug bar for drinkers on one side, and a main area devoted to food, which is served all day – a mixture of classic pub and slightly more adventurous dishes. They bake their own bread with flour from a nearby mill and source most other ingredients locally, including their own Brancaster Brewery, further up the coast. The garden has an outdoor play area for kids, and, in summer, they have a barbecue out here too to keep the adults occupied.

CONTACT Holt Rd, Letheringsett, Norfolk NR25 7AR • 01263 712 691 • kingsheadnorfolk.co.uk
HOW MUCH? Double rooms £120–£150 a night, including breakfast.

The Three Blackbirds

Situated in the pretty village of Woodditton, just outside Newmarket, it's third time lucky for this cosy Suffolk pub, which was refurbished a couple of years ago before suffering a devastating fire. It has been carefully updated since then, retaining the best of its original features, with bare brick walls, beams and ancient fireplaces, but with contemporary flourishes. There are 9 guest rooms in a purpose-built barn next door, some of which are dog-friendly: all come with super-king-size beds with high-quality mattresses, good-sized Smart TVs, fast wifi and tea and coffee-making facilities, and spacious bathrooms with rainfall showers and Bramley toiletries. As for the food, it's deliberately classic and rather delicious, focusing on local and seasonal produce, including hearty delights like pigs-head terrine and cider-braised pork alongside crowd-pleasing favourites like Newmarket sausage and mash with red onion gravy. Breakfast is an equally satisfying, plate-service affair, while there is even a menu for dogs, featuring various items to gnaw, chew and drink.

CONTACT 36 Ditton Green, Woodditton, Suffolk CB8 9SQ • 01638 731 100 • threeblackbirds.co.uk
HOW MUCH? Double rooms from £150 a night, including breakfast.

The White Horse

The White Horse guards its almost perfect position jealously, backing straight on to the marshes, lagoons and creeks of the North Norfolk Coast. It's a gastropub of long standing and has 7 en-suite guest rooms in the main building, and 8 more in the garden, with grass roofs to blend with the marshes beyond. All of the rooms are spacious and contemporary, with a blue-green décor inspired by the seascape beyond. Some have sea views and the top-notch 'Room at the Top', split over 2 levels, has its own viewing telescope. Whether you stay in the main building or the garden rooms, all have large comfy beds, Freeview TVs, digital radios, wifi and tea- and coffee-making facilities. It's a short stroll to the end of the garden to pick up the Norfolk Coastal Path, making the pub an ideal location for walkers, cyclists or indeed anyone who wants to make the most of this unique location. Food-wise, there's also no better place to return to after a day exploring the coast, with great fish, seafood and other locally sourced delights to enjoy while you watch the sun set over the sea.

CONTACT Main Rd, Brancaster Staithe, Norfolk, PE31 8BY • 01485 210 262 • whitehorsebrancaster.co.uk
HOW MUCH? Double rooms £160–£250 a night, including breakfast.

The Alma Inn

Bang in the centre of Harwich's port district, this salty old inn serves some of the best pub grub you'll find in East Anglia, yet it has lost none of its backstreet charm. Not only is the pub still a proper local, with plenty of folk stopping by for a drink, it's also a comfy place to stay if you're catching a ferry or just fancy a weekend away somewhere a bit different. There are 6 rooms to choose from, including a 2-bed family suite, and each has en-suite bathrooms with toiletries, a flatscreen TV, Nespresso machines, bottles of water and biscuits. The beds are comfortable and have luxury cotton linen, and the rooms have all been sympathetically renovated in line with the character of the building: re-purposed ships' timbers complement the beams and creaky floors, and the exposed brick walls and sea-faring charts place you firmly in maritime Essex. As for the food, there are Mersea oysters and local lobsters (sold by weight), fish and chips, and seafood sharing platters; and they also serve a variety of excellent local steaks – like the lobster, enjoyed very simply with chips and a choice of sauces.

CONTACT 25 King's Head St, Harwich, Essex CO12 3EE • 01255 318 681 • almaharwich.co.uk
HOW MUCH? Double rooms £80–£120 a night including breakfast. Family suite £155–£175.

The Bildeston Crown

This 15th-century coaching inn has been something of a local landmark for centuries, and a foodie destination for well over a decade. In its day Bildeston was one of the wealthy Suffolk wool towns, and although this is hard to discern in what is nowadays a peaceful village in one of the quieter corners of Suffolk, its comfortable upstairs rooms and excellent food mean the tradition continues to this day. There are 12 guest rooms, which come in all shapes and sizes – an individuality that the owners emphasize with a variety of decorative styles, from traditional to contemporary. All of them have baths (3 have walk-in showers as well) and all come with big comfy beds, tea-and coffee-making facilities, complimentary water, Freeview TVs and wifi – and, unusually, there's also a lift, so to that extent at least all are accessible if you have trouble with stairs. The same menu is served in the bar and the slightly more formal restaurant, and you can choose between an excellent selection of 'classics' – and the more seasonal, and more refined 'select' menu; or if you really want push the boat out, try the 7-course tasting menu.

CONTACT 104 High St, Bildeston, Suffolk IP7 7EB • 01449 740 510 • thebildestoncrown.com
HOW MUCH? Double rooms from £100 a night, including breakfast.

The Fritton Arms

Tucked away on the edge of the Norfolk Broads and Great Yarmouth, The Fritton Arms straddles the Norfolk-Suffolk border. It's a country house-cum-country inn that serves excellent food and has 9 rooms upstairs. It's deliciously comfortably and relaxed, with creaky floorboards, big fireplaces, random contemporary art and scatterings of books and magazines. There are squashy sofas in the lounge, easy chairs around a big open fire in the bar, and stripped-down pine tables mismatched with modish blue chairs in the restaurant, beyond which a big outside terrace and lawn stretches down to the lakeside. The pub is just one part of the Somerleyton Estate, which is in part a private members' club with loads of facilities and things to do – everything from boating, kayaking, SUP-ing and wild swimming in the lake or tamer stuff in a brand-new open-air, heated pool, to a spot of tennis on a choice of grass or clay courts. If you're staying at The Fritton Arms, you have access to all this, which should make it quite unlike any other country pub you might have ever stayed in.

CONTACT Church Lane, Fritton, Norfolk NR31 9HA • 01493 484 008 • frittonlake.co.uk/hospitality
HOW MUCH? Double rooms £160–£180 a night, including breakfast – minimum 2-night stay.

The Crown at Stoke by Nayland

Situated in the heart of Suffolk, The Crown is a relaxed foodie pub bang in the middle of what's commonly known as Constable Country – the picturesque hills and vales to the south of Ipswich where the 19th-century landscape painter lived and worked. Part of the Chestnut group, its rooms are in a purpose-built annexe that looks over the fields and woods beyond – country-style for the most part with a dash of contemporary flair on the ground floor. All rooms have tea- and coffee-making facilities, mineral water, fresh milk and biscuits and TVs; most have large bathrooms and the higher-end rooms are slightly bigger, with king-size beds, robes, separate baths and spacious walk-in showers. There's a 24-hour reception and the food is pretty good, served in a deliberately relaxed environment, with stripped pine tables and lots of locals happily making their way through crowd-pleasing lunch and supper menus. As well as pub classics like fish and chips, steaks and burgers, they serve interesting fish dishes and various sharing platters, along with an excellent breakfast each morning.

CONTACT Stoke By Nayland, Suffolk CO6 4SE • 01206 262 001 • crowninn.net

HOW MUCH? Double rooms £165–£245 a night, including breakfast.

The Lion Inn

This pub is popular locally but deserves to be better known beyond this corner of Essex. A self-titled 'gastropub' and 'deluxe auberge', it was the vision of local foodie entrepreneur Clive 'Spin' Thomson, who bought this rundown 15th-century pub and expanded it into a contemporary inn with boutique rooms, as well as a cool wedding venue. Spin's eye for detail is manifest in every aspect of The Lion, including the big American-style bar that's perfect for posing with a drink. It has 23 rooms (8 in a new extension), decorated in a crisp, contemporary style and equipped with fast wifi, Freeview TVs, DVDs, air-conditioning, mineral water and coffee and tea. The larger rooms have super-king-size beds and some have private patios or balconies. The bar and restaurant are enormous: residents can book but others can't, and despite its size there are still queues outside the door on a Saturday night or a Sunday lunchtime. The reason? Well, the food is very good but doesn't try to be too ambitious – fish-and-chips, excellent burgers, steaks and homemade pies supplemented by half a dozen more adventurous specials.

CONTACT Main Rd, Boreham, Chelmsford, Essex CM3 3JA • 01245 394 900 • lioninnhotel.co.uk

HOW MUCH? Double rooms £95–£175 a night, including breakfast. Bridal Suite £250.

The Pheasant

An award-winning country pub with good food and very comfy rooms.

Run by the very experienced and throughly warm and welcoming owner, Diana Donoghue, The Pheasant has pretty much everything you could want from a country inn – good, home-cooked food and a cosy place in which to eat it, and a handful of extremely comfortable and well-appointed rooms. Located in a peaceful part of rural north Essex, not far from the Suffolk border, it's not a grand operation at all. But it is an exceptionally cosy country pub, and Diana is a very hands-on owner, full of tips on the surrounding area and local sights and walks. A lot of the ingredients for the restaurant are grown in the large garden across the road, bees and hens provide the breakfast honey and eggs, and the pub even has its own smokehouse where they smoke not only fish but also the hops they pass on to local Norfolk brewer Woodforde's to produce their smooth signature Pheasant ale.

Their five rooms are housed in a building behind the pub and most have lovely views over the rolling countryside behind. They are all tastefully kitted out and spacious – a couple are huge! – and each is named after a local historical figure, for example Thomas Gainsborough, who lived in nearby Sudbury, and Captain Lawrence Oates (of Scott's doomed Antarctic expedition), who lived in the village and is commemorated in the local church. They all have big and comfortable beds with contemporary, colourful headboards, a mini-fridge with fresh milk and water, tea and proper coffee, flatscreen TVs with Freeview, local handmade toiletries and lots of reading material – plus there's wifi throughout and also in the pub. As for the restaurant, it serves locally sourced, seasonal food that's both well-priced and unpretentious and draws in lots of regulars: fish and chips, lovely homemade pies, and always roast beef on a Sunday, and usually half a dozen meat and fish main courses – duck breast, liver and bacon, shoulder of lamb – along with a couple of specials. Breakfast consists of a small buffet with yoghurt and other goodies, plus their own eggs and fabulous bacon and sausages from a nearby farm, which round off a visit very well.

And the location? Well, Gestingthorpe is a pleasant village, with its aforementioned church, St Mary's, which is worth a look not only for its memorials to the Oates family (all of whom seem to have died in foreign parts) but also an impressive double hammerbeam roof that dates from the late 15th century. There are also numerous circular walks you can do in the surrounding countryside, one of which takes in the ancient site of a Roman villa along the way.

CONTACT Gestingthorpe, Halstead, Essex CO9 3AU • 01787 465 010 • thepheasant.net

HOW MUCH? Double rooms from £125 a night, including breakfast.

ROOMS 5 en-suite double rooms.

The Gunton Arms

Situated in the 1000-acre deer park of Norfolk's Gunton Hall, The Gunton Arms has a reassuring country estate feel. But it's not a typical country pub by any means. Sure, its 8 guest rooms are comfortable and very homely, with the feel of your richest friend's country house, and the food they serve here is renowned for miles around. But as the project of London art dealer Ivor Braka, the walls of the inn are plastered with contemporary art – works by Tracy Emin, Gilbert and George and lots of other Brit-Art biggies – and it would be no surprise to trip over a Damian Hirst creation as you stagger off to your room. The food, too, is rather special: bar snacks like sausages, venison kofta and Yorkshire pudding with gravy, and main courses literally sourced from the fat of the land, with venison from the estate, local beef and lamb, Blythburgh pork and plenty of locally caught fish, much of it cooked on the vast French open fireplace in the main restaurant. The pub is also ideally placed for exploring North Norfolk, just a couple of miles from the coast at Overstrand and Cromer.

CONTACT Cromer Rd, Thorpe Market, Norfolk NR11 8TZ • 01263 832 010 • theguntonarms.co.uk
HOW MUCH? Double rooms £95–£185 a night, including breakfast.

The Packhorse Inn

City boy Philip Turner rescued his ailing local boozer about 6 years ago, turning it into a properly up-to-date country inn with food and rooms that was the first of his regional Chestnut pubs venture. It remains a good advert for the group, with an easy-going vibe and decoration that references the nearby horseracing at Newmarket. Food is very much at the centre of its offering, and although people do pop by for a drink the bar is more likely to be occupied by diners waiting for a table than locals necking pints. The menu changes regularly and features 3–4 starters and half a dozen mains that are well-chosen and seasonal and always take in a choice of local meat or game, fish and at least one veggie option. Of 8 very comfortable rooms, 4 are in the main building and 4 in the purpose-built 'Coach House' across the courtyard. There's not much difference between them, but those above the pub are slightly larger, with super-king-size beds and large baths as well as walk-in showers. They all have tea- and coffee-making facilities, complimentary water, homemade biscuits, Freeview TVs and decent wifi.

CONTACT Bridge St, Moulton, Suffolk, CB8 8SP • 01638 751 818 • thepackhorseinn.co.uk
HOW MUCH? Double rooms £100–£150 a night, including breakfast.

The Bucks Arms

Location, location, location. The Bucks Arms would be a nice pub wherever it was – a cosy old place serving excellent food to hungry locals and tourists, with 4 characterful rooms upstairs for those who want to stay over. In fact, it sits right outside the Jacobean splendour of Blickling Hall, North Norfolk, so is a very special place indeed, with 2 of its rooms enjoying unique views over the hall's serene frontage while the other 2 look out over the vast expanse of Blickling's country park and grounds. It welcomes dogs, and just as well: there are almost 5000 acres to explore on the estate, and there's bike hire next door in the hall. The rooms are simply furnished and generous in size. All of them have en-suite bathrooms, and 3 have 4-poster beds just to help you get into the spirit of the location; the largest room enjoys the best views of the hall. There's wifi throughout and each room has a flatscreen TV. As for the pub, it serves predictably excellent breakfasts and a full menu at lunch and dinner times – smoked haddock rarebit, a lovely Cromer crab salad or just great steaks, burgers and fish and chips.

CONTACT Blickling, Aylsham, Norfolk NR11 6NF • 01263 732 133 • bucksarms.co.uk
HOW MUCH? Double rooms from £105 a night, including breakfast.

The Waveney Inn

As one of only 2 pubs in this book that boasts its own pool, The Waveney Inn is a hard place to describe. It serves food and drink and has a collection of boutique-style rooms. But it's also part of the excellent Waveney River Centre, a camping, glamping and self-catering site that occupies a beautiful, almost secret spot in an untouched corner of the Broads National Park. The pub has 7 bedrooms: some have views of the river and marshes, and all are spacious and well kitted out, with flatscreen TVs, big comfy beds and large bathrooms with toiletries. Rates include the use of the Centre's indoor pool and the foot ferry across the river, plus an excellent breakfast in the pub, which the rest of the time serves a high-quality, varied pub menu. Best of all, the location is home to all sorts of outdoor activities. There is a nature trail for kids, bikes, canoes and day boats for hire, and the footpaths through the marshes on the far side of the river are lovely, leading eventually to the expanse of Oulton Broad. A perfect place to throw away the car keys and forget the rest of the world for a few days.

CONTACT Staithe Rd, Burgh St Peter, Norfolk NR34 0DE • 01502 677 343 • waveneyrivercentre.co.uk
HOW MUCH? Double rooms £99–£119 a night, pods £50, yurts £55; self-catering from £1000 a week.

The Ingham Swan

You couldn't ask for a more authentically Norfolk location than this popular local gastropub, recently back from the dead after a massive fire a few years ago. It has 4 very comfy rooms in the converted stable block to the side of the pub, and has added 3 more in a separate village house around the corner. They're all contemporary and ever-so-slightly retro, with exposed brick walls, cool greys and neutral tones, each with tea/coffee, kettles and Nespresso machines, complimentary water and biccies and Smart TVs, and bathrooms that are right up to date, with toiletries and powerful showers. But the food is the real deal here, overseen by chef-patron Daniel Smith: classic in style and inspiration, with big flavours based on high-quality, often local ingredients. The menu is tweaked daily, but their signature fillet of beef is usually on the menu, and you could start with fabulous Brancaster mussels or Cromer crab, before moving on to superb lamb rump – all before savouring the big dark skies of Norfolk on the way back to your room.

CONTACT Sea Palling Rd, Ingham, Norfolk NR12 9AB • 01692 581 099 • theinghamswan.co.uk
HOW MUCH? Double rooms £155–£195 a night, including breakfast.

The Guinness Arms

Located in the unassuming village of Icklingham, this old coaching inn is part of the Elveden Estate, which straddles the Norfolk-Suffolk border and has been in the hands of the Guinness brewing dynasty for over 100 years. They renovated the place a couple of years ago, turning it into a proper gastropub with guest rooms in various outbuildings. Like its sister pub, The Elveden Inn, its menus are based on produce from the estate, which covers around 20,000 surrounding acres and provides pork, game and venison along with never-ending supplies of fruit and vegetables. The result is a pub grub menu that hits the spot and is always beautifully presented and locally sourced. There are 8 rooms, each named after members of the Guinness family and styled accordingly – Alec's room is naturally full of actorish memorabilia and photos, while Lulu's room was designed by the fashion designer herself and has a hand-painted mural and a gorgeous 4-poster. Most importantly, all the rooms have good wifi, up-to-date bathrooms or wet rooms, robes and toiletries, Smart TVs and tea- and coffee-making facilities.

CONTACT The Street, Icklingham, Suffolk IP28 6PS • 01638 597 547 • guinnessarms.com
HOW MUCH? Double rooms £100–£150 a night including breakfast.

The Loddon Swan

Though neither a boutique inn nor a gastropub, The Swan makes a pretty good stab at both, delivering a combination of good food and comfortable rooms in a beautiful part of the Norfolk Broads National Park. It's first and foremost a proper village pub, full of locals propping up the bar or sipping drinks in the small patio garden. There are 10 rooms – 7 in 2 buildings behind the pub and 3 in the Victorian former council offices next door. Each has a contemporary yet deliberately homely feel, and all have up-to-date bathrooms, mostly with spacious separate showers, plus king- or super-king-size beds, good wifi, flatscreen TVs, complimentary still water, biccies and tea and coffee. There is a short and thoughtful menu, with a few dishes done well rather than a range of crowd-pleasing favourites; think confit chicken wings, pan-fried sardines or cod cheek scampi, baked plaice with samphire or loin of lamb with Provencal vegetables. The pub also does good sandwiches and a few pub classics. Service is excellent, and not at all affected – much like the pub itself!

CONTACT Church Plain, Loddon, Norfolk, NR14 6LX • 01508 528 039 • theloddonswan.co.uk
HOW MUCH? Double rooms £90–£100 a night, including breakfast.

The Cricketers

The creation of Trevor and Sally Oliver (yes, Jamie's parents), this pioneering gastropub was taken over recently by the local Chestnut group, but this hasn't made us think of it less fondly; indeed, it's still hard to beat the food they serve, which is several cuts above what you will enjoy elsewhere. The Olivers always hung their steaks, got their fish daily from Billingsgate, baked their own bread and insisted on using fresh local ingredients long before it was fashionable to do so, and the new owners have deliberately kept to the same important traditions. Yet prices are pretty much the same as in any decent gastropub, and you can stay overnight in one of 22 boutique rooms scattered between the pub itself, a couple of buildings next door and a bungalow across the road. Some of these are dog-friendly, and they have all been newly refurbished in a bright and contemporary style. All have tea and coffee,-making facilities, complimentary water and Freeview TVs – and a thoughtfully provided flashlight to help you find your way to the pub on dark nights!

CONTACT Clavering, Near Saffron Walden, Essex CB11 4QT • 01799 550 442 • thecricketers.co.uk
HOW MUCH? Double rooms £115–£130 a night including breakfast.

The Gin Trap Inn

A cosy North Norfolk 17th-century inn that specialises in delicious and local 21st-century food.

Just a mile from Hunstanton and the North Norfolk Coast, The Gin Trap Inn advertises itself as providing modern British food in a 17th-century inn. These are words to quicken the pulse of any pub lover, and we are happy to say that it delivers on both counts. Based in the village of Ringstead, this ancient inn is nowadays all about making the most of Norfolk's bounty to create great seasonal food. Not only that, it also has thirteen very comfortable bedrooms if you would also like to stay overnight, and has recently added a couple of two-bedroom cottages for those who prefer to self-cater.

First the food, which is focused on fish and seafood and locally farmed meat and game. They serve oysters harvested by a local fisherman, halibut with brown shrimp, local quail, pork and beef, on a regular changing menu that also features yummy bar snacks like sourdough focaccia and an ox-tongue mini Reuben sandwich. The pub is unusually family friendly too, with sourdough pizzas, pasta and cheesy chicken to appeal to younger tastes.

The rooms (and two split-level suites) meanwhile are cosy and comfy, each one different in size and shape but all furnished with a mixture of antiques and bric-a-brac that gives them real character while not dispensing with modern comforts. They all come with wifi, Smart TVs, luxury cotton bed linen and spacious en-suite bathrooms with robes and toiletries. They also have Roberts digital radios, tea- and coffee-making facilities and still and sparkling mineral water – all complimentary. Their two cottages are similarly well appointed, with two double bedrooms each and lots of living space, including a contemporary fitted kitchen and a balcony for summer evenings, and Smart TVs for cosy nights in. And, if you're feeling lazy, you can eat at the pub – breakfast is included in rates!

Dogs are welcome in most of the rooms and the cottages, and there's a garden with a play area for kids, but the chances are you will want to get out and explore. The pub is well positioned for visiting the nature reserves at Snettisham and Titchwell, and Holkham Beach and multiple other coastal attractions are not far away, including the nearby seaside resort of Hunstanton. You're also never far from some superb country walks, including a 7-mile loop you can do from the doorstep of the pub.

CONTACT 6 High St, Ringstead, Norfolk PE36 5JU • 01485 525 264 • thegintrapinn.co.uk

HOW MUCH? Double rooms from £120 a night, including breakfast, suites from £175 a night; 2-bedroom cottages from £240 a night, including breakfast.

ROOMS 13 guest bedrooms plus a couple of 2-bed self-catering cottages.

THE GIN TRAP INN

The Elveden Inn

This comfortable Thetford Forest country inn is perfect for families looking for adventure.

Midway between London and Norwich, just off the A11, The Elveden Inn is a proper country inn, a thoroughly inviting roadside hostelry with six comfortable rooms and a restaurant with a large patio and garden outside. It's part of the Guinness family's Elveden Estate, and, as such, is a complement to their impressive restaurant and retail offering across the road. Handily situated right on the edge of the large expanse of Thetford Forest, on the Suffolk-Norfolk borders, it attracts walkers, cyclists and families heading for the 'Go Ape' venue in the woods or the nearby Center Parcs location.

The pub reopened a few years ago after a complete refurbishment and has been cleverly and sensitively restored as a homely, family-friendly sort of place, with mismatched furniture and bare floorboards in its main public areas. The rooms are contemporary but cosy, decorated in neutral browns, creams and greys; there are two large family rooms at each end of the building, with super-king-side beds and sofa beds and bath/ shower, four doubles/twins with king-size beds and showers only, and two large annexe double rooms. All the rooms are provided with flatscreen Freeview TVs, tea- and coffee-making facilities, complimentary water, password-free wifi and Elveden's own-brand toiletries in the bathrooms.

It's worth knowing that Elveden is one of the largest arable farms in East Anglia, and also one of its most environmentally responsible, so you're in good hands when it comes to food and drink. The pub serves a menu that is a moderately priced, undemanding affair – just what you need after a full day in the forest, with fish-and-chips, burgers, sausage and mash and game and venison from the estate. Four of the rooms are dog-friendly, and, although dogs aren't allowed in restaurant areas, you can eat the same menu in the large garden or in the bar out the front. Eating in the windowed Garden Room, as the darkness gathers outside, is really not a bad way to end any day, but is even better if your kids are looking forward to their tree-swinging in the morning or if your bike is primed for the forest's trails.

CONTACT Brandon Rd, Elveden, Norfolk IP24 3TP • 01842 890 876 • elvedeninn.com
HOW MUCH? Double rooms £90–£110 a night, family rooms £100–£140 a night, all including breakfast.
ROOMS 8 double rooms, including family rooms that are large enough for a family of 4.

Lucky Dip

The Ramsholt Arms

Ramsholt is not so much a village as a handful of houses and this riverside pub, which enjoys a fabulous setting looking across the Deben Estuary. It's a homely, dog-friendly place with a large terrace, and serves decent food too. You can do a lovely circular walk up the river and then loop around inland – just the thing to work up a thirst for one of its guest ales. No rooms.

CONTACT Dock Rd, Ramsholt, Suffolk IP12 3AB • 01394 411 209 • theramsholtarms.com

The Fur & Feather

This is not only a nice boozer but also situated in one of the most picturesque villages in the Broads. As the brewery tap of Woodforde's brewery next door, it also serves the widest choice of their ales you'll find and tops this off with a menu of decent food: nothing fancy, but, like their beer, wholesome, honest and largely put together using local ingredients. No rooms.

CONTACT Slad Lane, Woodbastwick, Norfolk NR13 6SW • 01603 720 353 • woodfordes.com/the-fur-feather-restaurant-brewery-tap

King's Head

This pub is unusual in that it has no bar, just a room full of barrels where your server will disappear to fetch your drink while you get comfy in one of the pub's many panelled rooms. Also known as 'The Low House', it serves good food that you can enjoy in its large beer garden, and has a few guest rooms too.

CONTACT Gorams Mill Lane, Laxfield, Suffolk IP13 8DW • 01986 798 395 • lowhouselaxfield.com

The Butt & Oyster

This 17th-century pub was a favourite of Arthur Ransome, who kept his boat nearby and set 2 of his books here, and it remains a terrific riverside pub, with quarry-tiled bars, open fires and fabulous views over the Orwell River from its bay windows and terrace. Part of a small local pub group, it serves good food all day. No rooms.

CONTACT Pin Mill, Ipswich, Suffolk IP9 1JW • 01473 780 764 • debeninns.co.uk/buttandoyster

The Unruly Pig

This was Suffolk's 2021 'Pub of the Year' in the 'Good Pub Guide', and no wonder – the food they serve here is a magnificent blend of British and Italian that's worth travelling miles for. It was always a great foodie pub, even in its previous incarnation as 'The English Larder', and it makes a terrific stop-off on your way to or from the nearby National Trust site of Sutton Hoo. No rooms.

CONTACT Orford Rd, Bromeswell, Near Woodbridge, Suffolk IP12 2PU • 01394 460 310 • theunrulypig.co.uk

The Saracen's Head

This Georgian inn claims to be 'in the middle of nowhere but the centre of everywhere', and it's a reasonable claim in about as rural a location as you could imagine. It serves inventive and locally sourced food with seasonal variations, and the service is great and the vibe friendly and cosy. They have a few rooms upstairs too.

CONTACT Wolterton, Near Erpingham, Norfolk, NR11 7LZ • 01263 768 909 • saracenshead-norfolk.co.uk

The Duck Inn

Not far from the North Norfolk Coast and swanky Burnham Market, The Duck Inn is not really a drinkers' pub anymore, to be honest, but the food it serves more than makes up for it – locally sourced, high-end British cuisine that's the match of anywhere in the area (which is saying something in a region stacked to the gills with places to eat). No rooms.

CONTACT Burnham Rd, Stanhoe, Norfolk PE31 8QD • 01485 518 330 • duckinn.co.uk

The Stiffkey Red Lion

Right on the main coast road, The Red Lion in Stiffkey is a relaxing place for a pint but a good place to eat too. Food is excellent, based on seasonal and local ingredients, especially mussels and seafood. And just in case you can't resist sampling all the ales they have on tap, they have rooms upstairs and a self-catering cottage to rent.

CONTACT 44 Wells Rd, Stiffkey, Norfolk NR23 1AJ • 01328 830 552 • stiffkey.com

The Jolly Sailors

Once voted the nation's favourite family pub, this Norfolk coast boozer is a well-loved pub, partly for its food, which varies from stone-baked pizzas to tempting slow-cooked Texan barbecue specials. It also serves its own excellent Brancaster ales and stocks a huge selection of rums – all of which you can enjoy inside the cosy pub or outside in its kid-friendly beer garden. Dogs, sandy shoes and muddy boots all welcome. No rooms.

CONTACT Brancaster Staithe, Norfolk PE31 8BJ • 01485 210 314 • jollysailorsbrancaster.co.uk

(Top) The Ramsholt Arms; (middle) The Saracen's Head; (bottom) The Jolly Sailors.

The Victoria Inn

The pub of the Holkham Estate, just a few minutes' walk from the gates of the Hall, serving Estate-sourced food that you can savour in the bar, preferably after a day enjoying the glorious expanse of Holkham Beach and the pinewoods behind. It also has 20 bright and spacious bedrooms divided between the pub and the so-called Ancient House opposite, some of which are dog-friendly.

CONTACT Park Rd, Holkham, Norfolk NR23 1RG • 01328 711 008 • holkham.co.uk/stay-eat/the-victoria-inn

The White Horse Inn

A great village local that reinvented itself as a brewpub a few years ago and hasn't looked back, serving great local ales and excellent pub food to a happy crowd of both locals and boaters touring the Broads National Park. No rooms.

CONTACT The Street, Neatishead, Norfolk NR12 8AD • 01692 630 828 • thewhitehorseinnneatishead.com

The Nelson Head

If you've been spotting seal pups on the shore at Horsey or are strolling down from Waxham, this pub couldn't be better placed, a short walk from the shore and on the way to Horsey Windpump and Mere. It does its best to remain as unchanged as possible, full of Nelson-related memorabilia and serving up wholesome if unspectacular bar meals, lunchtimes and evenings. It's nice to sit across the road in the garden, or, if not, the front bar is a cosy place to eat, drink and fraternize with the locals. No rooms.

CONTACT Horsey, Norfolk NR29 4AD • 01493 393378 • thenelsonhead.com

The Station Hotel

It doesn't look much from the outside, but this old-timer is a real foodie haven, with a stripped-down main bar that serves some of the best food and drink in the area from a menu that takes in everything from a cheeseburger to guinea fowl with puy lentils or braised pig cheek with celeriac mash. Great food in short, chosen from a blackboard menu that changes daily – plus they fire up their wood-fired pizza oven at the weekend. No rooms.

CONTACT Station Rd, Framlingham, Suffolk IP13 9LE • 01728 723 455 • thestationframlingham.com

The Nutshell

This historic Bury St Edmunds pub claims to be Britain's smallest, and it is certainly pretty tiny – just about big enough for a dozen or so customers at a time to enjoy its antique, wood-panelled interior and gnarled old bar and benches. Look out for the mummified cat hanging from the ceiling! No rooms.

CONTACT 17 The Traverse, Bury St Edmunds, Suffolk IP33 1BJ • 01284 764 867 • thenutshellpub.co.uk

The Flitch of Bacon

Situated in a tiny Essex village, not far from Stansted Airport, this little beauty was conceived as a fine-dining pub with rooms by Daniel Clifford of Midsummer House in Cambridge, and it's still the ultimate high-end, cheffy pub with rooms, Michelin-starred and offering great food and all sorts of gourmet escapes.

CONTACT The Street, Little Dunmow, Essex CM6 3HT • 01371 821 660 • flitchofbacon.co.uk

The Oyster Smack Inn

This workaday waterfront town of white clapboard houses, sailing clubs and sea captains' mansions feels a bit frozen in time, but this high street pub, which was done up around a decade ago, certainly isn't – it's popular with locals and escapees from London mainly for its food, which is a good example of high-end pub food. Its 10 guest rooms are nothing fancy but perfect after blowing the cobwebs away on coastal and inland walks, or on seal or wildlife trips exploring the mysteries of the nearby coastal creaks and islands.

CONTACT 112 Station Rd, Burnham-on-Crouch, Essex CM0 8HR • 01621 782 141 • theoystersmackinn.co.uk

The Anchor at Walberswick

This seaside gastropub with rooms is very much in the image of its long-standing owners Mark and Sophie Dorber, with boutique rooms, excellent food and an impressive list of craft ales chosen by beer connoisseur Mark.

CONTACT Main St, Walberswick, Suffolk IP18 6UA • 01502 722 112 • anchoratwalberswick.com

The Locks Inn

This wonderful pub was recently rescued from the dead at the eleventh hour by the local community, who are hoping to revive its status as one of the Broads' most legendary riverside watering holes and music venues. You can get here on foot or by car but it's best reached on the iconic 'Big Dog' ferry from nearby Beccles. Let's hope it's open again by the time you read this.

CONTACT Lock's Lane, Geldeston, Near Beccles, Norfolk NR34 0HW • 01508 830 033 • thelocksinn.com

(Top) he Anchor at Walberswick; (middle) The Victoria Inn; (bottom The Oyster Smack Inn.

The Midlands

The heartland of the English Midlands is home to some of the most beautiful and diverse countryside in the UK, from the rolling hills of Shropshire, Herefordshire and the Welsh Borders to the gritty heights of the Pennines and flat-as-a-pancake farmlands of the Lincolnshire Fens. It's a stunning region to explore on foot, particularly in the peaks of Derbyshire and Staffordshire, where some of Britain's best gourmet inns have been taking care of visitors for decades.

The Duncombe Arms p.152

The Royal Oak

Even in the wilds of the Peak District, there aren't many places where you can wake up to the whistles of a shepherd, but that's what you get at this steadfast country pub. It occupies a solid stone building just up the hill from the Tissington and High Peak Trails – wonderful routes that follow the course of rail lines that once traversed the Peaks; you'll spot Hurdlow's former train station metres from the pub. This prime location makes The Royal Oak popular with cyclists and hikers, who give the place a lively, outdoorsy feel as they hunker down at the inn's 20-pitch campsite or in the bunk barn, which provides space for up to 34 in 5 dormitories, each sleeping 4–8 people. Toilets and hot showers are shared, and you can take advantage of an excellent breakfast each morning before yomping off into the distance. The pub itself is all beams, open fires and exposed stone walls with an extensive patio at the back. It serves good, homemade food all day, with ingredients largely sourced within a 20-mile radius, both traditional burgers, fish and chips and so forth, and tapas dishes.

CONTACT Hurdlow, Near Buxton, Derbyshire SK17 9QJ • 01298 83288 • peakpub.co.uk

HOW MUCH? Camping from £15 a pitch per night; bunkhouse beds from £20 a night.

The Bull & Swan

The Burghley Estate in the lovely old market town of Stamford, Lincolnshire, is best known for its annual horse trials. What it's not known for is the venerable old order of Bedlam, an aristocratic drinking club that used to take place in this nice old pub in the centre of town, and whose erstwhile members give the pub's 7 comfortable guest rooms their names. Each room is different in size and layout, but they're all very very pleasant, furnished in a style that's a successful blend of traditional and contemporary, and with decent-sized en-suite bathrooms. Downstairs, the pub is cosy and serves a blend of traditional food that's been beautifully updated and presented – everything from homemade Scotch eggs and doorstep sandwiches to expertly cooked steaks and fish and chips. As for Stamford, it's one of our favourite towns in all of England, and Burghley House itself, just outside, is one of the finest Jacobean houses in the country. Dogs are welcome and you're only a 15-minute drive from the large expanses of Rutland Water – which is perfect for sailing, cycling and walking.

CONTACT St Martins, Stamford, Lincolnshire PE9 2LJ • 01780 766 412 • thebullandswan.co.uk

HOW MUCH? Double rooms £105–£155 a night, including breakfast.

The Peacock at Rowsley

Owned by the local lords of the manor – in this case Lord and Lady Manners of nearby Haddon Hall – The Peacock at Rowsley is a perfect place from which to enjoy this beautiful part of the Peak District, and has been for decades. The building is firmly rooted in the 17th century, but the décor is a clever mixture of ancient antiques and modern touches, and there's an elegant restaurant and cosy bar downstairs that are a joy after a hard day's walking. Given the nature of the building, not one of its bedrooms is the same, but they all feature room service, tea and coffee, wifi and flatscreen TVs with Apple TV. There are 14 in all, plus one suite; most have large fireplaces, and comfy beds with big headboards (apart from a couple of 4-posters) and are furnished in a vaguely 'To-the-Manor-Born' style, but with splashes of colour and the same contemporary touches as the public areas. Dogs are welcome – and in this part of the world, where great walks abound, it would be a shame if they weren't. They certainly look the part flaked out in front of The Peacock's embracing hearths.

CONTACT Rowsley, Derbyshire DE4 2EB • 01629 733 518 • thepeacockatrowsley.com
HOW MUCH? Double rooms £150–£245 a night, including breakfast; suite from £350 a night.

The Fuzzy Duck

The Fuzzy Duck is a wonderful regeneration story – with all creature comforts attached. Back in 2013 Tania Fossey rescued her local pub in the appealing hamlet of Armscote, near Stratford-upon-Avon, and transformed it into an elegant venue. With her brother, Adrian Slater, she owns and runs the soap and bath product company Baylis & Harding, and her plan was to apply a similar ethos of affordable luxury to the pub, which she has done with some success. Step through the front door and you're in a slick, relaxing space painted in warming greys, with a welcoming bar and fireplaces. There's a large and sunny extension with bold art at the back, and an ample garden featuring stylish outdoor furniture in summer. Food is a big focus; the seasonal menu is mainly based on local ingredients and offers delights such as slow-cooked chicken breast with truffle and Parmesan fries, and wild mushroom and chive risotto. Upstairs are 4 sophisticated bedrooms named after ducks, all with big beds, fine linen and a host of Baylis & Harding toiletries, of course!

CONTACT Ilmington Rd, Armscote, Warwickshire CV37 8DD • 01608 682 635 • fuzzyduckarmscote.com
HOW MUCH? Double rooms £110–£130 a night; 2 family rooms from £140; prices include breakfast.

The George Townhouse

An updated coaching inn with stylish boutique rooms.

Located bang in the middle of the handsome north Cotswolds market town of Shipston-on-Stour, and by far the grandest building on the short high street, The George Townhouse is a historic 18th-century coaching inn that has been the heartbeat of the town for years. Given a major makeover at the beginning of 2016, it's now a medium-sized boutique inn, fitted out afresh for the 21st century, with a selection of comfortable rooms and good unpretentious food, while remaining an inviting place to stop by for a drink.

The George is part of the Brakspears group, and they have done a great job with the pub, updating it with flair and style while preserving the historic nature of the building. The rooms all come with king-size beds, high-quality mattresses and stylish bathrooms with rainfall showers, plus Temple Spa toiletries, flatscreen TVs, mineral water and Nespresso machines, and blackout curtains for insomniacs. There is plenty of choice too, with fifteen rooms in all, ranging from smallish 'Cosy' and 'Standard' rooms to larger 'Superior' and 'Deluxe' rooms, some of which have a freestanding bath and separate walk-in showers. There's also a large-ish Suite right at the top of the building.

The really nice thing about The George, though, is that it's a well-known venue for food and drink in the town, with non-residents popping in for breakfast, lunch and dinner to enjoy locally sourced food or just a pint or two, either in the main bar or restaurant or out on the popular terrace behind. The pub offers a shortish, moderately priced menu, with half a dozen starters and mains, plus good steaks and a few 'classics', including a great burger and fish and chips – and we challenge anyone to finish what is a generously portioned and delicious Full English breakfast. The atmosphere is good, and the welcome always warm, and there's a pride and enthusiasm for the town and its area that shines through in the service and surroundings. Not only that, there's plenty to do nearby in an area that straddles the Cotswolds and the Midlands, with everything from the Cotswold Distillery in nearby Stourton to Stratford-upon-Avon, which is only a 20-minute drive away.

CONTACT 8 High St, Shipston-on-Stour, Warwickshire CV36 4AJ • 01608 661 453 • thegeorgeshipston.co.uk

HOW MUCH? Double rooms from £100–£180 a night, including breakfast..

ROOMS 15 en-suite bedrooms – Classic, Superior, Deluxe and Deluxe Plus, plus one Suite.

THE GEORGE
TOWNHOUSE

The Duncombe Arms

Great food and rooms at this terrific Staffordshire country inn - if only all village locals were like this!

It was written that Johnny and Laura Greenall would take over this pub – not in the stars but on the pub sign itself, which bore Laura's mother's Duncombe coat of arms. The couple used to drive past the pub every day, which was formerly empty and rather neglected, and they dreamt of restoring it one day. That's exactly what they have done, taking this 1850s village boozer and turning it into a modern country inn renowned for the excellence of its food and the comfort of its rooms.

Just over the border from Derbyshire, The Duncombe Arms also enjoys a great location overlooking the Dove Valley, on the edge of the Peak District National Park. It's a ten-minute drive from Alton Towers, making it an excellent place to stay when visiting the resort, and not far from the pleasant country town of Ashbourne, renowned for its antiques dealers. The rooms - ten in total, in a separate building (Walnut House) behind the pub – are individually decorated in a contemporary country style that really works; think stylish artisan fabrics and wallpapers, mood lighting and bespoke art on the walls. They are large enough for a comfy chair or two and a writing desk, and the bathrooms are modern and well-conceived, some with spacious walk-in showers, others with a shower and bath, and all stocked with fluffy robes and fragrant Bamford toiletries. Each room also has a Roberts radio, a flatscreen TV with Freeview, tea and Nespresso coffee-making facilities, bottles of mineral water and homemade biscuits. The ground floor rooms open up on to a private patio area, while the junior suites are equipped with sofa beds and can accommodate a young family. Dogs are also welcome in two of the rooms, and they also offer a three-bedroom cottage for rent, Garden Cottage, on the nearby Wootton Hall estate.

The pub itself still has the feel of a village local but one where the emphasis is on good quality food, with a menu that features both well-established pub classics and more refined fare, using game and meat from nearby farms, local cheeses and seasonal produce. The food is delicious and pretty much everything in the kitchen is homemade, but the ambience is suitably pubby, with various different rooms, a roaring fire in winter and an outside terrace for warmer months. As for drinks, the pub serves its own Duncombe Ale, and the extensive wine list is carefully chosen by the veteran general manager James Oddy, who has also brought his love of craft gin to the pub, with over 28 different varieties on offer.

CONTACT Ellastone, Ashbourne, Staffordshire DE6 2GZ • 01335 324 275 • duncombearms.co.uk

HOW MUCH? Double rooms from £195 a night, Junior Suites from £225 a night, £20 a night for dogs.

ROOMS Ten rooms, including 2 family rooms, 4 large doubles with shower and 4 large doubles with bath and shower.

The Townhouse

This small boutique hotel is quite a venue. Right in the heart of Stratford, this 400-year-old building, just a few minutes' walk from pretty much everything you might want to see in town, has a buzzy pub and restaurant downstairs along with twelve very comfortable en-suite bedrooms on the upper floors, all of which have recently been refurbished in a highly contemporary style, with super-king-sized beds, crisp cotton sheets and deliciously fluffy duvets, and bathrooms with high-pressure rainfall showers and Noble Isle toiletries; some also have free-standing baths. All the rooms have tea- and coffee-making facilities, including Nespresso machines, mineral water, biscuits and – a nice touch – a small decanter of port! They also have TV/DVD players, wifi, and there's a small DVD library in reception. All in all, it's both a cosy and contemporary place to stay in what is a very convenient central Stratford-upon-Avon location. It also has the added bonus of the excellent bar and restaurant, which give a busy, urban feel to the place, with all-day dining from a brasserie-style menu.

CONTACT 16 Church St, Stratford-upon-Avon, Warwickshire CV37 6HB • 01789 262 222 • stratfordtownhouse.co.uk
HOW MUCH? Double rooms £125–155 a night.

The Devonshire Arms, Beeley

Another fine member of the Chatsworth stable, the 'Dev' is one of the Duke and Duchess's oldest pubs, and very handsome it is too, sitting squarely in the pretty hamlet of Beeley, just a mile or so from the stately pile. It's a pub that's moved with the times but is also strangely unchanged. You can sit in the stone-flagged bar with a pint or eat in front of the fire, but it also has a bright and modern brasserie these days, which serves the same menu – everything from wild rabbit pie to fish and chips and local game in autumn and winter. The pub is a cosy sort of place, giving you a warm feeling that continues right up to its bedrooms, 4 of which are upstairs while the others are scattered in various buildings around the village; one of these, Brookside House, is dog-friendly. All the rooms have wifi, Freeview TVs, tea- and coffee-making facilities and en-suite bathrooms with high-end toiletries, and are very comfortable, making this the perfect place for you to discover all the walks possible from the village, and, of course, on the Chatsworth Estate itself.

CONTACT Beeley, Derbyshire DE4 2NZ • 01756 718 111 • devonshirehotels.co.uk/devonshire-arms-beeley
HOW MUCH? Double rooms £159–£219 a night; suites from £239; all rates include breakfast.

The Barrel Inn

Set 1300 feet up on a ridge in the tiny Derbyshire hamlet of Bretton, where visitors often outnumber inhabitants in summer, this pub is a terrific place to get into the spirit of the Peak District and its outdoor delights. It's not only a cosy place to stay, with 5 lovely double bedrooms upstairs, but its hearty food and warm environment couldn't be more perfectly suited to the location, with inglenook fireplaces, beams, comfy settles and old-school horse brasses on rough plaster walls – just what you need after a hard day's hiking. The beer is great and the food is plentiful and good value for money, and to top it all off there's a brilliant flagged yard at the front to sit in on the odd warm day. It's pretty high here, so those days are rare, but hardy souls don't seem to mind, mainly because the view over Hucklow towards Buxton is stupendous. The gliding club is just over the hill and it's a chucking-off point for paragliders, so there's plenty to watch, and, not surprisingly, there are fabulous walks from here too. What better place to end a five-mile yomp?

CONTACT Bretton, Near Eyam, Derbyshire S32 5QD • 01433 630 856 • thebarrelinn.co.uk
HOW MUCH? Double rooms from £95 a night, including breakfast.

The Plough Inn

Nestled within the green confines of the Peak District National Park, the village of Hathersage has a relaxed and countrified air, and, at the heart of the village, the Plough is a country inn of ancient provenance, an attractive complex of stone buildings set back from the road with a slender courtyard at its centre. The hotel offers 7 immaculate bedrooms, each decorated in country-house pastel shades, and a handful of shepherds' huts – quaint, cute and simple wooden structures that are ideal for self-catering and come with a full range of equipment squeezed into their narrow confines. The Plough's restaurant is appealing, too, offering steaks, burgers, sharing boards and pizzas alongside the odd fancier dish, plus a choice of roasts on Sundays, all accompanied by the beers and ales of the local Bradfield and Abbeydale breweries. Hiking trails stretch out from Hathersage in all directions into the surrounding Peak District, drawing hikers from all over; dogs are allowed in every part of the inn, including all guest rooms and the pub area.

CONTACT Leadmill Bridge, Hathersage, Derbyshire S32 1BA • 01433 650 319 • theploughinn-hathersage.co.uk
HOW MUCH? Double rooms from £110 a night, including breakfast.

The Powis Arms

In the peaceful Shropshire village of Lydbury North, The Powis Arms is an old Georgian coaching inn, part of the Walcot Hall Estate and situated right by its main gates and drive. It's a friendly country pub and has a choice of accommodation options – a pop-up summer campsite and 4 very comfortable upstairs bedrooms (plus the estate has a multitude of glamping and self-catering options). The rooms are simple but well appointed, with decent beds and en-suite bathrooms, one of which features a bath and the other 3 showers. Each has tea-and coffee-making facilities and wifi but deliberately no TVs (they would spoil the peace and quiet). The rooms are quirkily furnished with furniture, objects and paintings plundered from Walcot Hall, giving each an individual, historic and cosy character. The campsite has 12 spaces for caravans and campervans, plus pitches for tents, and a heated shower block. Wherever you stay you can enjoy the excellent breakfasts served each morning, not to mention the well-priced food on offer the rest of the day.

CONTACT Lydbury North, Shropshire SY7 8AU • 01588 680 254 • thepowisarms.com
HOW MUCH? Double rooms from £80 a night, including breakfast. Camping pitches (April–Oct) £7.50.

The Cow

South Derbyshire doesn't come much more rural than the village of Lees, whose redbrick houses fan out from the village green and the pub, formerly known as 'The Black Cow', which has in recent years been updated as a smart gastropub and inn. It occupies a stalwart whitewashed 19th-century building with a lovely long bar and an open fireplace, wood-beamed ceilings and an assortment of period bric-a-brac. There is casual dining here, from a menu that sports a canny combination of pubby dishes that go well with the pub's selection of local ales – you are after all less than 10 miles from the brewing capital of England, Burton-on-Trent. To the rear of the pub there are 12 luxury bedrooms, each of striking modern design, some with heavy, luxurious drapes, others with imposing decorative bedheads, but all with everything you might need for a comfortable stay – king-size beds, Egyptian cotton sheets, Smart TVs, wifi, and coffee machines; the bathrooms have underfloor heating and walk-in showers. There are also electric charging-points in the carpark.

CONTACT The Green, Dalbury Lees, Ashbourne, Derbyshire DE6 5BE • 01332 824 297 • cowdalbury.com
HOW MUCH? Double rooms from £140 a night, including breakfast.

The Old White Hart

Deep in the Rutland countryside, Lyddington is a handsome hamlet, its charming limestone cottages fanning out from The Old White Hart, an ancient yet stylishly modernised country inn with 20 en-suite rooms, each decorated in contemporary style with shades of cream and fawn to the fore. Divided between the original limestone building and a neighbouring annexe, they vary from the cheapest annexe rooms to the most expensive 'King' rooms, but the main difference is size and location; all come with tea- and coffee-making facilities and biscuits. Downstairs there's a country-chic bar and restaurant, with stone-flagged floors serving the likes of duck and ginger spring rolls with hoisin sauce or chicken and broad bean risotto, and a famous Sunday Lunch, with generous portions of roast rib of beef with all the trimmings. If the sun is out, you will want to be outside in the garden, or you can wander along the village's main street to Bede House, the medieval wing of a palace that was once a retreat for the bishops of Lincoln and now in the possession of English Heritage.

CONTACT 51 Main Street, Lyddington, Rutland LE15 9LR • 01572 821 703 • oldwhitehart.co.uk
HOW MUCH? Double rooms with breakfast from £95 a night in the annexe to £120 in the main building.

The Olive Branch

Leafy and prosperous, the village of Clipsham sits prettily among the rolling fields of Rutland, its quiet charms giving little indication of the past importance of its limestone quarries, the stone from which was used to build scores of England's most important buildings. Nowadays its star-turn is The Olive Branch, a delectable gastropub housed in a stone cottage on the edge of the village. The décor, with its exposed wooden beams and bare walls, manages to be folksy and rural without being twee, and there is a good-sized patio, too. The food is outstanding, with a selection of tapas at lunchtime and a dinner menu featuring imaginative variations on traditional dishes. The owners are particular about where they source their food, using local suppliers and growing lots of veg in the neighbouring paddock. They also offer 6 elegant, individually decorated rooms in the attractively restored Beech House, across the road; bathrooms have double-ended baths and power showers and overnight stays are rounded off with a sumptuous breakfast in the adjacent barn.

CONTACT Main St, Clipsham, Rutland LE15 7SH • 01780 410 355 • theolivebranchpub.com
HOW MUCH? Double rooms with breakfast £145–£225 a night.

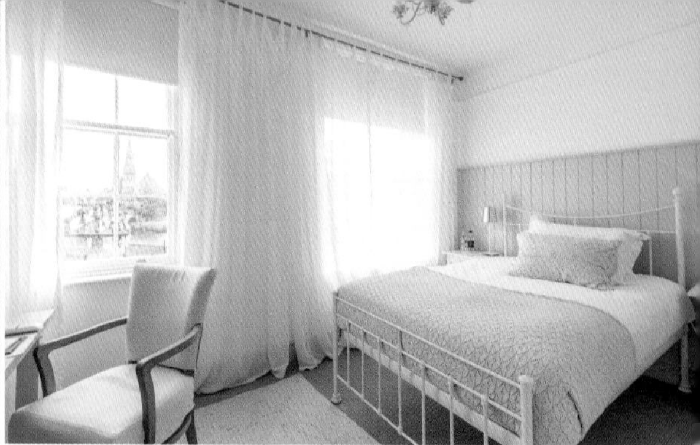

The Haughmond

On a quiet country road in the sleepy village of Upton Magna, The Haughmond is a modern coaching inn, owned and run by husband-and-wife team Mel and Martin. Dog- and cycle-friendly, it's a splendid place for good food, surroundings and service, with a restaurant that's a destination in itself, with 3 AA rosettes and a Michelin Plate award. The calming greens, stag-themed artwork and quality furnishings complement the building's original character, and you can relax with your drink in the newly redecorated Basil's Lounge, or adjourn to the peaceful garden and enjoy the extensive views over the surrounding countryside. There are 7 contemporary en-suite rooms, newly redecorated, with high-quality, modern oak furniture, white linen and deep pile carpeting that give the rooms a really luxurious feel. They all have wifi and flatscreen TVs, freshly ground coffee and bottled water. The inn also has a self-catering barn conversion for rent, and runs the Village Store & Café across the road, serving tea, coffee, cakes, sandwiches, ice cream and more.

CONTACT Pelham Rd, Upton Magna, Shropshire SY4 4TZ • 01743 709 918 • thehaughmond.co.uk
HOW MUCH? Double rooms £95–£130 a night, including breakfast. The Barn £360–£1100 a week.

The Lion + Pheasant

This attractive historic inn occupies a 16th-century building in a great position in the beautiful old town of Shrewsbury. With its friendly, relaxed ambience, it's a welcome oasis, with fresh and tasteful interiors featuring eclectic furniture and soft furnishings combined with charming original features – flagstone and wood floors, oak beams and fireplaces. The bar is a really nice space, and there's a popular and rather chic wine bar adjacent to the hotel, serving a wide range of wines and beers. You have a choice of eating spaces: a cosy restaurant downstairs and a more spacious one upstairs with rustic oak beams. The food is really good, using ingredients from local suppliers and producers, and a tapas menu is served in the wine bar. There are 23 en-suite bedrooms, where the building's original character is coupled perfectly with stylish contemporary design, with modern wooden furnishings, natural floorings, wrought iron and 4-poster beds, crisp white linen and large walk-in showers (some rooms have baths). In addition, there are 2 self-catering apartments with private entrances.

CONTACT 49-50 Wyle Cop, Shrewsbury, Shropshire SY1 1XJ • 01743 770 345 • lionandpheasant.co.uk
HOW MUCH? Double rooms £165-£230 a night, including breakfast. Apartments from £250.

The Pheasant at Neenton

The Pheasant is a delightful community-owned country pub with rooms, serving excellent food, in the sleepy village of Neenton, about a 10-minute drive from Bridgnorth. Bought and restored back in 2013, it is now managed by husband-and-wife team Sarah and Mark, from whom you'll receive a great, friendly welcome. Mark Harris's food is excellent, created and presented with immense care and talent. British classics with a unique, flavoursome slant are served in generous portions, using fresh local produce. It's food that brings a smile to your face, and you can enjoy it in the conservatory or Village Bar (both dog-friendly) or the Oak Room restaurant. Alternatively, relax outdoors on the dining terrace, which is possible in all weather due to integrated heaters, or in the orchard garden. There are 3 attractive rooms, each decorated in restful, neutral colours and furnished with super-king-sized beds and interesting industrial-styled lamps and lighting. There are spacious en-suite shower rooms, and tea, coffee and fresh milk are provided.

CONTACT Neenton, Bridgnorth, Shropshire WV16 6RJ • 01746 787 955 • pheasantatneenton.co.uk
HOW MUCH? Double rooms £90–£110 a night, including breakfast.

The Lion at Leintwardine

The Lion at Leintwardine is situated in a beautiful, quiet country setting, on the Shropshire-Herefordshire border, overlooking the Welsh Marches. Sitting peaceably at the spot where the rivers Clun and Teme meet, it offers tranquillity, a smiling welcome and a great choice of pleasurable spaces to eat, drink and relax. Owners William and Jane restored the building to its current form, and interiors are stylish, characterful and beautifully furnished, with leather sofas, tub chairs, eclectic coffee tables, chandeliers and lamps. The historic photographs on the walls and fresh flowers finish the look off nicely. There's a snug, a lounge bar, the dog-friendly top bar and the restaurant, while you can also enjoy the Modern British menu on the walled terrace or in the garden with benches on the bank of the river, overlooking the Grade II-listed Leintwardine Bridge. There's a superb apex-roofed, wooden-beamed breakfast room too. The 8 charming en-suite rooms are traditionally styled with dark-wood classic furnishings, ornate mirrors and lamps, and quality linens, while bathrooms are gorgeous and spacious.

CONTACT 7 High St, Leintwardine, Shropshire SY7 0JZ • 01547 540 203 • thelionleintwardine.co.uk
HOW MUCH? Double rooms £90–£130 a night, including breakfast..

The New Inn

When Mark and Julie Green bought The New Inn 5 years ago, it needed substantial updating. Fortunately, that wasn't a problem – the pub was the first one that Mark, now co-owner of 'Two Farmers' crisps, ever drunk in; and now this 16th-century coaching inn just outside Ross-on-Wye is back from the dead, with a superb bar, restaurant and a little snug for private parties. It still maintains a traditional look – all beams and plaster, but cleaned up and classy, with stripped-back, light oak beams instead of dark olde-worlde ones, and 3 very chic bedrooms, with cosy throws and robes, ultra-comfy beds, wifi and Smart TVs, tea and coffee. One room has a wow-factor glass-walled bathroom and free-standing bath – very romantic. The new New Inn is that sort of place – a pub for grown-ups (there's no kids' menu) with 21 wines by the glass and a great choice of ales, bespoke cocktails and an enormous list of gins. Food, too, is top-notch – think orchard pork, wild sea bass, blackberry soufflé – and, as well as the modern rustic dining room, there's a lovely secret terrace to enjoy it al fresco, too.

CONTACT St Owen's Cross, Herefordshire HR2 8LQ • 01989 553 387 • thenewinnherefordshire.co.uk
HOW MUCH? Double rooms from £150 a night, including breakfast.

The Saracen's Head

It pays to arrive early at this big, buzzing traditional pub with rooms if you want your pick of the tables, and you'll understand why as soon as you get here. Run by brothers Chris and Pete Rollinson, it sits beside the River Wye in the heavenly little beauty spot of Symonds Yat, a 10-minute drive from Ross-on-Wye. The best views are from the 2 large terraces literally feet from the water. Not surprisingly, it gets very busy, especially in summer. Of course, if you choose to stay overnight, you get it all to yourself in the morning. There are 9 rooms, unfussy and modern, the best of which are in the separate Boathouse. You may be pleased to know that no kids under 14 are allowed to stay, though they can come and enjoy the food, which is served in the laid-back bar or relaxed restaurant, or outside when you can bag a table. The menu mainly features pub crowd-pleasers, well cooked and nicely presented, while those overnighting can expect a generous brekkie before working off calories on a choice of activities nearby. The inn even provides free licences for angler guests.

CONTACT Symonds Yat East, Herefordshire HR9 6JL • 01600 890 435 • saracensheadinn.co.uk
HOW MUCH? Double rooms from £120 a night, including breakfast.

The Talbot

The oak-panelled dining room of The Talbot has a souvenir bullet in the wall from a skirmish between the Roundheads and Cavaliers. How much more historic can you get? Packed with character and cosiness, this handsome 16th-century black-and-white coaching inn is just off the high street in the Herefordshire market town of Ledbury – a handsome, timbered building with big doors, low ceilings, narrow corridors and creaky floorboards, and a warm, old-fashioned bar. There are 13 rooms, some of them olde-worlde and others more spacious with modern décor in the Old Stable Cottage. The Morgan Room has a huge bathroom/wet room and lots of space, so is particularly suitable for guests with disabilities. Lunch and dinner are served in the dining room, bar and courtyard, from menus that highlight local, seasonal, unfussy food - fish and chips with Wadworths beer batter is good, as is the steak and ale pie or their locally sourced beefburger. There are also lots of gluten-free and vegetarian dishes on offer and a good selection of wines by the glass.

CONTACT 14 New St, Ledbury, Herefordshire, HR8 2DX • 01531 632 963 • talbotledbury.co.uk

HOW MUCH? Double rooms £80–£120 a night, including breakfast.

The Riverside at Aymestrey

If foodie gems miles from anywhere are your thing, do not miss this one. The Riverside is a former coaching inn and sits surrounded by countryside right by the 1931 bridge over the River Lugg in the village of Aymestrey, 8 miles from Leominster. The gourmand bit comes from chef-patron Andrew Link, whose food is simply superb. He's into foraging, so expect extraordinary flavours such as wild garlic, as well as ultra-fresh herbs and veggies from the kitchen garden. Delights include battered Herefordshire snails, braised pheasant stew, truffle chips and blue cheese ice-cream. To cap it all, the bar offers hand-pulled real ales and ciders, and a brilliant wine list. The warm, cosy bar and restaurant has low ceilings and dark beams dressed with garlands of hops, and the inn has 6 upscale rooms, including 2 spacious suites in an annexe. They have sublimely comfortable feather-and-down beds, high-end bathrooms with Nobel Isle toiletries, wifi, flatscreen TVs and minibars, tea and coffee and homemade biscuits – and pets can stay overnight in a couple of the rooms.

CONTACT Aymestrey, Herefordshire HR6 9ST • 01568 708 440 • riversideaymestrey.co.uk

HOW MUCH? Rooms from £95 a night for a snug double; from £120 for a suite. Breakfast included.

The Kilpeck Inn

With so many locals closing down, The Kilpeck Inn, 10 miles from Hereford, is a good news story. Boarded up and abandoned for 5 years, it reopened in 2010 and is nowadays a warm and welcoming country inn serving great food. Its flagstone floors and walls were built from stones collected from the local castle, torn down during the English Civil War, and walls feature old photos and works by local artists. Elsewhere, the look and feel is 'modern country', with light wood tables and chairs and a cosy bar with sofas and chairs with sheepskins. There's also a garden, plus 4 fresh and modern bedrooms with all the trimmings. Food is not typical pub grub, even if it sounds like it: the burgers are made from scratch, hake comes with homemade tartar sauce, chips are handcut and there's a cracking venison Sunday lunch in winter. Thirsty patrons come for Herefordshire Butty Bach, Robinson's cider, grapefruit gin from the Chase Distillery down the road and Welsh wine. Ollie, the friendly black spaniel, is in charge of low-level waste management, and pets are welcome in the bar.

CONTACT Castle Park, Kilpeck, Herefordshire HR2 9DN • 01981 570 464 • kilpeckinn.com
HOW MUCH? Double rooms £90–£120 a night, including breakfast.

The Greenman

Drive through the Herefordshire village of Fownhope and you can't miss the large lemon and beige building that houses this superb pub and restaurant. The inside may be rustic but it's chic, too, with thumping great wooden tables, warming fireplaces, blackboards and beams: classy with cool touches. When owners Sean and Sarah Mason took over the pub and renovated it, they made sure locals had their own designated Drinkers' Table, with no food allowed. Beer aficionados come from miles around to sup Greenman bitter, specially brewed by Wye Valley Ales. But, really, it's a shame to come and not try the tempting food – pan-fried pigeon breast, black pudding Scotch egg, a trio of chocolate doughnuts... come on! The Herefordshire beef is particularly succulent. Cheese fiends will adore Stinking Bishop, Slack-ma-Gurdle and Hereford Hop, and, when you're done, it's nice to know that there are 17 beautifully furnished, boutique-style rooms spread over the property, including 5 rooms in the Old Cottage that can accommodate self-caterers.

CONTACT Fownhope, Herefordshire HR1 4PE • 01432 860 243 • thegreenman.co
HOW MUCH? Double rooms £80-£120 a night, including breakfast.

The Crown at Woolhope

The Crown is a proper, down-to-earth country pub, serving both locals and visitors to this beautiful apple-growing area of Herefordshire. Given the location, it's no surprise the bar stocks 26 ciders and perries, including the inn's own 'King's Cider', and to go with them the pub serves unpretentious, delicious food – including popular choices like Cornish fish and chips, cider-steamed mussels, award-winning Sunday lunches, and pizzas from a new wood-fired oven. There's a large bar, real fires, a dartboard and a small porch called 'Pond Life' – so called, says landlord Matt, because that's where the misbehaved folk hang out. Out front, The Crown has a public terrace and garden, while next door there's an extension for self-catering rental that comfortably sleeps 14 and is connected to the pub by a secret door. It's a fabulous property, with 5 bathrooms to go with its 7 bedrooms, a games room and huge kitchen/diner and a private garden with a barbecue. Can you think of any other self-catering property that is attached to its own pub?

CONTACT Woolhope, Herefordshire HR1 4QP • 01432 860 468 • crowninnwoolhope.co.uk
HOW MUCH? Self-catering accommodation from £40 per person per night, not including breakfast.

The Kilcot Inn

Parents will tell you that all a pub needs to be über-cool is a dirty great space out the back where the kids can run wild; better still if there's a mini-playground and some benches where mum and dad can perch. Step forward The Kilcot Inn, a pretty, privately owned country pub bang on the Herefordshire-Gloucestershire border, 7 miles from Ross-on-Wye. Inside, there's a small bar if you want just a drink and a chat, or a larger restaurant if you're making a night of it. The food has flair, with daily specials and a menu of favourites, such as fish and chips and Herefordshire steak, plus unusual fare like ostrich burgers or bean and leek burgers. Children, vegetarians and vegans are well catered for. The bar serves local beers and ciders, and the wine list includes vegan and organic wines. Upstairs are 4 nicely furnished, modern en-suite rooms with all the trimmings – tea and coffee, TV, sofa and bathroom toiletries. Thoughtful touches include a covered cycle shed, so guests can store their bikes safely, and pet-friendly areas with water bowls and dog biccies.

CONTACT Ross Rd, Newent, Gloucestershire GL18 1NA • 01989 720 707 • kilcotinn.com
HOW MUCH? Double rooms from £99 a night, including breakfast.

Lucky Dip

The Chequers Inn

Perched on the densely wooded hillside above Carver on the precipitous moors road to Sheffield, this handsome 16th-century inn, once a series of farm workers' cottages, is brimming with character. Inside are polished wood floors, exposed stone walls, gleaming oak furniture and cottagey textiles and prints. The food is wholesome and beautifully presented and local ales include brews from Peak Ales and the Bradfield Brewery. There are 7 boutique rooms upstairs in case you want to make a night of it, while outside the terraced garden is a great place for a pint or the starting-off point for a fabulous walk up to Froggatt Edge.

CONTACT Froggatt Edge, Hope Valley, Derbyshire S32 3ZJ • 01433 630 231 • chequers-froggatt.com

The Saracen's Head

The Saracen's Head dates back to 1791 when it was run as a farm and hostelry, and while owners Robin and Terri Hunter have retained lots of original features, they've cleverly brought the place up to date with no small amount of pizzazz. Inside is a mixture of old and new, with lovely vintage pieces next to contemporary chunky tables and chairs. Robin is no slouch in the kitchen, so expect the likes of hake with wilted spinach and mash or spicy Goan style monkfish. Yet the well-kept local beer and a dartboard ensures that this still feels like a proper pub. They also have their own deli. No rooms.

CONTACT Church Lane, Shirley, Derbyshire DE6 3AS • 01335 360 330 • saracens-head-shirley.co.uk

The Strines Inn

This handsome stone pub is on the stunning Strines road, which runs from Penistone into Derbyshire, and is a no-nonsense sort of place, with horse brasses, open coal fires, swirly carpets and battered mismatched furniture. The welcome is warm, though, and the homemade food will raise a smile – not a frozen lasagne in sight, but giant Yorkshire puddings and pies for carnivores and homemade butter bean stew for veggies. It prides itself on well-kept real ale, and there's tons of room to sit outside and enjoy the views – and, in case you can't tear yourself away, they have rooms upstairs, all with 4-poster beds.

CONTACT Mortimer Rd, Bradfield Dale, Derbyshire S6 6JE • 01142 851 247 • thestrinesinn.co.uk

The George

You're disposed to liking this place as soon as you clap eyes on it: the pub sits on the edge of the green, a handsome, mellow stone building with a garden to sit in on good days. Inside, the polished tiled floors gleam and old oak tables beckon, and the food is bang up to date, with the likes of goats' cheese beignet, confit jersey royals with bone marrow crumb, braised hogget with smoked aubergine, poached chalk stream trout – and, for afters, Earl Grey pannacotta or blueberry cheesecake with honey, lemon and lavender. Stunning Dovedale and Milldale are just down the road; you'll kick yourself if you don't take a walk after lunch. No rooms.

CONTACT Alstonefield, Derbyshire DE6 2FX • 01335 310 205 • thegeorgeatalstonefield.com

The Red Lion

Ask a child to draw an old pub on an oak tree fringed green in a sleepy village and chances are this is what they'd come up with. Litton is one of the prettiest and least-known High Peak villages, and The Red Lion's been a pub since the late 1700s, when it was converted from 3 farm cottages. Not much has changed inside – wonky stone floors, metre-thick walls and hearty walkers' fare from the kitchen – one-piece beef stew, steak & ale pie and some brilliant traditional puddings. They're dog-friendly and have 2 lovely en-suite double rooms upstairs in case you want to stay over.

CONTACT Church Lane, Litton, Derbyshire SK17 8QU • 01298 871 458 • theredlionlitton.co.uk

The Samuel Fox

Samuel Fox Esq, son of Bradwell, is credited with inventing the modern steel-ribbed umbrella, which became a worldwide success in the 19th century – not bad for a local lad. The eponymous pub has nothing to do with him but it's a fitting memorial, a nice mixture of old-school and contemporary, with a bright, spacious bar gussied up in contemporary style, and fancy food rustled up by chef-patron and ex-Gordon Ramsey acolyte James Duckett. If you fancy making a night of it, book into one of the bedrooms, all with great views across the hills. 'Bradder', as it's known locally, is a bit of a hidden gem in the Peak District, so steal a march and head here.

CONTACT Stretfield Rd, Bradwell, Derbyshire S33 9JT • 01433 621 562 • samuelfox.co.uk

(top) The Samuel Fox; (middle) The Red Lion;
(bottom) The Strines Inn.

The Anglers Rest

One of the country's best examples of many previously distressed pubs that have been rescued over recent years by local communities and are now being run as a going concerns, mostly not for profit. Being a community pub isn't necessarily just about surviving. This one is a great village pub that stocks a wide range of local ales, serves excellent food and also hosts regular live music: just like any other pub, in fact. Unlike most other pubs, though, it also runs the local Post Office, café and gift shop! No rooms.

CONTACT Main Rd, Bamford, Derbyshire S33 0DY • 01433 659 317 • anglers.rest

The Kean's Head

Owned and operated by Castle Rock, a small pub group and brewery based in Nottingham, the Kean's Head is a popular city-centre spot standing in the shadow of Nottingham's finest medieval church, St Mary's. The premises date back to the 19th century, if not before, and have been sympathetically modernised in an informal Victorian style, with bare wood floors and exposed wooden beams. The one-room pub's highlight is its range of craft beers, with the varied brews of Castle Rock taking pride of place – don't miss the delectable Harvest Pale – but there are guest beers, too, and a stand-up assortment of whiskys. The menu is classic bar food, with the likes of corned beef hash, burgers and pies in substantial helpings. No rooms.

CONTACT 46 St Mary's Gate, Nottingham NG1 1QA • 0115 947 4052 • castlerockbrewery.co.uk/pubs/keans-head

The Full Moon Inn

The pretty village of Morton sits in tranquil countryside between a branch railway line and the fast–flowing River Trent. The main reason for venturing out here is to seek out the Full Moon Inn, a tastefully modernised country pub that offers outstanding British food focused on local produce and traditional dishes, albeit cooked with a contemporary eye towards presentation. The pub also has one splendid large double room upstairs in case you want to stay, with a super-king-size bed and a sofa bed too.

CONTACT Main St, Morton, Near Southwell, Nottinghamshire NG25 0UT • 01636 830 251 • thefullmoonmorton.co.uk

The Kangaroo Inn

If there is a local pub in England that's as welcoming as The Kangaroo then we have yet to find it. Just a few miles outside Craven Arms in the heart of the Shropshire countryside, this is quite simply a terrific pub, rooted in the community, with a great choice of ales, an annual summer beer festival and a menu of hearty pub grub. We always stop by if we're in the area! No rooms.

CONTACT Clun Rd, Aston on Clun, Shropshire SY7 8EW • 01588 660 263 • thekangarooinn.co.uk

The Fox & Hounds

Right on the green in the pretty Rutland village of Exton, The Fox & Hounds ticks all the boxes that a country pub should. Good food? Tick! Roaring fires? Tick! Warm welcome? Tick! Close to good walks? Tick! Dog-friendly? Tick! Plus it also has some cosy rooms upstairs in case you want to stay over and make the most of its idyllic location not far from Rutland Water.

CONTACT 19 The Green, Exton, Near Oakham, Rutland LE15 8AP • 01572 811 032 • thefoxinexton.co.uk

The Berkeley Arms

Situated in the sleepy Leicestershire village of Wymondham, not far from Melton Mowbray, this pub offers much more than just a pork pie – in fact, it has a long and deserved reputation as a place to eat. Its menu takes in everything from local game terrine and salmon gravadlax to superb steaks and fish dishes; and if you just fancy a snack they offer good bar nibbles, too – black pudding Scotch eggs, duck spring rolls or crispy whitebait with tartare sauce. No rooms.

CONTACT 59 Main St, Wymondham, Leicestershire LE14 2AG • 01572 787 587 • berkeley-arms.co.uk

The Finch's Arms

The location's the thing at this family-owned pub, which sits in the almost impossibly picturesque cul-de-sac Rutland village of Hambleton, just a short stroll from the banks of Rutland Water. Good food and some slick en-suite rooms make it the budget alternative to the Michelin-starred fare at posh Hambleton Hall, which overlooks the water from its perch on the edge of the village.

CONTACT Oakham Rd, Hambleton, Rutland LE15 8TL • 01572 756 575 • finchsarms.co.uk

The Bridge Inn

This lovely beamed old pub isn't the sort of place you stumble across by accident, tucked away as it is deep in Herefordshire border country. But it occupies a stunning riverside setting, serves excellent food and even has its own brand of gin – trust us, you won't want to leave. Just as well, then, that they have 4 B&B rooms available in a nearby farmhouse plus a self-catering yurt and a handful of camping pitches.

CONTACT Michaelchurch Escley, Herefordshire HR2 OJW • 01981 510 646 • thebridgeinnmichaelchurch.co.uk

(top) The Full Moon Inn; (middle) The Finch's Arms; (bottom) The Bridge Inn.

Yorkshire and the Northeast

There's perhaps no region that has embraced the UK's food revolution more than Yorkshire, and no wonder. It has always been home to some legendary pubs and restaurants, but the beauty of the landscape and its natural bounty also makes it easy for chefs to get inspired. The results are plain to see: numerous superb country inns across Yorkshire, Durham and Northumberland that make terrific bases for exploring the hills, dales and coastline of this unique corner of Britain.

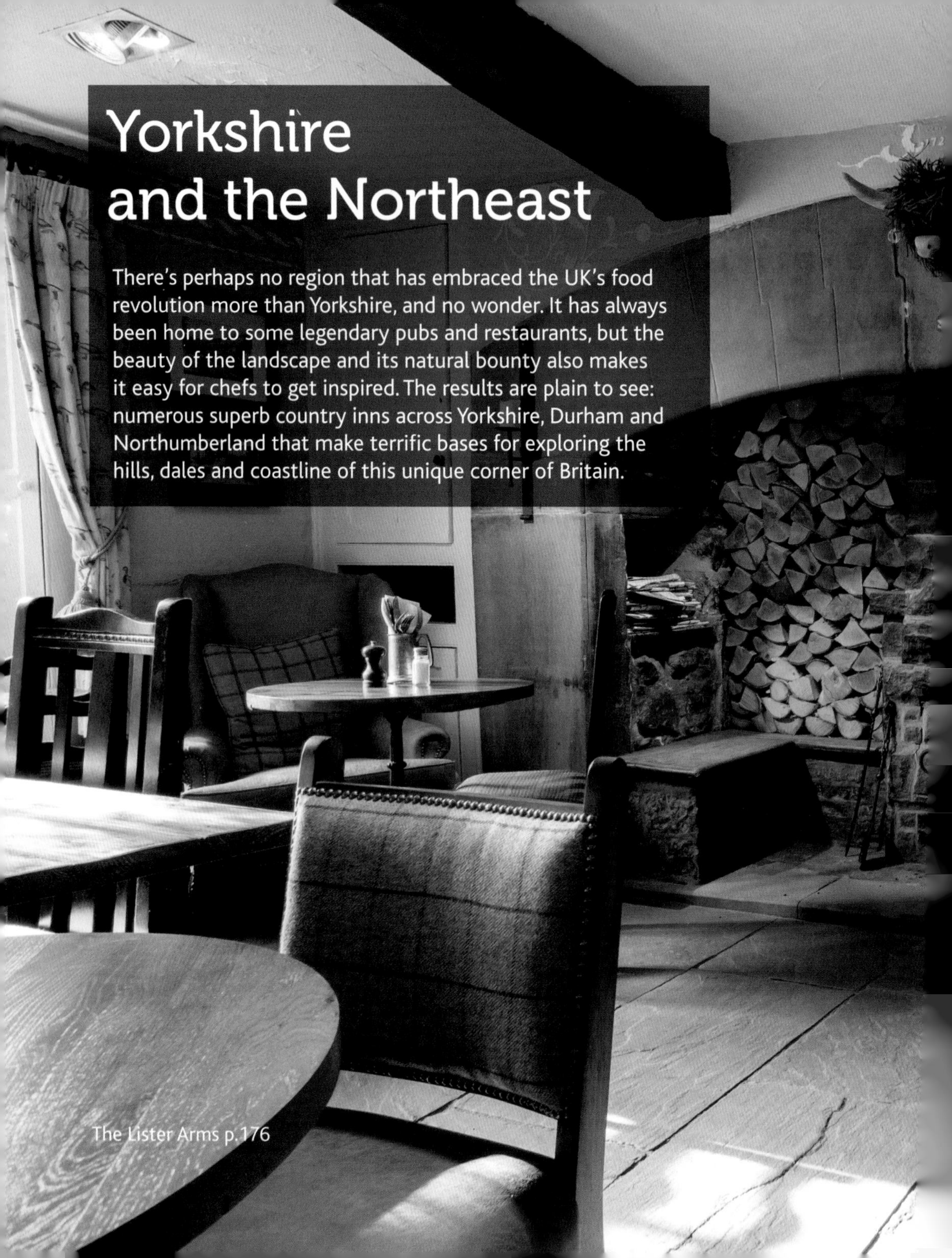

The Lister Arms p.176

DRY
LOGS

The Star Inn

Pretty much everyone will point you towards the Star at Harome if you tell them you're looking for a proper country pub with great food. The old thatched inn dates back to the 14th century and certainly looks the part, with a vintage interior of low beams, wood panelling and rough plastered walls. Chef and owner Andrew Pern roots his seasonally changing menus firmly in North Yorkshire, where he grew up, from Scarborough-caught fish with samphire and brown shrimps to estate game and local lamb, pork and beef, all enhanced by their own herbs and veg. It's modern cooking at its best, but relaxed and fancy-free – so the same menu is available in bar or restaurant. To turn a meal into a memorable night, stay over in their accommodation across the road, where 8 highly individual beamed rooms offer a select experience, from a roll-top bath at the foot of a handmade bed to a piano or even a snooker table in your room. There's a private lounge and terrace, while breakfast is served under a magnificent wooden wheelhouse ceiling.

CONTACT High St, Harome, North Yorkshire YO62 5JE • 01439 770 397 • thestaratharome.co.uk

HOW MUCH? Double rooms £190–£250 a night, inckuding breakfast.

Woolly Sheep Inn

Let's start with breakfast – the very best finish to any stay at the Woolly Sheep Inn, a Timothy Taylors' pub near the foot of the High Street in the bustling North Yorkshire market town of Skipton. Locally sourced sausage and bacon, homemade black pudding, muffins, real bread to slice yourself, barista coffee, made-to-order omelettes, French toast, orange juice on ice served in old-fashioned stopper bottles – you can see where we're going with this and why we like it so much. It's of a piece with the rest of the well-presented, well-cooked food they serve at the pub, and it sets you up heartily for a day exploring the nearby Yorkshire Dales. And the rooms? Don't worry, they're grand as well – perhaps a bit on the small side, but all 12 are ship-shape and furnished with modern country pine and earthy tones mixed with pastel colours. All the guest rooms have flatscreen TVs, bottled water and tea- and coffee- making facilities. There is more space in the superior rooms, plus a fold-down sofabed, and some of the rooms are dog-friendly.

CONTACT 38 Sheep St, Skipton, North Yorkshire BD23 1HY • 01756 700 966 • woollysheepinn.co.uk

HOW MUCH?.Double rooms £95–£125 a night, including breakfast.

The Blue Lion

With the gorgeous Yorkshire Dales surrounding it, The Blue Lion is one of the area's finest stays – a Grade-II-listed building with a history as long as your arm, including being the last public house in England to have a 6-day licence, thanks to a previous landlady. Current owners Paul and Helen Klein have built a stunning reputation for the pub, not just for its 15 boutique rooms, some of which are dog-friendly, but for the food too, which has won them a 'Dining Pub of the Year' award on more than one occasion. The rooms are split between the main house and the converted stable building, and vary from 'Petite Doubles' to 'Classics' or 'Large Classics'. Our choice would be the Large Classic, which not only offers views over the Dales but also a bath as well as a shower, while all rooms have flatscreen TVs, wifi and tea- and coffee-making facilities as standard. Meanwhile the countryside of the Yorkshire Dales beckons outside – and, as it happens, the team have a series of 6 walking maps available at the reception to help you plan your day.

CONTACT Main Rd, East Witton, North Yorkshire DL8 4SN • 01969 624 273 • thebluelion.co.uk
HOW MUCH? Double rooms £105–£155 a night, including breakfast.

The Angel at Hetton

As one of the Dales' most celebrated dining destinations, and perhaps the North's original gastropub, The Angel at Hetton has long been a destination for both good food and comfortable accommodation. But this legendary Yorkshire Dales establishment has been breaking new ground of late, with the 2 Michelin-starred chef Michael Wignall taking over as chef-patron a couple of years ago. He and his wife Johanna have lifted this lovely old inn to a new level, with 15 individually designed and refurbished guest rooms that are split between the main building and Fell View Barn's 5 individual luxury suites across the road, which boast magnificent views over Rylstone Fell. Next door, another building, Sycamore Bank, also has 2 studios and 2 suites. Attention to detail is spot-on, and as a guest you have a guaranteed reservation for dinner. As a romantic retreat, or for a big gesture or celebration, The Angel is hard to beat – as Steve Coogan and Rob Brydon famously found out all those years ago in the the first of the popular TV series 'The Trip'.

CONTACT Hetton, Near Skipton, North Yorkshire BD23 6LT • 01756 730 263 • angelhetton.co.uk
HOW MUCH? Double rooms from £295 a night, including breakfast and dinner.

Lord Crewe Arms

A cosy country pub in a glorious location, with heaps of history to spare.

Part of the 'Calcot Collection', which mostly runs high-end boutique hotels further south, this much-loved inn on the Durham-Northumberland border is an extraordinary building with an extraordinary history – a 12th-century former abbot's lodgings that dominates the impeccably preserved village of Blanchland, at the foot of the local moors.

Inside the main building, it's all stone corridors, soaring ceilings, heraldic shields, hidden nooks and majestic fireplaces – including one that hides a secret 'Priest's Hole', where Jacobite rebels once sheltered. There are guest rooms in the old abbot's residence and the restored miners' cottages that flank the adjacent cobbled square, and while no two are the same, you can count on a certain updated country-chic style. They're classed as 'Cosy' (the smallest), 'Canny' or 'Champion' (the best), though all feature king-sized beds, robes, aromatherapy toiletries and carefully selected art and furniture. The Champion rooms and the two suites also boast Nespresso machines, and the suites are particularly lovely, especially Blackdene, an utterly charming cottage duplex with an open log fire and a winding staircase to an upstairs boudoir. Colours throughout are earthy and muted – restful in other words, just like the peaceful surroundings, where the loudest sound you'll hear in the morning is the birdsong. Breakfast is a sophisticated and welcome start to your morning, with home-baked bread, locally smoked salmon, eggs benedict or an excellent Full English fry-up to set you up for the day.

Later in the day you will be needing sustenance, and drinking in the medieval, vaulted Crypt Bar, which doubles as the village pub, and eating in the Bishop's Dining Room, is as atmospheric at it sounds, the latter a very handsome space of country tweed, rustic wooden floors, flower-filled vases and big windows looking over the grounds. An enormous fireplace – big enough to stand a rugby team in – is used for roasting chickens on a spit, and the menu as a whole is a real delight of roasting, smoking and grilling, with robust English flavours and ingredients balanced by seasonal produce from the kitchen garden.

The Lord Crewe is a perfect place from which to explore either County Durham or Northumberland – over the lonely moors in either direction, to Stanhope in Weardale or to Hexham and Hadrian's Wall. The area is a bit of a venue for country sports and outdoor activities, too, whether it's shooting and fishing, or just enjoying the local walks and bike rides. It's a sensational place to stay, summer or winter, with its private gardens, palatial rooms, roaring fires and traditional air.

CONTACT The Square, Blanchland, Northumberland DH8 9SP • 01434 677 100 • lordcrewearmsblanchland.co.uk
HOW MUCH? Double rooms from £209 a night, including breakfast.
ROOMS 21 rooms including 2 top-of-the-range suites and a family suite.

The Olde Ship Inn

This classic old (sorry, 'olde') pub above the harbour at Seahouses is an homage to the sea. It doesn't look like much from the outside, but walk inside and prepare to be amazed as pretty much every inch is covered in nautical nick-nacks, maritime models, curios and mementoes. With a floor made from ships' decking and various cosy stained-glass and panelled snugs resembling little cabins, there's no doubt that it's a thirsty mariner's dream. There are also plenty of real ales, and a beer garden with harbour views, and the food is really popular – the sort of stick-to-the-ribs menu that you need for a bracing day on the coast. For the best of the local catch, go for a fresh crab salad, smoked fish chowder or Craster kippers. It's worth staying over, too, – not least for the trips you can make up and down the coast from here and out to the Farne Islands and elsewhere – so it's good to know that upstairs there is a range of guest rooms, some with 4-posters, and several suites, which boast tempting sea views all the way to the Farne Islands and beyond.

CONTACT Main St, Seahouses, Northumberland NE68 7RD • 01665 720 200 • seahouses.co.uk
HOW MUCH? Double rooms from £100 a night, including breakfast.

The Golden Lion

This traditional coaching inn, in the heart of the handsome Yorkshire market town of Settle, is not only a handy halt if you're passing through on the magnificent Settle-Carlisle railway or exploring the joys of the Yorkshire Dales National Park. It's also a successful blend of old and new, with an old panelled bar and big stone fireplace with the original Golden Lion fire brasses combined with an open-plan contemporary eating and drinking joint that's as handy for a cappuccino as it is for a Saturday night dinner or drink. The locally sourced menu serves what might be called modern Yorkshire bistro fare – bangers and mash, chargrilled steaks, tapas, pasta dishes – which you can eat in the snug bar, dining room area or (weather-permitting) the outside courtyard, while upstairs there are 14 refurbished rooms offering comfortable overnight accommodation. Divided between doubles and twins, they all come with en-suite bathrooms and big comfy beds, Smart TVs, tea and coffee and fresh milk and biscuits; 'Character' rooms have a bit more flair décor-wise and are more spacious.

CONTACT Duke St, Settle, North Yorkshire BD24 9DU • 01729 822 203 • goldenlionsettle.co.uk
HOW MUCH? Double rooms £155-£180 a night, including breakfast.

Queen's Arms

A new lease of life for a back-country inn has put the heart back into the tiny hamlet of Littondale. The route here is a beauty, down a single-track road through countryside that gets prettier until Litton trumps the lot, with its ancient roadside inn and rolling hills beyond. The food is worth the journey itself but it's the guest rooms upstairs that convince you to stay – welcome comfort shoehorned into 4 oddly named, oddly shaped rooms that reflect the age and character of the inn. Earthy greens, browns and oatmeals predominate, the furniture is antique pine, and the bathrooms – squeezed in where they can – nice and modern. A cushioned window seat here, a padded bed-head there, and everything is nice and dandy. Skirfare has the biggest bathroom, while Potts has humorously low, bang-your-head oak beams and a side-passage into a second room that's perfect for kids. Two other rooms share a shower room and make up a self-contained suite. There are very few distractions, save a great pub and some fine food downstairs, and arguably the Dales' finest scenery on the doorstep.

CONTACT Litton, Near Skipton, North Yorkshire BD23 5QJ • 01756 770 096 • queensarmslitton.co.uk
HOW MUCH? Double rooms £79–£119 a night, including breakfast.

The Carpenters Arms

Located in pretty little Felixkirk, just outside Thirsk, The Carpenters Arms is a clever marriage of country inn and destination restaurant – we love that you can turn up in country casuals and wellies or a Little Black Dress and be made just as welcome. It's a village pub with a twist, with a warm, welcoming feel, from its oak beams and stone floors to the sparkling place settings. The enticing menu offers bistro classics, grills and game in season, aged beef, fish and seafood from the coast. Most of the veg and herbs – not to mention the flowers throughout the pub – come from the pub's own kitchen garden, while service is bright and slick. The cosy beamed pub is just one dining space; there's also a garden room with log-burner or – for lazy summer lunches or warm evening dinners – tables on an outdoor deck. If you feel like you don't want to leave after enjoying a meal, wait until you see the rooms – glamorous garden suites, arranged around a landscaped courtyard, looking down over the sweeping Vale of York. They'll probably have to prise the key from your hands after a night here!

CONTACT Felixkirk, Thirsk, North Yorkshire YO7 2DP • 01845 537 369 • thecarpentersarmsfelixkirk.com
HOW MUCH? Double rooms £145–£165 a night, including breakfast.

The Angel of Corbridge

Don't be in too much of a hurry to get to Hexham and Hadrian's Wall – the gorgeous village of Corbridge springs a real surprise if you're thinking it's all a bit wild and windswept in this neck of the woods. The honey-stoned buildings and old centre have a real charm, and The Angel has been here for hundreds of years in various guises. Nowadays, it's a gussied-up country inn with a great bar and plenty of nooks, crannies and comfy chairs to settle down in around a wood-burning stove. There's a great beer selection too, with plenty of local brews. When the weather allows, you can sit out front and watch the well-heeled world of Corbridge go by. The food's a hit, including pub and bistro classics and a Sunday lunch that draws diners from miles around. They even have their own gourmet chippy around the back. The guest rooms are a real mixed bag, and some rooms are quieter than others, but they've done a nice, contemporary job on the décor and this would be a great base for touring the Roman sites that make this part of the world so unique.

CONTACT Main St, Corbridge, Northumberland NE45 5LA • 01434 632 119 • theangelofcorbridge.com
HOW MUCH? Double rooms with breakfast from £120 a night. Family rooms £200.

The Lister Arms

With a Dales village as iconic as Malham, in the heart of rugged Yorkshire walking country, you hope the pubs are going to be up to scratch, and The Lister Arms does not disappoint. It's exactly the right kind of old-stone, ivy-clad, walkers-welcome sort of place – an updated country inn basically, with stone-flagged floors and big old fireplaces. Dogs are welcome in the bar while you revive yourself with a pint of Thwaites, the house beer. But you also get a bit more country-chic style in the restaurant, and nicely presented food – all the pub classics, lots of it locally sourced, including homemade pies that should put some zip back into tired walkers' legs. Some of the finest walks in England are accessible right from the door – the breathtaking circuit of Malham Cove being the obvious one – so if you were thinking you might need to stick around a while, you're in luck. There are some pretty, warmly decorated rooms upstairs – no 2 the same, given it's a 17th-century building – and more in a light-filled, converted barn that also has a lounge and private garden.

CONTACT Malham, Skipton, North Yorkshire BD23 4DB • 01729 830 444 • listerarms.co.uk
HOW MUCH? Double rooms with breakfast from £100 to £140 a night.

The Red Lion

It's quite something to maintain a reputation for as long as The Red Lion has, especially in a region known for its age-old pubs and inns. Sure, it looks the part, but the pub, which is the mainstay of Burnsall, a couple of miles outside the honeypot village of Grassington, has built a loyal following around its food for the last 30 years or so. The feel is more restaurant than pub, more creative than straight-up classic, so expect changing seasonal choices, local meat and game, fish from the coast and inventive ways with veg and other special dishes. You'll probably want to book, unless you're just dropping by for a drink, which is no bad thing in itself. Burnsall is a gorgeous spot on the River Wharfe – largely unchanged – which makes a night at this old coaching inn a bit of a treat, certainly if you're after some real country peace and quiet. There are rooms in the pub or in the associated Manor House B&B, most with the sort of views over river and fells that make you want to bound out of bed and head off to work up an appetite for another go at the menu.

CONTACT By The Bridge at Burnsall, North Yorkshire BD23 6BU • 01756 720 204 • redlion.co.uk
HOW MUCH? Double rooms £90–£140 a night, including breakfast.

The Lion Inn

'Food served all day' – words to warm the cockles of any hungry hiker's heart. And they really mean all day too, from noon until 10pm, which makes the Lion an absolute winner on any big day out, tramping around the wilder corners of the North York Moors. We're talking an old-school menu of steaks, ham and eggs, pub curry, fish and chips, pies and the like, all dished up with an eye on the outdoorsy clientele, hence served with proper homemade chips or rice 'or both'. Summer days and Sunday lunches see the pub packed at meal times, though exhausted Coast-to-Coast walkers pretty much drop by at any time – cosy nooks in front of warming fires, real ales and candlelit dining areas soon revive the spirits. There are guest rooms, too, on the simple side but comfortable enough and accompanied by the sort of breakfast that Desperate Dan would approve of. If it snows overnight don't be surprised if your country mini-break turns into a lengthy lock-in – the high moorland road outside is one of the most exposed in England, and the next nearest places are 6 miles in either direction.

CONTACT Blakey Ridge, Kirkbymoorside, North Yorkshire YO62 7LQ • 01751 417 320 • lionblakey.co.uk
HOW MUCH? Double rooms £80–£110 a night, including breakfast.

Pipe & Glass Inn

Inspired cooking and gorgeous rooms make this an essential East Yorkshire stopover.

A picture-perfect country inn with its own kitchen garden didn't have to look far for inspiration when it came to naming its rooms. The celebrated Pipe & Glass Inn has five select boutique suites that it calls 'Lovage', 'Mint', 'Rosemary', 'Sage' and 'Thyme' – glamorous garden pads that soften you up for the Michelin-starred dining experience at the inn. They are each gorgeously decorated, and highly individual – Sage is a sleek silver and black, Thyme more of a gold and aubergine affair, while Rosemary is done out in dramatic red and cream. All the rooms have king-sized or super-king beds, plus all the bells and whistles you might expect, from bluetooth speakers to graciously appointed bathrooms, plus there are now four additional rooms and one enormous suite in the 'Old Lambing Yard', just a few hundred metres from the pub. Romance-seeking couples will find all of these to be perfect for a sumptuous weekend of wining and dining, broken up by saunters through the parkland of the Dalton Estate, which you gaze over from the rooms' private patios.

As regards the food, chefs and owners James and Kate Mackenzie's menu is a beacon of rustic style, garnering East Yorkshire's first Michelin star in 2010 and keeping it ever since by sticking to first principles. Local, seasonal produce is at the heart of a sensibly priced menu that celebrates proper English cooking. Dishes are rooted in the region, and while the cooking's clever, it's not pretentious, so regular favourites like the unmissable fish pie sit alongside things like slow-cooked lamb with cumin lentils, or bangers, bubble and squeak. Vegetables and herbs are from the kitchen garden, and there's a proper menu for children that treats them as serious little diners. You can eat in the clubbable bar like an average punter or make a reservation and dress up a bit for the cheerful restaurant – the menu and the polite, attentive service is just the same. There is also a conservatory and outdoor dining in decent weather.

The inn itself is lovely and olde-worlde, and a nice place just to have a sandwich and a pint, if that's what you're after – they serve their own specially brewed pale ale, made by the local Wold Top brewery, which you can also enjoy in a shady garden. It fits right in to pretty-as-a-picture South Dalton, an estate village with blue-doored estate cottages, a handsome church and a duckpond. Indeed, the inn stands right at the entrance to the Dalton Estate, so there are some fine parkland walks to hand, either to work up an appetite first or walk off dessert.

One thing to note – the inn is closed on Mondays, so the rooms aren't available on either Sunday or Monday nights, and they normally only take room bookings with a table reservation.

CONTACT West End, South Dalton, Beverley, East Yorkshire HU17 7PN • 01430 810 246 • pipeandglass.co.uk

HOW MUCH? Double rooms £200–£250 a night.

ROOMS Large luxury double rooms divided between the Pipe & Glass and the Old Lambing Yard a short walk away.

The Black Swan

First things first. Is it a pub? Well, yes and no. This 16th-century country inn has the ambience, ales and rolling rural views that are de rigueur in these parts. But the truth is you are probably only here to worship at the table of Tommy Banks, the local chef who has turned his family's Black Swan pub into a Michelin-starred destination of some renown. It regularly features in the 'world's best' lists, with a field-to-fork ethos that starts in the kitchen gardens, dives into the local hedgerows and plunders nearby artisan outlets and farms for the produce. Dinner is a celebrated tasting menu, and while dishes can't be predicted, you should expect the sort of foraging, fermenting, preserving and experimenting that comes with Michelin recognition. Settle in too – this is an all-night, multi-course affair. The guest bedrooms, just a few yards from the main building, are all gorgeous and come with table reservations, making the point that the meal is very much the experience you are signed up for. Reservations otherwise have to be made up to a year in advance.

CONTACT Oldstead, North Yorkshire YO61 4BL • No phone bookings • blackswanoldstead.co.uk
HOW MUCH? Room, tasting dinner and breakfast, £240–£300 per person.

The George & Dragon

Step back in time on a stroll into one of the most atmospheric of the Yorkshire Dales' villages, complete with whitewashed stone cottages, ancient church, cobbled streets and a general ye-olde air of the sort that graces calendars and chocolate boxes. (We say Yorkshire Dales, but the postal and SatNav address is Cumbria – don't get the locals started!) Pick of the pubs is the very traditional George & Dragon, where you can sink a pint from the local Dent Brewery, including a feisty Dales Way IPA, which celebrates the long-distance walk that runs right through the village. That also gives you a flavour of the visiting clientele, as does the hearty menu of pub meals that should fuel a good day's hiking or biking hereabouts. The countryside is stunning, and at Dent station (actually 4 miles away from the village) you have access to the incomparable Settle to Carlisle Railway, one of Europe's great train routes. Overnight stays are possible in the pub's cosy-country guest bedrooms, and if you take a late-night walk down the cobbles you'll be able to enjoy dazzling night skies.

CONTACT Main St, Dent, Cumbria LA10 5QL • 01539 625 256 • georgeanddragondent.co.uk
HOW MUCH? Double rooms from £80 a night, including breakfast.

Holly Bush Inn

A proper little pub – the sign above the door says it all. The farming hamlet of Greenhaugh has one of the best-kept inns in the whole of Northumberland, a charming and ancient drovers' inn of old stone walls, cosy, contemporary en-suite rooms and a garden with glorious valley views. There's no TV signal and no mobile reception – do we hear cheering? – but there are 3 very nicely turned-out en-suite rooms in the pub itself (one above the bar, which closes at midnight – fair warning), and 4 more rooms in the adjoining cottage, which includes their one single room. This is 'Dark Sky' country, so night-time star-gazing is pretty much compulsory, and you're just a short drive from Kielder Water and Forest for a taste of the outdoors. If the rooms get a lot of plaudits, then so does the food – really good locally sourced, posh pub grub, including lots of veggie options. You'll need to book ahead if you want to eat as it's not that big, or you can always just call in for a warm-up in front of the old black-leaded range with a pint of ale...

CONTACT Greenhaugh, Hexham, Northumberland NE48 1PW • 01434 240 391 • hollybushinn.net
HOW MUCH? Double rooms from around £100 a night, including breakfast.

The Station Inn

Gourmet destination? Idyllic location? Ancient inn? Well, not especially. Wonderful sight after slogging around the Three Peaks for hours, or a welcoming shelter after a wind-buffeted visit to Ribblehead Viaduct? God, yes! The remote Station Inn at the top of Ribblesdale does what it says on the tin (it's an inn, near a station) and we're glad to say it does it extremely well. The pub has been updated quite recently by new and enthusiastic owners and there's a bar with local brews, an extensive pub menu (proper pies, gammon, lamb shank, fish and chips) sourced from local ingredients where possible, and each of the 6 rooms has been spruced up in a bright modern style and offers spectacular views of the surrounding countryside. There's cheaper bunkhouse accommodation for individual hikers and groups – short on frills (shared facilities and you need to bring your own sleeping bags) but a handy location for exploring some of the Dales' most dramatic scenery. You don't even need a car to get here; the station is a stop on the Settle to Carlisle railway line.

CONTACT Ribblehead, Low Sleights Rd, Cumbria LA6 3AS • 01524 241274 • thestationinnribblehead.com
HOW MUCH? Double rooms £100–£110 a night, including breakfast, bunk barns £20–£30pp.

The Black Horse

Everyone has their favourite Whitby pub, like everyone has their favourite Whitby fish and chip shop, and if you haven't checked out The Black Horse yet you might want to update your list. It's in the heart of the old town and is a classic of its kind – 2 tiny bars awash with stained glass and original features, and a roster of craft beers, gins and rums with amusing names and alluring back-stories. There's barely room to swing a cat; even so dogs are welcome in both bars. Grab a table if you can and then you can sample what we will forgive them for calling 'yapas' – Yorkshire tapas – which runs the gamut from local cheeses and pork pie to mussels, cockles and prawns. Disentangle yourself from dogs' leads and other people's limbs and stroll out and up the famous 199 Steps to the ancient abbey on the headland for windswept views. If you fancy staying longer, there are 4 comfy rooms upstairs – again, there's not much space; but they're equipped with all you need and have recently been redecorated. Breakfast isn't available but that hardly matters in Whitby, where every second place is a café.

CONTACT 91 Church St, Whitby, North Yorkshire YO22 4BH • 01947 602 906 • the-black-horse.com
HOW MUCH? Double rooms from £70 a night, not including breakfast – 2-night minimum stay.

Shibden Mill Inn

One of Yorkshire's hidden secrets reveals its pleasures slowly – a drink on the charming patio, a wander through the oak-beamed interior, and a leisurely gastropub meal. All right, it's not really a secret any more, but there is something special about discovering this pub for the first time, tucked away in a valley by a stream that used to power the 17th-century mill. Turned into a pub in the 1890s, it's kept its vintage look and backdrop but the ambience and experience is definitely contemporary. Take the lunchtime sandwiches – trout pastrami with mustard creme fraiche, anyone? – or the up-to-the-minute mains such as miso-glazed hake. There is also a seriously cosy bar and a sunny, shrub-filled patio on which to enjoy your drinks, and the rooms are absolutely lovely, modelled around the quirky corners and exposed brickwork of the original building. At first glance this might not be the most obvious weekend-away territory, but this is 'Gentleman Jack' country, with Shibden Hall and the beautiful Calderdale valley on the doorstep and Halifax just a 10-minute drive away.

CONTACT Shibden Mill Fold, Shibden, Halifax, West Yorkshire HX3 7UL • 01422 365 840 • shibdenmillinn.com
HOW MUCH? Double rooms £140–£165 a night, including breakfast.

The Rose & Crown

There's a certain type of bar that puts you right at ease – whether it's the oak beams and open fire, the cheery welcome or the range of beers. That's certainly the case at The Rose & Crown, a former coaching inn on the route into Teesdale and the North Pennines. The scenery gets wilder beyond here, which makes Romaldkirk a decent stop in any case: a charming village set around its handsome pub and historic church. The food is worth pausing for too, though you'll need to book as it's a well-known dining destination and the menu reflects the surroundings: hearty country food, strong on local produce. You can stay the night in one of 14 spacious rooms (the ones in the main building are more in-keeping with the overall tenor, with their old beams and exposed stonework). If all you're after is a walk and a pint, though, the pub is perfect – either for a local riverside stroll or a short drive upstream to rugged waterfalls. And though it might seem as if you're way off the beaten track, it's only 6 miles to Barnard Castle – famous now for all sorts of reasons!

CONTACT Romaldkirk, Barnard Castle, County Durham DL12 9EB • 01833 650 213 • rose-and-crown.co.uk
HOW MUCH? Double rooms £135–£160 a night, including breakfast.

The Joiners Arms

The Northumberland coast doesn't just have beaches, it has amazing beaches, in all their rolling-dune, white-sand glory. And in the same way, the dog-friendly Joiners Arms is so much more than just a pub. It describes itself as a 'gastropub and luxury 5-star inn', and this converted village inn is pretty handsome all round – think rustic-chic, with a dramatic stone-flagged bar and potted plants everywhere. They've done great things with the rooms – high-end boutiquey, with more than a bit of glam – and if you're thinking of a romantic coastal weekend away, they certainly would hit the spot. The food is fancy pub-style grub (local lamb, fish and chips, steak-frites, pasta) and pretty good value, while outside tables soak up the passing drinkers' trade in summer. Ultimately, though, the surroundings are the main draw: it's just half a mile to the local beach, where you can potter all day, or a little further to the breezy hilltop ruins of Dunstanburgh Castle and the scenic harbour at Craster; the mighty castles of Bamburgh and Alnwick are just a short drive away.

CONTACT Newton-by-the-Sea, Northumberland NE66 3EA • 0191 933 7409 • joiners-arms.com
HOW MUCH?. Double rooms from £155 a night, including breakfast.

The Black Swan

A destination country pub for rooms, food – and a collection of yurts!

Right on the border between Cumbria and its Lake District and Yorkshire and its Dales, The Black Swan, just outside the pleasant market town of Kirkby Stephen, delivers everything we expect of a country pub with rooms. It's in a fabulous rural location, close enough to both national parks to explore them comfortably, and it's also very easy to reach, just ten minutes' drive from the M6. The rooms are cosy and comfortable without being ostentatious, and they also welcome dogs, so you can make the most of the vast array of walks in the immediate area, most notably the beautiful Howgill Fells, which are right on your doorstep.

The Black Swan is also a destination for food. It has a homely downstairs bar and the food it serves in the dining room is appealingly hearty and homemade, locally sourced and from a changing seasonal menu that features plenty for vegetarians. Think pork schnitzel and steaks, along with classic bouillabaisse or an onion and mushroom tart, all well priced and a cut above regular pub grub.

There are seventeen guest rooms in all, including four double rooms, three rooms with king-size beds, and seven superior rooms and suites with super king-size beds. They have all the amenities you need, with comfortable beds with Egyptian cotton sheets. Wifi, flatscreen Freeview TVs, tea- and coffee-making facilities with fresh milk, and en-suite bathrooms equipped with extra-large towels, organic handmade toiletries. Six of the rooms are dog-friendly and one is kitted out specifically for disabled access, with a properly adapted bathroom and room for wheelchairs, while several others are on the ground floor.

Uniquely, there are also three yurts set up in the lovely riverside garden – Yorkshire-built roundhouses actually, which stand up better to the Cumbrian weather and, thanks to their log-burning stoves, offer year-round accommodation. They have king-size beds, towels, robes and slippers are included, and there are tea- and coffee-making facilities too. Indeed it's only the compost loo and the open-air woodland shower that separates them from the indoors – and a babbling beck with a little bridge that separates them from the pub garden. There's also outdoor seating and a communal fire pit for al fresco dining, and a rope swing for a bit of active play.

As for Ravenstonedale, it is a lovely village that deserves a wander, with some monastic ruins along with tennis courts and mini golf for those interested in more active pursuits. Or just get your walking boots on – there are any number of footpaths to explore from the village.

CONTACT Ravenstonedale, Kirkby Stephen, Cumbria CA17 4NG • 01539 623 204 • blackswanhotel.com
HOW MUCH? Double rooms and suites from £135–£175 a night. Yurts £125–£135 a night.
ROOMS 17 rooms, including 4 double rooms, 3 king-size rooms, and 7 superior rooms and suites, plus 3 yurts, each sleeping 2 people.

The Pheasant Inn

Deep in Northumberland National Park, pubs and inns are few and far between, so when you happen upon places like The Pheasant you dive in gratefully – and then are doubly grateful that you did. Set in a clearing close to Kielder Water, the inn is right out of central casting, with an ivy-covered façade and an interior that rolls back the centuries, all sepia-toned photos, stone walls, old beams, timeworn tables and polished brass. People return again and again for a slice of real old English country charm, eating in one of two bars or the restaurant from a menu strong on local meat and game, with fish from the coast. The garden is particularly lovely: a grassy haven with tables by a small brook; while in winter, the inn is the sort of place where you can hunker down in front of an open fire. Converted rooms in what was formerly the barn and hayloft provide a quiet night in what is already a tranquil part of the world – the night skies are magical hereabouts, in one of the darkest places in the UK, and there's an observatory and night-sky events up at Kielder Forest.

CONTACT Stannersburn, Falstone, Northumberland NE48 1DD • 01434 240 382 • thepheasantinn.com
HOW MUCH? Double rooms from £110 a night, including breakfast.

Tan Hill Inn

Few pubs in Britain are as famous as the Tan Hill Inn, which is the UK's highest pub – over 1700 feet up in the Yorkshire Dales – and this means it's a place of pilgrimage as much as anything else. To get here, you have to negotiate twisting single-track roads to what they describe – with only minimal exaggeration – as 'the top of the world'. Cut off by deep snows in winter, and blowing a gusty breeze most times of the year, despite the middle-of-nowhere vibe there's nothing barebones about it. A hiking and biking crowd keeps things convivial, the food is excellent value (and meals are served all day, so there's no rushing against the clock to get here) and half a dozen cask ales oil the chat and good cheer. Add to that riotous music nights – by definition, 'the highest gig in Britain' – and the Tan Hill Inn makes for a brilliant detour, wherever you're headed for in the Dales. No one is likely to be turned away, either: as well as guest bedrooms and bunk-rooms, there's parking for motorhomes and a wild campsite from where the views go on forever.

CONTACT Reeth, Swaledale, North Yorkshire DL11 6ED • 01833 533 007 • tanhillinn.com
HOW MUCH? Double rooms with breakfast from £175 a night.

The Fauconberg

If we had to go for one word to describe the Fauconberg, we'd say 'genteel', and that's no bad thing. It's certainly in keeping with Coxwold, which is a well-to-do village on the western edge of the North York Moors. Once the home of literary great Laurence Sterne (of 'Tristram Shandy' fame), whose family home lies just up the road, the Fauconberg fits right in – beautifully picturesque, with tables outside on the cobbles overlooking period cottages, and an interior that looks every inch the traditional village inn. You should probably book if you want to eat – Sunday lunch especially – while a pint and a walk is a delight at any time. Ruined Byland Abbey is only a mile or so away (it was one of Sterne's favourite walks), or you can head up to the dramatically sited White Horse of Kilburn on Sutton Bank for some glorious panoramas. The rooms are all different – updated country farmhouse in style, one with wood-panelling and a 4-poster – while an absolute charmer of a summer-only garden room in the grounds makes the most of the local views.

CONTACT Thirsk Bank, Coxwold, North Yorkshire YO61 4AD • 01347 868 214 • fauconbergarms.com
HOW MUCH? Double rooms £130–£200, including breakfast.

The Black Horse

More than 300 years old, The Black Horse Beamish is a country pub within walking distance of the world's oldest railway bridge, Causey Arch, and Beamish Museum, where staff in period costume convey aspects of northeastern life in bygone times. The pub's beer garden overlooks undulating greenery along the boundary of County Durham and Gateshead. It's a spacious and welcoming pub, and a popular dining spot. The kitchen sources ingredients from local farms and its varied menu includes a range of steaks plus a masterful sticky toffee pudding. Farmhouse-style furniture, exposed stonework and a sizable conservatory foster an airy yet cosy vibe. The accommodation encompasses 5 guest rooms in a stone-built terrace, with oak furniture, copper bathtubs and artworks depicting local scenes, plus walk-in showers stocked with White Company toiletries. They also offer 2 luxury suites and 2 additional rooms in the Red Row Retreat, which you can book individually or as a group, along with the estate's Huckleberry Cottage, which you can rent as self-catering or as a B&B.

CONTACT Red Row, Beamish, County Durham DH9 0RW • 01207 232 569 • blackhorsebeamish.co.uk
HOW MUCH? Double rooms from £180 a night, including breakfast.

Twice Brewed Inn

Less than a mile west of the Roman Army Museum at Vindolanda, the cosy Twice Brewed Inn is ideally placed for an overnight stay on the southern fringe of the Northumberland National Park. A short walk from Sycamore Gap, the much-photographed dip in what was the Roman Empire's most northerly frontier, the region's dark skies are reason enough to stay here – and to prove it the inn has an observatory with telescopes for viewing the stars, and runs astrophotography workshops, among other events. But the real reason is for its 19 comfortable and modern bedrooms, which make the most of the landscape and are equipped with tea and coffee, flatscreen TVs and en-suite showers. Superior rooms give the best views, and staying gives more opportunities to sample Twice Brewed house beers in its taproom. Booking a tour is an option, should you be interested in details of the beermaking process, which uses water drawn from an onsite well. There's a terraced beer garden, and excellent steak pies and pizzas baked in a wood-fired oven feature among the comfort food on the menu.

CONTACT Bardon Mill, Hexham, Northumberland NE47 4AN • 01434 344 534 • twicebrewedinn.co.uk
HOW MUCH? Double rooms from £110 a night, including breakfast.

The Impeccable Pig

This well-regarded pub and restaurant sits in the heart of the small Durham town of Sedgefield and has a pleasantly quirky vibe. Comfy leather armchairs and booths are ranged around the ground floor bar, a chandelier hangs from the exposed wooden beams of the ceiling, and the pub offers a bistro-style menu that includes a selection of steaks, fish and pizzas made with focaccia dough. You can order a plate of the Lindisfarne oysters, and roasts are by no means the only options on their weekly 'Sunday Pig-Out' menu. There are 10 opulent, boutique-feel guestrooms in the coach house, all with playful pig-related names. With parquet flooring and eye-catching ceiling lights, the rooms have huge 7-foot-wide beds with Egyptian cotton sheets, minibars and copper bathtubs that allow guests to wallow in comfort. The ground floor rooms also have their own hot tubs and a private garden, while booking the suite gets you a sauna too. Treats include Duck Island toiletries, Illy coffee machines and some very imaginative welcome packs for guests!

CONTACT Front St, Sedgefield, County Durham TS21 3AT • 01740 582 580 • impeccablepig.co.uk
HOW MUCH? Double rooms from £250 a night, including breakfast.

The Dirty Bottles

Located between Alnwick's marketplace and the bailey of the castle (home to the Duke of Northumberland and the set of Hogwarts in the first 2 Harry Potter films), this pub's grubby-sounding name shouldn't put you off. The dusty glassware in its windows is associated with a grisly tale from centuries ago, when moving the bottles reputedly caused the sudden death of the innkeeper. His widow suggested that a similar misfortune would befall anyone who dares shift them, explaining why they remain untouched. Elsewhere, the interiors are impressively clean, and all 4 bedrooms have an opulent look and feel, with gilt headboards, leather armchairs and vintage-style patterned wallpaper; they also have Nespresso machines. Smart TVs, and all but one has a bathtub as well as walk-in showers. Downstairs, the atmospherically illuminated pub, with stone walls, beer barrels and exposed floorboards, serves a selection of regional ales and an eclectic menu that includes a variety of hot dogs and American-style barbecue dishes, with brisket, pulled pork and sweet potato fries.

CONTACT 32 Narrowgate, Alnwick, Northumberland NE66 1JG • 01665 606 193 • thedirtybottles.co.uk
HOW MUCH? Double rooms £150–£170 a night, including breakfast.

St Mary's Inn

Occupying a clocktower-topped redbrick building with mullioned windows that was formerly the administrative centre of a sprawling hospital campus, this contemporary inn is a new addition to the lovely Northumberland town of Morpeth's accommodation options, with 11 airy, comfortable bedrooms whose décor mixes modern fittings and vintage furniture. Original works by local artists provide colour and character and bathrooms feature Grohe fittings and Villeroy & Bosch porcelain. The rooms are quiet despite being above a sizable pub and restaurant, which downstairs features wood-burning stoves, parquet flooring and farmhouse-style tables in high-ceilinged rooms. Temporary art exhibitions often adorn the walls, and the result is a welcoming place to enjoy a pint of locally brewed beer and pub favourites such as burgers and fish and chips, along with more refined fare like cheese souffle and butternut squash risotto. Breakfasts are hearty, sausage or bacon sandwiches made with stottie cake featuring alongside an excellent Full English.

CONTACT St Mary's Lane, Morpeth, Northumberland NE61 6BL • 01670 293 293 • stmarysinn.co.uk
HOW MUCH? Double rooms £109–£139 a night, including breakfast.

Lucky Dip

The Jolly Fisherman

This refurbished Craster pub has a fabulous harbourside location where Northumberland's finest crabs are landed and its finest kippers smoked, and tradition dictates that walkers pop into the Jolly, with its barebones floors, low beams and open fires, for crab soup and sandwiches. The menu is strong on the local seafood, and if you head on out to the harbour-top beer garden you're rewarded by a simply stunning view up the coast towards Dunstanburgh Castle and the beaches beyond. No rooms.

CONTACT Haven Hill, Craster, Northumberland NE66 3TR • 01665 576 461 • thejollyfishermancraster.co.uk

Birch Hall Inn

Pretty Beck Hole is made up of half a dozen cottages, one farm, one old bridge and one pub – old-fashioned and idiosyncratic, and loved for its quirky ways. Basically, we're talking 2 age-old bars with a fully stocked sweet shop in the middle and a terrace garden out back, serving real ales to walkers, locals and in-the-know visitors. The menu is simple and fancy-free – locally made pork pie with pickle, big flat butties known in these parts as 'stotties', scones, jam and cream, and the moreish 'Beck Hole Beer Cake'. A joy all round, and unmissable if you're in the area. No rooms.

CONTACT Beck Hole Rd, Beck Hole, Near Whitby, North Yorkshire YO22 5LE • 01947 896245 • beckhole.info/bhi.htm

Blacksmith's Arms

If ever a pretty village had a pretty pub, it's Lastingham and the undeniably quaint Blacksmiths Arms – basically a row of old cottages with low beams, leading from a bar with a roaring fire into 2 separate dining areas. The food is on the posh side but the ales are solidly northern, served in a keep-your-elbows-to-yourself bar covered in beer mats and hanging tankards. They're used to walkers and they have 3 simple rooms for those who want to stay over.

CONTACT Lastingham, North Yorkshire YO62 6TN • 01751 417 247 • blacksmithsarmslastingham.co.uk

The Hayburn Wyke Inn

The secluded inn above the old smugglers' beach of Hayburn Wyke is a no-nonsense kind of place, with regulation pub food and 6 simple rooms. When it's sunny, it's lovely, with outdoor tables, a grassy garden and a separate children's playground. Above all you visit for the footpath down to magical Hayburn Wyke, through a wooded ravine and by a twin waterfall, to a remarkable bay filled with millions, possibly billions, of variously coloured pebbles and rocks, and seaweed-covered boulders that are the size of human heads.

CONTACT Newlands Rd, Cloughton, North Yorkshire YO13 0AU • 01723 870202 • hayburnwykeinn.co.uk

The Moors Inn

If you're in the mood for an easy walk with a decent pub at the end, this one should fit the bill nicely – a traditional village inn on the southern edge of the North York Moors, with a nice line in regional ales and homecooked food. Dishes are hearty, the suppliers local, and lots of the veg and salad is grown on the owner's allotment up the road. Two 5-mile circular walks run right from the front door: north to Lastingham and its church, or south to Sinnington, both of which have a great pub, so there's no danger of unrequited thirst. They have 8 really nice, dog-friendly bedrooms upstairs too.

CONTACT Appleton Le Moors, North Yorkshire YO62 6TF • 01751 417 435 • moorsinn.co.uk

The Ship Inn

Is there a better pub in Northumberland than the ship-shape, seriously stunning Ship? Set at the back of a cute green surrounded by fishermen's cottages, just yards away from the fabulous beach at Low Newton, the Ship does everything right, from the barebones maritime interior to the in-house brewery to a shortish food menu that plays to local strengths – locally caught fish, crabs and lobster, organic lamb koftas and other meat sourced from local farms. There really is nothing finer than a pint and a fresh crab sandwich outside on the grass; and there are regular music nights from great musicians. Oh go on then, another pint of 'Red Herring' it is!

CONTACT Low Newton, Near Alnwick, Northumberland NE66 3EL • 01665 576 262 • shipinnnewton.co.uk

(Top) The Jolly Fisherman; (middle) Birch Hall Inn; (bottom) The Hayburn Wyke Inn.

Barrels Alehouse

A quirky bar that sums up the independent spirit of Berwick, The Barrels is the town's best real ale pub. But it's also more than that, with a laid-back, continental feel that encourages long afternoons and late nights. It serves half a dozen real ales from a front bar with vintage paraphernalia and iconic music images, and hosts live acts down in the cellar. If it's a beer you want in Berwick, look no further. No rooms.

CONTACT 59–61 Bridge St, Berwick-upon-Tweed, Northumberland TD15 1ES • 01289 308 013

The Adelphi

A drink in the wonderfully fancy Adelphi is a step back into the Victorian age, with 4 separate snug bars resplendent with carved wood, decorated tilework, swagged velvet drapes and etched glass. Drinks and food are thoroughly up to date, though, with a changing roster of indie brewery ales and local Leeds Brewery tipples, along with a seasonally changing gastropub menu available day and night. No rooms.

CONTACT 1–3 Hunslet Rd, Leeds, West Yorkshire LS10 1JQ • 0113 245 6377 • theadelphileeds.co.uk

House of Trembling Madness

Secreted away above its craft beer shop, this atmospheric pub occupies the oldest medieval hall in York and serves an amazing selection of microbrews and guest ales of varying provenance and percentages. Food is in the same vein – and the décor is suitably medieval, with old wooden beams and solid oak benches and tables.
No rooms.

CONTACT 48 Stonegate York, North Yorkshire YO1 8AS • 01904 640 009 • tremblingmadness.co.uk

Ye Olde White Harte

Calling something 'ye olde' doesn't usually impress us, but we're prepared to make an exception for Hull's oldest pub, which has been a fixture here since the late 18th century. Earlier, when it was a private house, Hull's governor took to the upstairs room now known as the 'Plotting Parlour' and resolved to deny King Charles I entry to the town – upon which all heck broke loose as the English Civil War erupted. Old wooden panels, vintage tiled fireplaces, a shaded alley courtyard – oh, and a secret tunnel and a mysterious skull – all add up to a proper 'ye olde' atmosphere, which for once is thoroughly appreciated. No rooms.

CONTACT 25 Silver St, Hull, East Yorkshire HU1 1JG • 01482 326 363 • yeoldewhiteharte.com

The Three Acres

High on the bleak Pennine moors, this old drovers' inn has been a beacon of fine pub dining for 40 years. It's a breezy drive to get here and the inn must have been a welcome sight for wayfarers in days gone by, though now it's a special occasion kind of place, with a traditional interior, a restaurant vibe and a tempting 'modern Yorkshire' menu.

CONTACT Roydhouse, Huddersfield, West Yorkshire HD8 8LR • 01484 602 606 • 3acres.com

The Buck Inn

The best pub in Malham for the hardcore hiking crowd, or indeed anyone with mud on their boots and a pint in mind. There's a dedicated walkers' bar, where dogs and filthy children are always welcome, and good-value meals do the job after a day in the outdoors – as do the rooms.

CONTACT Cove Rd, Malham, North Yorkshire BD23 4DA • 01729 830 317 • thebuckmalham.co.uk

The Fox & Hounds

Just 4 miles outside Pickering, this is one of those well-kept village pubs that you'd be happy to have as your local. There's a traditional bar at its heart, with a double-sided log-burner, but it's more of a contemporary dining pub these days, with nice oak tables set throughout the place. Portions are Yorkshire-sized and suppliers are resolutely local, most from within just a few miles. There is also a selection of beautifully furnished 'Cottage', 'Garden' and 'Classic' rooms to choose from.

CONTACT Sinnington, Near Pickering, North Yorkshire YO62 6SQ • 01751 431577 • thefoxandhoundsinn.co.uk

The Old Hill Inn

Halfway between Ingleton and Ribblehead, this old place presents a charming rustic interior, with exposed stone walls, ancient beams, a big pine dresser, and a large wagon wheel separating a couple of booths in the bar. It also serves food that is on the gastro side of things – and puds that are almost an art form, overseen by resident pastry chef and sugar sculptor Colin Martin. It's also on the Three Peaks route and has a couple of B&B rooms upstairs, and an adjacent caravan site.

CONTACT Chapel-le-Dale, Ingleton, North Yorkshire LA6 3AR • 01524 241 256 • oldhillinningleton.co.uk

(Top) Barrels Alehouse; (middle) The Adelphi; (bottom) The Buck Inn.

The Northwest

For many people, England's Northwest means the peaks and fells of Cumbria and the Lake District; and it's true that a number of memorable pubs occupy some truly beautiful spots in this fabled region. But Lancashire and Cheshire have their moments too, and offer an equally enticing prospect for anyone wanting to break out for a weekend from the nearby metropolitan areas.

Wild Boar Inn p.196

Wild Boar Inn

Away from the lake – and thus off the radar for many – the über-rustic Wild Boar at Windermere springs a surprise, especially for those expecting a traditional lakeland inn. Yes, there are stone floors, oak beams, a real-ale bar and some lovely rural surroundings, but a keen sense of style – especially in 'Feature' and 'Luxury' rooms – brings things bang up to date. Designers have gone to work on the bathrooms, so you might get a free-standing copper bath and a walk-out balcony overlooking the woods, where only the birds (and bees) can see you in the altogether; other rooms have bespoke wallpaper, canopy beds, cast-iron wood-burners and Smart TVs, while outside you can work up an appetite in the 70-acre woodland, complete with 'gym exercise trail'. And appetite you will need to tackle the excellent restaurant, which makes a justifiable song-and-dance about its on-site smokehouse. The pub also has its own microbrewery, and guests get to choose from a range of fun activities in the grounds, from archery and clay pigeon shooting to, yes, knife-throwing!

CONTACT Crook, Windermere, Cumbria LA23 3NF • 01539 445 225 • englishlakes.co.uk/the-wild-boar
HOW MUCH? Double rooms from around £165 a night, including breakfast.

Woolpack Inn

We love this successful update of one of Cumbria's most historic inns as one of the region's best eating and drinking spots. It's one of its best places to stay, too, with 7 en-suite guest rooms in calming colours, with Herdwick wool carpets, stylish furnishings and fabrics and cool, updated bathrooms that manage to raise eyebrows and soothe aches at the same time. All rooms have wifi, tea and coffee, and toiletries, and one room has a double jacuzzi. There is also a cabin for rent, a motorhome site and a large self-catering house – Stanley House (where you can also rent individual rooms) – and the pub itself is as cosy as can be. Once you've worked up an appetite, you'll want to try something from the extremely eclectic menu, which ranges from pizzas and inventive snacks to burgers, Middle Eastern shawarmas and an array of more traditional local dishes like 'Cumbrian Tattie Pot'. It's a beautifully peaceful spot, with high mountains all around, at the top of Eskdale and the bottom of Hardknott Pass, and at the foot of Scafell Pike.

CONTACT Hardknott Pass, Eskdale, Cumbria CA19 1TH • 01946 723 230 • woolpack.co.uk
HOW MUCH? Double rooms with continental breakfast £80–£110 a night; cabin £175 a night.

Cuckoo Brow Inn

A gloriously cosy hideaway, buried away in Far Sawrey, just a hop, skip and a jump from Beatrix Potter's old home at Hill Top and a shortish stroll down to the ferry to Bowness. Yet you will truly feel as if you are a million miles from the modern world. The rooms are smart and contemporary, with deep baths and plenty of big fluffy towels to wrap up in afterwards. There is a range of rooms available to choose from, including double rooms with super-king-size beds to family rooms with bunk beds; all have flatscreen TVs and tea- and coffee-making facilities. Dogs are positively encouraged and allowed everywhere. On winter afternoons, as the frost nips the air outside, the bar is a snug retreat with an open fire and assorted dogs snoozing around the legs of the nearby tables. During summer, an outside seating area offers tranquil views of the surrounding fells. Dining is relaxed and the ingredients locally sourced on a menu that features traditional pub classics as well as more contemporary options. Breakfasts are excellent, and again all made using local produce.

CONTACT Far Sawrey, Ambleside, Cumbria LA22 0LQ • 01539 443 425 • cuckoobrow.co.uk
HOW MUCH? Doubles rooms from £95 a night, including breakfast. Family rooms £149.

The Inn at Whitewell

If you're looking to escape the hustle and bustle of modern life and simply get away from it all, then this is the place for you. Situated in the heart of the Forest of Bowland, The Inn at Whitewell is a lovely spot to escape to for a while, surrounded by miles of stark, stunning moorland. It feels like it's in the middle of nowhere, but the reality is that it's in the middle of everywhere – the nearest village, Dunsop Bridge, has a phone box which officially marks the geographic centre of the UK! The Inn dates back to the 14th century and is warm and inviting. During the winter months fires blaze in assorted hearths; in summer there is a stunning patio area on which to sit back, relax and take in the magnificent views. Each of the 15 bedrooms is unique, with its own style and décor, ranging from cosy and historic to sleek and modern, and they also rent a 3-bed cottage, The Piggeries, to those who would rather self-cater. With plenty of walks right from the door and wholesome, hearty meals to come back to, this is a perfect, dog-friendly retreat any time of the year.

CONTACT Whitewell, Near Clitheroe, Lancashire BB7 3AT • 01200 448 222 • innatwhitewell.com
HOW MUCH? Double rooms with breakfast £140–£240 a night. Dogs free. Piggeries £1740 for 3 nights.

Drunken Duck Inn

Situated on a rustic hill between Ambleside and Hawkshead, the Drunken Duck Inn offers a real mix of experiences, with a very appealing set of rooms and the benefit of a top-notch gastropub on the premises. Contemporary colours and boutique furnishings are standard, even in the most basic rooms – it's a 400-year-old building, so these are a bit tight on space, though you'll never be anything less than comfortable. Other rooms are bigger, some located in a separate building across the courtyard, and most have great views over the fells, not least the stunning open-beamed Garden Room with its own balcony. As for the food, people drive from far and wide to eat at here, which serves contemporary gastro fare that's strong on local sourcing and seasonal dishes and flavours – think rabbit, leek and bacon terrine or Lancashire cheese soufflé followed by chalk stream trout or venison suet pudding. Meanwhile, the really welcoming bar specialises in the inn's own Barngates Brewery beers, most quirkily named after the old pub dogs (Tag Lag, Cracker, and so on).

CONTACT Barngates, Ambleside, Cumbria LA22 0NG • 01539 436 347 • drunkenduckinn.co.uk
HOW MUCH? Double rooms from £165 a night, including breakfast.

The Bay Horse

Canal Foot in Ulverston is one of Cumbria's best kept secrets. Perennially popular with locals, with far-reaching views across Morecambe Bay, this gentle 2-mile walk along the canal is hard to fault. And in a world of identikit pub chains, The Bay Horse is unique and welcoming, with a cosy pub area, a gorgeous conservatory/dining section and glorious year-round views. It's a 'proper' pub, at the heart of the local community – open from 9am serving coffee and breakfast and usually buzzing with people enjoying the newspaper over a freshly made brew, often with a dog snoozing at their feet. The rooms are smart and comfortable, and they have plenty of homely touches along with outstanding sea views. The inn is steeped in local history: before the arrival of roads and railways it was a start/end point for cross-bay commuters, and the walls of the pub are a tribute to its many colourful regulars. The food is home cooked – chef-patron Robert trained under celebrity chef John Tovey – and is always plentiful and locally sourced, wherever possible.

CONTACT Canal Foot, Ulverston, Cumbria LA12 9EL • 01229 583 972 • thebayhorsehotel.co.uk
HOW MUCH? Double rooms from £100 a night, including breakfast.

The Cavendish Arms

When it comes to finding the perfect English village, Cartmel is pretty hard to beat, with tiny, winding streets, an ancient village centre and picture-postcard cottages. But there is more to the village than that. In addition to the stunning Priory, there's a famous racecourse, the Michelin starred L'Enclume restaurant, and The Cavendish Arms, tucked away down a quiet street, a stone's throw from the village centre. It's the perfect base for exploring the Southern Lakes – a 450-year-old coaching inn that oozes history from every exposed oak beam – and is the perfect southern Lakeland hideaway. There is a range of rooms available to suit most budgets, and each room is modern, fresh and stylish, from the quirky Cavendish Loft to a standard double; attention to detail matters at The Cavendish and it shows. In the restaurant, they pride themselves on offering a contemporary selection of seasonal English dishes – including Cartmel's local delicacy, Sticky Toffee Pudding! – and a wine list that goes far beyond what you normally expect in a pub, with plenty available by the glass.

CONTACT Cavendish St, Cartmel, Cumbria LA11 6QA • 01539 536 240 • thecavendisharms.co.uk
HOW MUCH? Double rooms £75–£125 a night, including breakfast.

White Horse Inn

This pub is a hiker's paradise, with fabulous food, a warm and inviting bar, basic but spotless rooms and Blencathra (or Saddleback) right on the doorstep – literally, the pub is on the lower flanks of the mountain. Many hikers will no doubt have their sights set on bagging a number of its summits – there are so many routes up Blencathra you could comfortably fill a weeklong stay exploring the different options and never get bored. And the food they serve here is precisely what you need after a good day out on the fells – piping hot, served in good-sized portions and properly tasty (seriously, you HAVE to try the black pudding and haggis croquettes with pepper sauce!). The atmosphere is relaxed, the welcome warm and friendly and the dormitories in the old stable blocks offer comfy beds with a shared shower and toilet, a communal kitchen area and bed linen by prior arrangement. Throughout the cooler months there's a real fire to hunker down next to, and, during the summer, there's plenty of outdoor seating for long evenings as the sun sets over the nearby fells.

CONTACT Threlkeld, Near Keswick, Cumbria CA12 4SY • 01768 779 883 • thewhitehorse-blencathra.co.uk
HOW MUCH? £14pp a night in the bunk room, £240 a night for the entire bunk room. Linen/towels extra.

The Plough

A country inn where the food and rooms are a cut above the rest.

A country inn that's a cut above, The Plough at Lupton might look like a straightforward roadside pub – Kirkby Lonsdale is just five miles down the road, Kendal, nine miles away, and it's just a couple of miles off the M6 (junction 36). But the surprises are all inside.

A really handsome makeover a few years ago turned it into a wonderful, sweeping open-plan bar and restaurant under majestic oak beams. Informality is the key here, from squishy sofas by the log-burner to family-sized dining tables, and the food follows suit – a pick-and-mix menu of 'sharing boards', starters and main courses that's far more restaurant than pub. If the food is locally sourced, the inspiration is largely Mediterranean, hence courgette fritters with Lancashire cheese and honey, or local lamb with Mediterranean vegetables and Feta cheese, and the relaxed style means you're just as welcome to call in for a glass of prosecco and some salt-and-pepper squid rather than going the whole hog. The wine list is good – there's lots by the glass, and open-to-view wine cellars are a nice touch – and beers are local and hand-pulled. The kitchen is open all day, too, par for the course at such an on-the-ball establishment, and they serve a simpler brasserie-style menu from noon onwards, which features pub classics like fish and chips, sausage and mash and fish pie, along with burgers and pizzas. Finally there's a selection of roasts on Sunday, with a choice for kids.

The five boutique rooms upstairs are in the same classy vein as the food. Indeed it isn't fair to have to choose a room at the Plough – they are all gorgeous, in an earthy, stylish, Farrow & Ball kind of way, with handsome country furniture and big bouncy beds. And when they say 'fabulously large bathroom', they mean it; indeed in the rooms named Torsin and Redman in particular, you could pretty much hold a conference while soaking in the lovely roll-top baths, and artfully arranged old-fashioned bottles, high-end toiletries, soft lighting and rainfall showers the size of dinner plates complete the picture. All the rooms have wifi, Illy coffee machines, DAB radios and fluffy towels and dressing gowns.

In the end, however, choice might not come into it, because there are only six rooms at The Plough, and it's a well-known getaway, so if you want to stay, book ahead is our advice – just remember to bring your SatNav to navigate your way around the bathroom.

CONTACT Cow Brow, Lupton, Cumbria LA6 1PJ • 01539 567 700 • theploughatlupton.co.uk

HOW MUCH? Double rooms with breakfast from £155 a night; suites from £205.

ROOMS 6 individually designed double rooms and suites.

The Derby Arms

A little bit different, and off the main tourist track, this pub is full of delights for those who visit. With a cosy and inviting bar and quirky mismatched furniture, it's definitely a place to relax and feel comfortable. At the bar you'll discover a good range of local beers on tap, and the menu offers a solid selection of pub food with plenty of choice – plus you can sample their famous 'design your own' Derby Burger. There are only 6 bedrooms, and each one is spacious, comfortable and full of quirky and interesting furniture. And if one of your days happens to be a bit drizzly, then you can hide away in the games room and enjoy a game of pool, or simply curl up with a good book. After breakfast, you can try a walk up Whitbarrow Scar; it's not exactly flat, but it's not too adventurous either, and the views from the top are stunning, from the Lake District fells in the north all the way to Morecambe Bay. For a more sedate excursion try a visit to the garden nursery at Halecat House, or the delightfully Georgian town of Grange-over-Sands, just a short drive away.

CONTACT Witherslack, Near Grange-over-Sands, Cumbria LA11 6RH • 01539 552 207 • thederbyarms.co.uk

HOW MUCH? Double rooms from £85 a night.

The Pheasant

The perfect place to use as a base to explore the popular northern lakes, The Pheasant is hidden well away from the main road and surrounded by woodland, but it is very easy to access. The bar area is open and airy with plenty of nooks and crannies, and there are plenty of local brews to choose from, not to mention gins and liqueurs from the nearby Lakes Distillery. And their Sunday roasts are legendary. There is a selection of rooms including twins, doubles and family rooms, all with a crisp, fresh feel, plenty of thoughtful touches and wonderful peaceful views of the surrounding fells and woods. They all have wifi, tea- and coffee-making facilities and TV; some are dog friendly and there's a pet-friendly area in the bar, well stocked with water and treats. As for things to do, there is high-octane mountain biking in nearby Whinlatter Forest, the ever-popular town of Keswick, just a short drive to the south, and – an equally short drive west – Cockermouth, a busy market town that was the birthplace of William Wordsworth and Fletcher Christian.

CONTACT Bassenthwaite Lake, Cockermouth, Cumbria CA13 9YE • 01768 776 234 • inncollectiongroup.com

HOW MUCH? Double rooms £134 a night, including breakfast .

The Brown Horse Inn

Winster is an area popular with locals and well tucked away from the busy spots, but this quiet valley has so much to offer – and The Brown Horse is a good place to base yourself, with some lovely walks right from the door and plenty of other places to explore nearby. Situated on an old trading route, The Brown Horse was once an important coaching inn for traffic and goods travelling between Kendal and Windermere. It has 9 rooms that are contemporary and comfortable with the occasional fun, quirky feature; all have solid oak king-size beds, wifi, flatscreen TVs and well-appointed modern bathrooms. All of them boast wonderful views, but the 4 housed in a separate building with their own patio area have perhaps the best views of all. The dining area is spacious and well laid out; even on a busy night, it doesn't feel cramped, and the food is classy, imaginative and plentiful (their chef was 'Pub Chef of the Year 2020'!). The cheeseboard, in particular, is a thing of beauty, containing a good selection of classic and local cheeses to choose from. Be sure to leave room!

CONTACT Winster, Near Windermere, Cumbria LA23 3NR • 01539 443 443 • thebrownhorseinn.co.uk
HOW MUCH? Double rooms £105–£125 a night, including breakfast.

Kirkstile Inn

Situated in a highly under-visited corner of the Lakes, and great for a hideaway stay, the Kirkstile Inn is a sympathetically restored 400-year-old pub and brewery, specialising in great food and drink and terrific accommodation, with 8 guest rooms both upstairs and in a nearby annexe. The rooms in the main building have been modernised but retain their old beams and plaster walls, plus there are a number of more contemporary premium rooms, along with 2 self-contained family suites that can sleep up to 2 adults and 2 children; one room even has a 4-poster. All the rooms are simply but stylishly furnished and come with flatscreen TVs, tea- and coffee-making facilities and up-to-date en-suite bathrooms. It's a terrific location too, with picturesque Loweswater just a step away, and the peak of Melbreak towering above both the lake and inn. Climb up that and you'll have earned a decent night's sleep and a choice of dishes from the inn's hearty menu, featuring local lamb and good steaks, which goes down well with a pint of their own Loweswater Gold!

CONTACT Loweswater, Cumbria CA13 0RU • 01900 85219 • kirkstile.com
HOW MUCH? Double rooms from £120 a night, including breakfast.

Pentonbridge Inn

Beautiful rooms and superb food and wine feature at this cosy inn on the England-Scotland border.

Less than a mile from Liddle Water, whose meandering course marks the England-Scotland border, and a couple of miles west of Kielder Forest Park, the Pentonbridge Inn has a reputation for serving well-presented, flavourful British food that warrants an overnight stay. The inn has nine elegant bedrooms divided between the main original building and a converted barn that is connected to the hotel. Their décor makes use of tweed, wood and slate to reinforce its Cumbrian countryside location. Cushioned seats on window ledges in some of the rooms offer views of the surrounding landscape, and Egyptian cotton bedding and modern bathroom fittings bring a hint of luxury. It's nice to know also that dogs are welcome in the three barn rooms, and receive a bowl and bed to go with the edible treats left for their lucky owners.

Each of the bedrooms bears the name of a local family – border folk who long ago rustled livestock and conducted cross-border raids. Staying means you're welcome to visit nearby Netherby Hall, whose owners redeveloped the Pentonbridge Inn from a country pub in which farmers would gather to catch up over a pint or two to the gourmet destination it is now. The country house is less than ten minutes' drive away and encompasses a Pele Tower that once provided protection from raiders, while its walled garden supplies the vegetables and herbs prepared in the inn's highly regarded kitchen.

Back at the hotel, food is served in a chic and airy bar and dining room, with exposed honey-coloured stonework. What are you likely to eat? Locally sourced meat and fish feature on an impressive menu with imaginative suggested wine pairings, often from the New World – say, starting with shorthorn beef tartare with a rich Argentinian red followed by local Herdwick lamb with an Australian Fiano or pan-fried cod loin with a Canadian pinot noir; or you could try Whitehaven lobster with a fresh Aussie Viognier followed by Cartmel Valley red deer with a robust red from Tuscany. They also offer a 'signature' ten-course tasting menu if you really want to go to town, and even the drinks are exotic – pickled martinis or milk punch vodka, anyone?

CONTACT Penton, Near Carlisle, Cumbria CA6 5QB • 01228 586 636 • pentonbridgeinn.co.uk

HOW MUCH? Double rooms with breakfast £150–£205 a night, including breakfast.

ROOMS 9 beautifully furnished bedrooms divided between the original inn and a connected converted barn.

PENTONBRIDGE INN

The Sun Inn

The lovely Lakeland village of Hawkshead has 3 or 4 old inns, all offering rooms and food, but The Sun is the pick of the bunch since it added a dollop of modern flair to its 17th-century interior. They've kept the exposed stone, oak beams, open fires and panelling, and there's a vintage bump-your-head feel as you make your way around upstairs. But there are designer fabrics and locally made items of furniture in the rooms (and an impressive 4-poster bed in one), and a contemporary look to the bar, where decently priced meals – local crab and scallops, local lamb and fish, along with a handful of veggie dishes – are served. The rooms are all different but they're cosy and make the most of the old stone walls of the inn, with handmade furniture, flatscreen TVs, tea and coffee and new bathrooms with toiletries. Not only that: the cobbles and inclines of Hawkshead are on your doorstep, and you're not far from key Lakes attractions like Tarn Hows and Grizedale Forest, Wray Castle, Windermere and Coniston Water, and the ever-popular World of Beatrix Potter.

CONTACT Main St, Hawkshead, Cumbria LA22 0NT • 01539 436 236 • suninn.co.uk
HOW MUCH? Double rooms £115–£145 a night, including breakfast.

Wasdale Head Inn

English country inns don't come more end-of-the-road than the Wasdale Head, sited under England's highest mountains, just past Wast Water, the country's deepest lake. Celebrated as the birthplace of British climbing, it's still a draw for mountaineers and hardcore walkers, and offers a taste of the rugged country hereabouts for more casual visitors. There's a hearty, hiker-friendly menu featuring steak and ale pie, fish and chips, bangers and mash and house burgers, and 9 smallish rooms – all with amazing views – while a converted cottage and stone barn have larger rooms and self-catering apartments. Everything has been nicely refurbished in a modern-rustic style and the only complaint people have is that they've put TVs in the rooms where there used to be none – which tells you all you need to know about the kind of clientele they're used to here. The inn also operates the very basic hike-and-climb campsite in the field across the lane – punters here will be your drinking buddies in Ritsons bar at night, though there is also a rather lovely wood-panelled residents' bar with your own peep-hole on to the action.

CONTACT Wasdale Head, Near Gosforth, Cumbria CA20 1EX • 01946 726 229 • wasdale.com
HOW MUCH? Double rooms £120–£140 a night, including breakfast; apartment short breaks £250–£450.

George & Dragon

Clifton's George & Dragon makes a great base for touring around Penrith, Ullswater, the Eden Valley and the northern Lakes. This old Georgian inn – part of the local Lowther Estate – looks age-old traditional from the outside, but inside it's had a zippy designer makeover, with 11 lovely guest rooms that mix pretty fabrics, mod cons and paintings and antique furnishings from the Lowther collection to great effect. All the rooms come with flatscreen TVs and wifi, minibars and tea and coffee and bijou bathrooms, many with either walk-in showers or roll-top baths – the 'Deluxe' rooms have both. All in all, it's a very handsome space throughout, while for great food and drink the downstairs bar is as pubby and atmospheric as ever but also a real country gourmet's delight, serving produce grown or reared on the estate or from within 20 miles of the pub. Dogs are welcome in the bar, although not the restaurant, but the same terrific menu is served in both – and in summer you can also enjoy your food in the outside courtyard and garden.

CONTACT Clifton, Penrith, Cumbria CA10 2ER • 01768 865 381 • georgeanddragonclifton.co.uk
HOW MUCH? Double rooms £100–£160 a night, including breakfast.

The Punch Bowl Inn

Sat enticingly in the pretty village of Crosthwaite, The Punch Bowl Inn is the very model of an updated country inn, serving excellent food and every day with a selection of 9 warmly furnished rooms to retire to at the end of the evening. There are gentle colour tones throughout, country cottage furniture and chic fabrics, and some have 4-posters made from reclaimed elm and free-standing clawfoot tubs, while one, Noble, sits under oak eaves and takes up the whole top floor. So comfortable will you be that you may never want to leave your delightful room but, if you do, it will probably only be to toddle down for the scrumptious meals they serve in the downstairs bar and restaurant – the menu is a diverse Franco-British affair powered by some terrific local suppliers and could feature anything from steak tartare and black pudding to local lamb and twice-baked Lancashire cheese soufflé. Outside, you're in the glorious rolling countryside of the Lyth Valley and just a short drive from Windermere.

CONTACT Askham, Penrith, Cumbria CA10 2PF • 01931 712 443 • punchbowlinnaskham.com
HOW MUCH? Double rooms £100–£120 a night, including breakfast.

The Roebuck Inn

In the heart of the leafy village of Mobberley, Cheshire, not far from Tatton Park, the Roebuck Inn was a rather sad affair a few years back – empty and in desperate need of some care and attention. Luckily for us, a major refurbishment 5 years ago saw the iconic building transformed into a stylish and extremely welcoming gastropub, with 6 individually decorated boutique bedrooms for those who want to prolong their stay. Dating back to 1708, it's lost none of its pubby charm, and the bedrooms – they are named after grape types (Malbec is the cheapest, Picpoul the most expensive) – are full of character and charm: natural wood sits alongside leather and plaid while free-standing baths, open fires and antique and ornate French beds make each one truly individual. There are deliberately no phones or TVs in the rooms, making it a real retreat from the hustle and bustle of daily life, and the food served downstairs is excellent, with an international menu that features all sorts of delicious dishes, from fresh fish tacos to massaman curry and beef bourguignon.

CONTACT Mill Lane, Mobberley, Cheshire WA16 7HX • 01565 873 939 • roebuckinnmobberley.co.uk
HOW MUCH? Double rooms £115–£145 a night, including breakfast.

The Watermill Inn

Midway between Kendal and Windermere, the Watermill Inn is tucked away in a quiet spot just a few hundred yards from the A591, in the tiny village of Ings. You're within easy striking distance of dozens of beautiful walks – in the nearby Kentmere Valley or up on Scout Scar near Kendal – while the pub itself offers all-day dining, and benefits from being attached to the excellent Windermere Brewery, whose ales you can sup in the bar. There are 8 bedrooms, all very homely, and decorated in keeping with the age of the building, although taller guests will need to watch out for the odd low beam. There are 6 doubles, 1 single and a family room, all with tea- and coffee-making facilities, TV and wifi and bathrooms with toiletries and decent showers. The Watermill is also one of the lakes' most dog-friendly pubs, with dogs welcome in all rooms and the bar and snug, dog portraits on the walls and even a special page in the bar menu dedicated to canine treats. For every dog that stays with them, The Watermill makes a donation to The Dogs Trust!

CONTACT Ings, Near Windermere, Cumbria LA8 9PY • 01539 821 309 • lakelandpub.co.uk
HOW MUCH? Double rooms £100–£115 a night, including breakfast.

The Royal Oak

The place to stay in Keswick, this welcoming and historic coaching inn has kept up with the times with updated guest rooms and a downstairs bar and restaurant that serves good, locally sourced food and local ales. The rooms are crisp, smart and modern, with big comfy beds, heavy curtains and colourful throws, plus wifi and flatscreen TVs, tea and coffee (with fresh milk), and a tray for your boots after a muddy mountain hike. There's also a welcome tray with lots of local treats, and well-appointed bathrooms with rainfall showers. Downstairs, the bar area is relaxed and comfortable, with plenty of local beers, and the restaurant serves a menu that combines classic pub food with more refined dishes. It's worth knowing, also, that Keswick enjoys a reputation for being one of the most dog-friendly towns in Britain and it's clear from the moment you arrive here that they truly love dogs, with water bowls on one side of the porch and a bag of towels on the other. Dogs can also enjoy a special 'Sausage Breakfast' to set them up for the day before taking on one of numerous walks from the town up into the surrounding fells.

CONTACT Main St, Keswick, Cumbria CA12 5HZ • 01768 773 135 • royaloakkeswick.co.uk
HOW MUCH? Double rooms with breakfast £160 a night, including breakfast.

The Bridge

It's arguable that The Bridge is more of a restaurant with rooms than a pub, but it displays all of the characteristics that we love in the best British pubs. It has a welcoming bar that serves food all day but is just as appropriate for a crafty pint as a full meal; it occupies a lovely riverside location in a picturesque village – in this case Prestbury in Cheshire; and it features 20-odd comfortable yet affordable rooms to flop into at the end of the night. It is, in other words, the very essence of a modern pub, with stylish interiors in both public areas and rooms that blend contemporary and vintage styles. All rooms have big comfy beds, Smart TVs, en-suite bathrooms with rainfall showers and fast wifi; some are accessible, some dog-friendly, while one room has a 4-poster bed. The restaurant serves an all-day menu that is deliberately casual, with burgers, skewers and pasta, local steaks and lots of cool snacks and sides - salt & pepper squid, Scotch eggs, loaded sandwiches and lots of vegan and veggie fare, which you can enjoy in the bar or outside in their riverside gardens.

CONTACT The Village, Prestbury, Cheshire SK10 4DQ • 0330 137 3770 • flatcaphotels.com/the-bridge
HOW MUCH? Most double rooms £114–£179 a night – not including breakfast.

Lucky Dip

The Bitter End

Cockermouth is home to Jennings brewery, whose beers are found all over the Lakes, so all hail The Bitter End, a fab little independent microbrewery and pub, hidden away up a Cockermouth side street. It might be Cumbria's smallest brewery, but the beers are excellent, as is the food, with local steaks and gourmet burgers a popular draw. No rooms.

CONTACT 15 Kirkgate, Cockermouth, Cumbria CA13 9PJ • 01900 828 993 • bitterend.co.uk

Badger Bar

Some of the best walks in the Lake District start from this awesome hotel bar, 2 minutes' walk from Rydal Water, with open fires, super-friendly staff, real ales and great food at great prices tempting locals and visitors alike. There is also a selection of comfy rooms too, some of which are dog-friendly.

CONTACT Glen Rothay Hotel, Rydal, Cumbria LA22 9LR • 01539 434 500 • theglenrothay.co.uk/the-badger-bar

Old Dungeon Ghyll

Run by Neil and Jane Walmsley for almost 40 years, the Old Dungeon Ghyll, situated at the top of the Great Langdale Valley, is a classic Lake District walkers' pub – indeed a visit to the hiker's bar here is a rite of passage for anyone in the Great Langdale area, and its 12 comfortable, traditionally furnished rooms upstairs have for decades provided a cosy refuge for walkers after a long day on the Fells.

CONTACT Great Langdale, Ambleside, Cumbria, LA22 9JY • 01539 437 272 • odg.co.uk

Hole in 't Wall

The best pub in Bowness is also the oldest, named after the hole through which pints of ale were passed to the horsemen in the days when this was a coaching inn. It's a proper Lakeland pub, with plenty of character inside and out, and on a summer's day the sun-trap terrace fills quickly with hikers, tourists and not a few bemused Japanese visitors on their way to the nearby Beatrix Potter attraction. No rooms.

CONTACT Robinson Place, Bowness-on-Windermere, Cumbria LA23 3DH • 01539 443 488 • holeintwall.co.uk

Dog & Gun

A dog-friendly, real-ale kind of pub, with ancient wooden benches, roaring fires and a changing selection of beers. Bar meals here are popular – hearty dishes with lashings of potatoes, rice and fresh veg, including the house special goulash, which is filling enough to get you up Everest and back. No rooms.

CONTACT 2 Lake Rd, Keswick, Cumbria CA12 5BT • 01768 773 463 • greeneking-pubs.co.uk/pubs/cumbria

The Mortal Man

Plan a hike up to rugged Troutbeck and you'll have earned a welcome pint at The Mortal Man, a fine old pub with roaring fires, filling bar meals and regularly changing ales. There are bedrooms too, and staying over means you have the chance to try out the pub's own walking guides, which take you on energetic local routes right from the front door.

CONTACT Troutbeck, Windermere, Cumbria LA23 1PL • 01539 433 193 • themortalman.co.uk

Hawkshead Beer Hall

The slickest of Cumbria's independent breweries has a taproom attached in the Mill Yard at Staveley – a big, open-plan, contemporary bar where you can look right on to the brewing vats and staff are happy to offer tasters and tips. Tapas and bar meals are matched to beers, and there are regular gigs and other events, so it's a cracking place all round. No rooms.

CONTACT Mill Yard, Staveley, Cumbria LA8 9LR • 01539 825 260 • hawksheadbrewery.co.uk

The Britannia Inn

The picture-perfect hamlet of Elterwater has a picture-perfect pub, the Britannia, with a large slate terrace overlooking the green. It's on the footpath that leads further up into Langdale, so it gets a steady stream of hikers, happy to freshen up with a big mug of tea or a pint of real ale. Bar meals are good – homemade pies, Cumberland sausage, fish and chips, slow-cooked lamb – and rooms upstairs are cosy and traditional, with lovely views and a real sense of peace and quiet.

CONTACT Elterwater, Ambleside, Cumbria LA22 9HP • 01539 437 210 • thebritanniainn.com

(Top) Badger Bar; (middle) Old Dungeon Ghyll; (bottom) Hole in 't Wall.

The Wainwright

The Wainwright is perfect for anyone looking for a proper Cumbrian pint. The owners, John & Kate, set out to create the sort of pub they'd want to visit themselves and the walls are crammed with local information, there's a TV in the bar with a silent video loop of stunning Lake District walks and the food is proper hikers' grub – well cooked, and plenty of it! The pub also serves a huge array of Cumbrian beers. No rooms.

CONTACT Lake Rd, Keswick, Cumbria CA12 5BZ • 01768 744 927 • thewainwright.pub

Ennerdale Brewery

Trust us, this is a brewery tap room with a difference: Ennerdale Brewery is very much a family business, started by dad, with mum still in charge of the food and the siblings now running the day-to-day business. It's a hub of the local community: from the outside it may look like an industrial unit (with plenty of parking), but step through the doors and you're in a huge English tearoom, with a well-stocked bar and spectacular food. No rooms.

CONTACT Chapel Row, Rowrah, Cumbria CA26 3XS • 01946 862 977 • ennerdalebrewery.co.uk

The White Lion

A solid coaching inn since 1657, and although it's had quite a few licks of paint since then, the ancient flagged floors, stone fireplaces and wood panelling combine well with its comfortable and stylish interior. The beautiful big open fire at the far end of the bar hasn't been tampered with, and a crowd-pleasing menu ranges from sandwiches to 'Infamous' beef stew and a 'right and proper pork pie'. For many years, various writers, poets and painters have colonised a corner of this comfortable pub; why not pull up a chair with a pint of Timothy Taylor, Copper Dragon or Black Sheep and wait for the muse? Or try one of the pub's 10 crisp and neat guest rooms for size?

CONTACT Bridge Gate, Hebden Bridge, West Yorkshire HX7 8EX 3RR • 01422 842 197 • whitelionhotel.net

Pump & Truncheon

It's a tall order finding a pub in Blackpool where you won't be forced to sing karaoke, join in a drinking game or remove items of clothing, but may we tentatively suggest this independently owned, real-ale haunt at the back of Blackpool's Golden Mile that was formerly a rozzers' drinking den, hence the name. If it's not exactly a quiet old traditional pub, it's not a pumping party venue either, and a decent pool table and budget bar meals might persuade you to stick around for longer than one drink. No rooms.

CONTACT 13 Bonny St, Blackpool, Lancashire FY1 5AR • 01253 624 099

The Windmill

Situated in the pleasant village of Parbold, nor far from Ormskirk, this canalside pub is owned by the same people as The Plough in Lupton and is every bit as good, with ancient floors , stripped tables and log fires and serving good food to a mixed crowd of walkers, anglers and dog-walkers. The perfect stop-off on the Leeds-Liverpool canal. No rooms.

CONTACT 3 Mill Lane, Parbold, Near Wigan, Lancashire WN8 7NW • 01257 462 935 • thewindmillparbold.co.uk

The Vicarage

Sister venue to The Bridge in Prestbury, and situated just outside the fashionable market town of Knutsford in Cheshire, this is a very comfortable place both to drink and to eat, with lots of sofas, fireplaces and a bar that's always buzzing. It also has no less than 26 elegant and contemporary bedrooms upstairs, so you can stay over too, leaving you free the next day to enjoy an excellent breakfast and explore Knutsford's historic and undeniably attractive town centre.

CONTACT Knutsford Rd, Cranage, Holmes Chapel, Cheshire CW4 8EF • 0330 137 3770 • flatcaphotels.com/the-vicarage

Eltermere Inn

Perhaps it's more of a hotel than a pub, but the Eltermere Inn is nonetheless a great Lakeland place to stay, with a deliberately relaxed atmosphere and wonderful food. Views from its rooms are stunning, while inside is all high ceilings and tasteful décor, with nicely decorated bedrooms. Dogs are allowed in the bar, which is comfortable and cosy with a large fire roaring away in the hearth throughout the winter months, and a range of local beers and spirits to warm you from the inside out. The food is good too, and for something a little special, all guests also have free access to the spa at Langdale Estates, just five minutes' drive down the road, where you can enjoy a swim in the pool or a steam in the, er, steam room.

CONTACT Elterwater, Ambleside, Cumbria LA22 9HY • 01539 437 207 • eltermere.co.uk

(Top) Pump & Truncheon; (middle) Eltermere Inn; (bottom) The Vicarage.

Wales

As one of Britain's most inspiring natural playgrounds, not many people come to Wales to go to the pub. But, in fact, some of its inns are among the UK's most historic – much like the country, stacked full of myths and legends and literary references. What's more, Wales has seen a big food revolution in recent decades, with the result that it's home to the country's biggest food festivals and some of its very best foodie pubs.

The West Arms p.224

Browns Hotel

Dylan Thomas's old watering-hole is a terrific boutique venue, with stylish rooms and excellent food.

Flanked by some of the more popular areas of Pembrokeshire and Swansea, you might be forgiven for overlooking Laugharne. But to do so would be to miss one of Wales's most appealing small towns, and one of its finest and most historic hotels – Browns. Known for being one of Dylan Thomas's favourite watering holes – allegedly he used to give the pub's phone number as his own! – the hotel closed down in 1959, and, although the pub stayed open for another 47 years, it too closed in 2008.

However, both the hotel and pub re-opened a few years ago and are back in their rightful place at the centre of village life. Each of Browns' boutiquey bedrooms is different, varying from cosy doubles to luxury suites, but they are all stylish, characterful and comfortable, decorated with contemporary artworks in a cool palette of greys and blues. Named after a local historic feature or location, each has a sturdy king- or super-king-size bed furnished with high-quality linen and premium Welsh woollens, air-conditioning, flatscreen Freeview TVs and digital radios. Each room also has a mini fridge filled with filtered bottled water and homemade treats, and tea- and coffee-making facilities, including Nespresso-style machines. Bathrooms vary but come with eco-friendly toiletries, and some with double roll-top baths. All but three rooms are dog-friendly, and for groups of up to seven people there's also a self-catering unit, Dylan's Den.

There is good wifi throughout the pub and hotel and it also has parking, with two electric car-charging points. The bar is an inviting place to have a drink, with a few Dylan Thomas volumes to leaf through and a pleasant beer garden for sunny days. The restaurant – Dexters – is a destination in itself, specialising in superb Dexter steaks from nearby Llyn Farm, served simply with triple-cooked chips and a secret sauce, but also with a small handful of other dishes to choose from.

Perhaps the best thing about Browns, however, is its location. Laugharne is a mesmerising village and is easily explored on foot. Cool things to see include Dylan Thomas's boathouse and writing shed, Laugharne Castle and the stunning surrounding Teifi Estuary, which inspired so much of Thomas's finest work and is home to a variety of birdlife. Thomas is buried in the churchyard of the medieval church of St Martin's, which is itself worth a look, while other writers associated with Laugharne include Kingsley Amis, who wrote 'The Old Devils' while staying here, and Mary Wollstonecraft, who spent time in Laugharne as a child. The annual Laugharne Weekend makes the most of the village's literary leanings and is a great time to visit, but really Laugharne – and specifically Browns – is a terrific venue at any time of year.

CONTACT King St, Laugharne, Carmarthenshire • SA33 4RY • 01994 427 688 • browns.wales

HOW MUCH? Double rooms £110–£160 a night, including breakfast

ROOMS 14 en-suite double rooms and suites.

The Felin Fach Griffin

There's no better place for a country weekend away doing nothing much amid glorious surroundings.

'The simple things in life done well' is the motto of this rather special inn – and we reckon it's perfectly suited to this gastropub with rooms, situated in the hills between the Black Mountains and the edge of the Brecon Beacons National Park. It lives up to its billing in every way possible, with seven very comfortable guest rooms above a restaurant that is one of the best in the region. It's also a proper pub, with all that implies, serving well-priced, well-kept local ales – a bit of a haven for local drinkers and a welcoming place for everyone else, with a roaring fire in winter. And dogs and children are most definitely welcomed.

The rooms are all different in size and style, but all have big beds, Roberts radios, homemade biscuits, fresh flowers and posh toiletries. There are no TVs, and they make a thing of that, so embrace the good old days and read a book. Breakfasts are delicious (scrambled eggs and smoked salmon if you prefer, local apple juice, homemade soda bread), and a good indicator of the quality of the dinner you'll enjoy – namely seasonally influenced dishes and ingredients from the Welsh borders, whether it's beef or lamb, local cheese, or herbs and veg picked from the inn's own kitchen garden.

There are lovely short menus for lunch and supper, featuring half a dozen starters and mains, that change every day and are full of tempting dishes often based on local, seasonal ingredients – think Black Mountains smoked salmon followed by local Middle White sausages, or pork rillettes followed by Cornish sea trout,. You can eat in the bar, the Library or the 'Tack Room', where there is a log fire, or there are larger tables in the Aga Room. As for drinks, there are always at least four real ales on tap, mostly from local brewers like Brecon Breweing, Wye Valley and Monty's, and staff are also keen to talk up their wonderful selection of sherries, not to mention a highly individual wine list made up of interesting blends you won't easily find elsewhere.

There is no shortage of things to do during the day to work up that appetite, from a hard day's walking to book-browsing in Hay or just pottering around nearby Brecon, Abergavenny or Crickhowell. Really there's no better place for a Welsh country weekend away; and if you like their style, it's good to know that the owners use the same motto for the other pubs they run, in Cornwall – the Gurnard's Head near Zennor and Old Coastguard in Mousehole.

CONTACT Felin Fach, Brecon, Powys LD3 0UB • 01874 620 111 • felinfachgriffin.co.uk

HOW MUCH? Double rooms £140–£185 a night, including breakfast. DB&B £207.50–£247.50 a night. No charges for cots or dogs.

ROOMS 7 double/twin en-suite rooms, with dogs welcome in all the rooms.

The Fox & Hounds

Just half an hour from Cardiff, this pub is an attractive base from which to explore the Glamorgan Heritage Coast, whose 14-mile path runs west from nearby Aberthaw to the seaside resort of Porthcawl. The dog-friendly bar is a cosy spot to relax with a beer after a walk, particularly if you can bag the antique settle next to the wood-burner. Outside, a terrace overlooks 13th-century St Cadoc's Church, noted for its medieval wall murals and one of many listed buildings in this time-passed, rural village. However, most visitors come to The Fox & Hounds for the food. Lunch and dinner menus are not extensive, but local, seasonal produce is turned into the likes of Rosedew Farm burger topped with Welsh Cheddar, or wild mushroom arancini. Sunday lunch, which includes fish and vegetarian options, is always popular and there is a good wine list too. Accommodation consists of a standard double, a larger double/twin and a superior double with a sofabed (suitable for children); all are decorated in cottage style and equipped with tea and coffee, homemade biscuits and bathrobes.

CONTACT Llancarfan, Vale of Glamorgan, CF62 3AD • 01446 781 287 • fandhllancarfan.co.uk
HOW MUCH? Double rooms from £85–£100 a night, including breakfast.

The Brit

The steel-producing town of Port Talbot used to be somewhere you'd pass on the way to the beaches of Gower or West Wales. But the home town of actors Richard Burton, Anthony Hopkins and Michael Sheen has had a renaissance in recent years after a Banksy mural – 'Season's Greetings' – appeared on someone's garage (it's now on display in Ty'r Orsaf, opposite the train station). The other reason tourists head here is for the mountain bike trails in nearby Afan Forest Park, often spending a night at The Brit, an award-winning gastropub in an attractive riverside setting a couple of miles northeast of 'The Port'. It has 3 rustic but comfortable rooms – a large en-suite double and 2 bunk rooms sleeping 4 people – a garage for your bikes, and a stylish bar-restaurant whose quirky modern décor attracts drinkers and diners from all around. The pub was Swansea CAMRA's 2019 'Pub of the Year', and, although the food menu has an international flavour, it uses local specialities like Glamorgan sausages (cheese and leek). Meals are served in the bar, restaurant or in the tree-shaded garden.

CONTACT London Row, Cwmavon, Port Talbot, Vale of Glamorgan SA12 9AH • 01639 680 247 • thebrit.wales
HOW MUCH? Double rooms from £60 a night, bunk rooms £25pp, including a basic self-service breakfast.

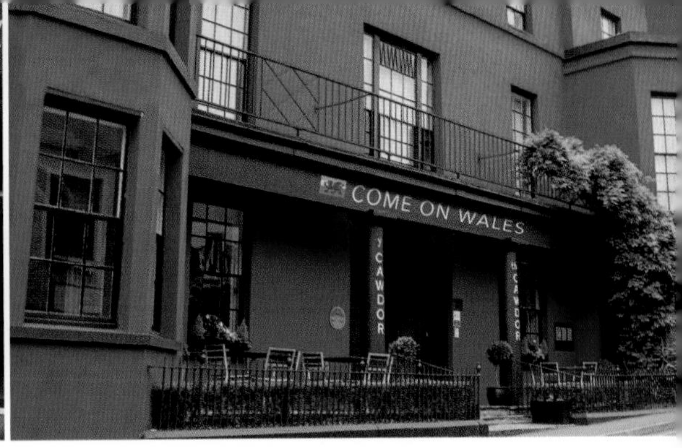

Billycan

A welcome addition to Tenby's often rather traditional accommodation, Billycan sits amid the pastel townhouses of this busy Pembrokeshire seaside resort, a former British Legion club that has been successfully turned into a contemporary pub and restaurant. The décor throughout has a nautical feel, in keeping with the town's past as a major port during the Middle Ages, along with wood-lined feature walls, leather banquettes and the odd touch of zinc. Locally made Melin Tregwynt soft furnishings add a touch of luxury in the otherwise minimalist bedrooms, of which there are 5, plus a 2-bedroom penthouse apartment complete with jacuzzi. Billycan's owners also run fish and chip shops in the Rhondda Valley, so it comes as no surprise that this is one of the star dishes on the menu, sitting alongside good-quality burgers and grills, while vegetarians can feast on items like Puy lentil and sweet potato pie or goat's cheese and walnut salad. The bar has a few street-side tables and chairs for fine days and there's a large selection of beers.

CONTACT Lower Frog St, Tenby, Pembrokeshire SA70 7HS • 01834 842 172 • billycan-tenby.co.uk
HOW MUCH? Double rooms with breakfast from £115 a night; apartment from £520 (2-night minimum stay).

The Cawdor

The Carmarthenshire market town of Llandeilo is a good base from which to explore the western side of Brecon Beacons National Park, home to the Black Mountains – one of the wildest parts of Wales. The Cawdor, on the town's main road, has been welcoming travellers since 1765, and in recent years has become one of the best places to stay in the area, with 24 rooms and 2 penthouse apartments. All are individually and tastefully decorated with upmarket furnishings and are provided with locally made Myddfai toiletries. The downstairs bar, with its Chesterfield sofas and roaring fire, is a popular place to stop for lunch after browsing the indy stores of this handsome Georgian town. Dishes are made with local produce, served in the bar or dining room, and feature the likes of Carmarthen Ham (air dried, salt cured) or shepherd's pie made with pulled lamb – accompanied by local ales like Tomos Watkin and Evan Evans. There are several reasons to spend a couple of nights in Llandeilo, not least a visit to the National Trust's Dinefwr, a 17th-century manor house with grounds designed by Capability Brown.

CONTACT 72 Rhosmaen St, Llandeilo, Carmarthenshire SA19 6EN • 01558 823 500 • thecawdor.com
HOW MUCH? Double rooms with breakfast £95–£150 a night, apartments £200–£250.

Pontcanna Inn

If you've ever been to Cardiff for a sports or music event, chances are you've stayed in a workaday B&B on Cathedral Road, about 15 minutes' walk west of the centre. One of the many Victorian villas that line this street, the Pontcanna Inn is named after its location in the Welsh capital's most fashionable district and is all about sports – matches are shown on big screens and the cricket, football and rugby grounds are all within walking distance. Food is good-quality pub grub, such as burgers, sausage and mash and fish and chips, but vegetarians and vegans won't go hungry either, while ales are by the Newport-based craft brewery 'Tiny Rebel' – the only Welsh brewery to win 'Champion Beer' at the Great British Beer Festival. There are 10 bright rooms, decorated with florals and botanicals, with iron beds that give a Steampunk vibe. Some of the rooms can be on the small side, and those at the back may be a problem for light sleepers when the beer garden is full, but they are very comfy and equipped with wifi, TVs and tea and coffee, and there's free onsite parking.

CONTACT 36 Cathedral Rd, Cardiff CF11 9LL • 02920 232 917 • pontcannainn.com
HOW MUCH? Double rooms from £79 a night, including breakfast.

King's Head Inn

At the tip of the Gower Peninsula, Britain's first designated Area of Outstanding Natural Beauty, this ancient pub has long been a favourite with surfers who come to ride the waves at the north end of Rhossili – a 4-mile stretch of golden sand that regularly features in lists of the world's best beaches. There are 2 beamed bars in the ivy-clad 17th-century inn, and the drinks served are solidly local: the top bar has more than 100 whiskies, including Wales-made Penderyn; and the dog-friendly bottom bar is the place to sample gins, including those from nearby Gower; most of the beer comes from the Gower Brewery. Traditional pub food and stone-baked pizzas feature on the menu, and even the 'Dragon's Breath' lamb curry has a local touch. They have 27 spacious, contemporary-rustic rooms, in 3 buildings, including 2 barn conversions; dogs are welcome and there's a lockup for surfboards. But it's not just about watersports: the pub organizes trail running and rambling weekends on the Gower Coast Path, and there are myriad other activities, from archery to bushcraft.

CONTACT Llangennith, Swansea SA3 1HX • 01792 386 212 • kingsheadgower.co.uk
HOW MUCH? Double rooms £125–£200 a night., including breakfast.

Stackpole Inn

Tucked away just a pebble's throw from Barafundle Bay – a broad sweep of sand that is hands-down one of Wales' loveliest beaches – the ivy-swathed Stackpole Inn has scooped a string of awards over the years, and it's not hard to see why. Stay the night and you'll properly relax in one of 4 seasidey rooms, done up in soft blues, greys and whites, with hardwood floors, handmade cushions, DVD players and desks. Two of them have sofabeds that pull out to accommodate families. Owners Gary and Becky extend a warm welcome in the bar-restaurant downstairs, where exposed stone, a wood-burner and cheek-by-jowl wooden tables lend a rustic feel. Provenance matters here, so you can expect an impressive line-up of Welsh beers, and the food emphasises local sourcing, whether you go for simply cooked seafood or the signature pan-roasted rump of Welsh lamb with pearl barley, charred onions and wild garlic. You're also within easy reach of some of the country's most dramatic coastlines, and the village itself edges the Stackpole nature reserve, with its woods, coastal dunes and the Bosherston Lakes lily ponds.

CONTACT Jasons Corner, Stackpole, Pembrokeshire SA71 5DF • 01646 672 324• stackpoleinn.co.uk
HOW MUCH? Double rooms from £120 a night, including breakfast; family rooms from £130.

The Bell at Skenfrith

A deft fishing rod flick from the English border on the banks of the River Monnow, The Bell is one of the establishments that helped Monmouthshire get its tag as a foodie Mecca – a whitewashed 17th-century hostelry with views of either the pea-green hills behind or the murmuring river out front. Its 11 delightful rooms are country-mansion in style, large and light with Farrow & Ball colours, claw-foot baths and other antique furnishings. Especially striking are the elegant mustard-tinted Coachman, the 2-level Lough Arrow and Heckham Peckham with its curving beams and semi-4-poster. There are 2 bar areas – the Dog & Boot Bar for the many muddy hikers and anglers the inn receives and another snug area with a wood-burning stove and sofas – and an excellent restaurant where you can feast on roast pork tenderloin enveloped in Parma ham and braised pork cheek, or beetroot and goats' cheese risotto. The wine list is standout too, and in summer you can take your drink out to the sloping grassy beer garden. Whenever you are here, try some local walks. The Bell has mapped and marked the best.

CONTACT Skenfrith, Monmouthshire NP7 8UH • 01600 750 235 • thebellatskenfrith.co.uk
HOW MUCH? Double rooms £150–£250 a night, including breakfast.

The West Arms

This one-time haunt of cattle drovers is bang up to date, with special bedrooms and superb Welsh food.

In such majestically rugged surroundings as those around Llanarmon Dyffryn Ceiriog (or Llanarmon DC, as most people thankfully abbreviate this charming but lengthily-named village) this whitewashed old inn comes as a very welcome, gentle surprise. Dating back to the 16th century, and a one-time haunt of cattle drovers, the pub was taken over by Nicky and Mark Williamson a couple of years ago and they have devoted bundles of attention since then to bringing it bang up to date. The result? A fabulous gastropub with rooms that you won't want to leave.

The beamed interior is super-inviting, with a snug lounge with a wood-burning stove and a more formal slate-floored dining room with an inglenook fireplace, while at the back the wide, grassy beer garden is almost the only level ground around beneath the Berwyn Mountains' undulating uplands. Of the fifteen bedrooms, there are 'Character' rooms, with big old beams, king-size beds and views over the village, newly refurbished and slightly more contemporary 'King Valley' rooms, with super-king-size beds and offering wonderful views over the mountains; and 'Classic' rooms either in the main pub or the converted stables. There are also rooms with one double and single that are suitable for small families, and a couple of suites. The Bunny Warren Suite is quirkily spread over three levels and has a chunky brace of timber encasing the sleeping area, while the beamed Howard Room is centred around its amazing four-poster king-size bed. But you can find beams, fireplaces, beautifully exposed stonework and gorgeous countryside views throughout all the accommodation. And all the rooms come with en-suite bathrooms and wifi, and all of them welcome dogs, which is just as well as you couldn't be in a better location for walkies.

Above all, the inn has a reputation for sensational cuisine, and it's nice that the menu mentions by name the people supplying many of the ingredients, confirming that providing food of this quality is a team effort, with a cast of hundreds. Eating here is a a celebration of Welsh food: the butchers from nearby Llanrhaeadr provide much of the meat, including succulent Berwyn lamb, and you can supplement that with a divine leek and Caerphilly tart or the pub's own mustard, chutney and churned butter.

As for things to do, just get outside! Hiking in the Berwyn Mountains includes the walks around breathtaking Pistyll Rhaeadr waterfall, one of Wales' highest and one that may be familiar from the Timotei shampoo advert. Search out also medieval Chirk Castle and Chirk Aqueduct and Tunnel, which carries the Llangollen Canal across the Ceiriog river.

CONTACT Llanarmon Dyffryn Ceiriog, Wrexham LL20 7LD • 01691 600 665 • thewestarms.com

HOW MUCH? Double rooms from £155 a night, including breakfast. Dogs £10.

ROOMS 16 guest rooms and suites, which are divided between beamed 'Character' rooms, more contemporary 'King Valley' rooms with great views and super-king-size beds and 'Classic' rooms, also with good views and cast-iron beds.

WEST
ARMS

The Bear Hotel

Exuding charm from every creaking beam and wonky staircase, The Bear is quite possibly the coaching inn of your dreams. Situated in biscuit-tin-pretty Crickhowell, there has been a pub here since 1432, and it's not hard to imagine the horses and coaches pulling through its gated archway. In summer, the whitewashed façade is a riot of hanging baskets, while in winter log fires blaze away in grates. The pub's 35 rooms vary considerably in style. Done out in neutral tones, with modern bathrooms featuring shower or bath, the compact 'cosy' and 'good' categories are comfortable but by no means fancy. By upgrading to the more spacious 'best' rooms it's easier to appreciate the pub's historic features, from oak beams to antique furnishings. Or to ramp up the romance, opt for a suite with a 4-poster and free-standing bath. Book a table for dinner, allowing time for a pint in the beamed bar before choosing from an unfussy menu that plays up regional sourcing. Outside, the Brecon Beacons unfurl, including Crickhowell's own Table Mountain, 451m Crug Hywel, reached on a 3-mile ramble.

CONTACT Crickhowell, Powys NP8 1BW • 01873 810 408 • bearhotel.co.uk
HOW MUCH? Double rooms with breakfast from £123 a night; with spa bath from £209; suite from £248.

Harbourmaster

There's always a good buzz at this cornflower-blue Grade II-listed pub on the quayside in Aberaeron, and those wishing to stay will find 13 boutiquey rooms spread across 3 harbourside buildings. The original rooms in the harbourmaster's residence have sea views, palettes of breezy blues or lavenders, eye-catching fabrics, and period details. All have tea and coffee, robes, slippers and contemporary bathrooms with Molton Brown toiletries. Top billing goes to the chic warehouse rooms with roll-top baths, and the attic 'Madonna' suite, with its dreamy bay views. Score a table for dinner and you won't be disappointed: the restaurant delivers some of the region's most inventive food – dishes like Cardigan Bay crab linguine, and slow-roasted short rib of Welsh beef with sweet potato purée. A pint of Cardiff Pipes ale or seaweed-infused Da Mhile gin is a perfect accompaniment to crispy cockles and salt-and-pepper squid. Breakfast is right up there, too, from a Full Welsh with laverbread to organic halloumi with the Harbourmaster's own riff on beans. You'll need a hearty start for the terrific walks on the nearby Ceredigion Coast Path.

CONTACT Pen Cei, Aberaeron, Ceredigion SA46 0BT • 01545 570 755 • harbour-master.com
HOW MUCH? Double rooms with breakfast from £175 a night; attic suite from £195; warehouse rooms £260.

The Brigands Inn

The hills start getting steeper as you approach Mallwyd from the south or east, and one of Gwynedd's finest coaching inns is almost the first sight you see: an impeccably-preserved 15th-century gem with whitewashed walls, buckled beams and open fires to warm any wayfarer's heart. Named for the outlaws who once roamed the region, the beams and antique furniture not only grace common areas but also 9 individually-designed rooms, each of which has an air of rustic refinement, with solid oak beds (some 4-posters) and Egyptian cotton sheets, while bathrooms have baths and either monsoon or separate walk-in showers. The food is exactly what you need after a day in the outdoors: pub classics done to high standards – 28-day-aged steaks from grass-fed Hereford cattle and salmon with a poached egg and cider rarebit sauce; and it's worth staying overnight for the breakfast alone (the chef is a former National Breakfast Awards winner). Local activities include fishing on the nearby river, walking in the Snowdonia foothills or making the jaunt to charming nearby village Dinas Mawddwy.

CONTACTMallwyd, Machynlleth, Powys SY20 9HJ • 01650 511999 • brigandsinn.com
HOW MUCH? Double rooms from £115 a night, including breakfast.

Llanthony Priory

Like a mini Tintern Abbey, Llanthony Priory sits buried in a little-known spot in the Black Mountains, in the heart of the Brecon Beacons National Park. It's far less of a tourist attraction than its better-known cousin, but, unlike the great ruins of Tintern, it has its own pub attached – made up of a bar in the crypts of the abbey and a hotel occupying the Llanthony Priory's former lodgings, Court Farm, plus a field reserved for camping. The guest rooms are homely and simply furnished – rather monkish in fact, with thick stone walls and beams; 2 are reached by a spiral staircase and a couple have 4-poster beds. None have en-suite facilities, but they do share a couple of up-to-date bath and shower rooms, and, just to emphasise the feel of retreat, there's no wifi or phone signal either – though rooms do include tea- and coffee-making facilities and rates include a decent breakfast. The bar is as rustic as it gets, housed in the undercroft of the original abbey and serving good local ales and a varied and inexpensive menu at lunch and dinner.

CONTACT Llanthony, Monmouthshire NP7 7NN • 01873 890 487 • llanthonyprioryhotel.co.uk
HOW MUCH? Double rooms £100-£110 a night, including breakfast.

Y Star Inn

Less a settlement than a scattering of houses spread-eagled around old mineworkings high in the Cambrian Mountains, you have to be an adventurer just to make it to Dylife. So naturally the 17th-century Y Star Inn attracts lovers of the outdoors, including bikers (it's on Sustrans Route 8) and hikers (it's on legendary long-distance trails the Cambrian Way and Glyndŵr's Way). Although the pub has just changed hands, we're hoping the new owners don't change it too much. Its 8 bright and comfortable rooms are simple and spacious, with wifi, flatscreen TVs, tea and coffee and en-suite bathrooms (4 of which have baths), and dogs are welcome in selected rooms. The views are the truly jaw-dropping, especially if you scoop a room facing the green mountainside across the road. Do not go to sleep too swiftly though: the hills here are one of the UK's best dark-sky zones and star-gazing can be phenomenal. Down in the bar and restaurant, staff are used to serving hearty portions to famished walkers, whether it's locally-caught trout or Welsh lamb and mint pie.

CONTACT Dylife, Llanbrynmair, Powys SY19 7BW • 01650 521 345 • starinndylife.co.uk
HOW MUCH? Doubles from £110 a night, including breakfast.

Groes Inn

Welcome to the oldest licensed pub in Wales, which opened its doors in 1573, and whose rustic bar, with its low beams, rough-stone hearth and fire, feels little changed since then. This family-run coaching inn has 14 rooms, all light and peaceful, with a sense of space and proportion, and tastefully decorated in a palette of olives, dove greys and taupes, with painted wainscoting, patterned wallpaper and vintage dressing tables, and complimentary tea, coffee and water. The best have terraces overlooking the hills, while Tesla charging-points ramp up the inn's sustainable credentials. After a bracing hike you'll want to pull up a chair in the bar, where you'll find an excellent selection of local brews and the pub's own Dragon's Fire ale. The vine-draped conservatory serves well-presented pub classics, including their signature cheese and onion pie with chunky chips and staples like lamb shank and pork belly. The setting is pretty special, with the peaks of Snowdonia to the west and the river twisting north to Conwy, Britain's most impressive medieval walled town, capped by one of Edward I's phenomenal castles.

CONTACT Llanrwst Rd, Conwy LL32 8TN • 01492 650 545 • groesinn.com
HOW MUCH? Double rooms £95–£145 a night, not including breakfast.

The Old Black Lion

Pick of the pubs with rooms in Hay-on-Wye, The Old Black Lion has an endearing old-world vibe. Legend has it that Oliver Cromwell sojourned here while the Roundheads besieged Hay Castle, and you can't blame him for making himself comfortable among the inn's dark beams and oak tables worn by many a pint glass. There are no airs and graces: 'boots and paws' are welcome, and the crowd is an interesting mix of walkers, cyclists, canoeists, music lovers and book-browsers. The guest rooms – 6 doubles, 2 twins, 2 singles – each have individual flourishes (some have ruby-red walls and oil paintings, others vintage furnishings and florals) but far and away the most atmospheric is The Cromwell Suite, with its sagging beams, antiques and soft lamplight. Downstairs you can sample Wye Valley Old Black Lion Ale, and the food is uncomplicated but good, with starters like smoked salmon and mackerel with pickled cucumber and pea shoots followed by hearty mains like roast lamb rump with garlic and chive mash. Come on a Friday evening and you might even be treated to a spot of live jazz.

CONTACT26 Lion Street, Hay-on-Wye HR3 5AD • 01497 820 841 • oldblacklion.co.uk
HOW MUCH? Double rooms £130–£145 a night, including breakfast.

The Harp at Old Radnor

The country lane ends in an expanse of green sloping away to the Radnor Valley. But this is one backwater dead-end where you don't want to reset the GPS, due to the presence of this ancient tavern, all oak beams and slate floors and dripping in character. With the Offa's Dyke Path passing close by, hikers as well as locals visit to take in the views from the tree-shaded garden, and some are sensible enough to stay over in one of 5 guest rooms that look out over the hills or the garden. They're country farmhouse-elegant, with fabrics lending either a blackberry or iceberg-blue tone, and all have en-suite or private bathrooms, flatscreen TVs and wifi. The thoughtful food that's on offer reaches far beyond standard pub classics, featuring dishes such as Gressingham duck with fennel cassoulet, garlic and pepper sausage, pancetta and butterbeans. Local producers are evident throughout the menu, from Welsh cheeses to Herefordshire ciders, and Herefordshire's Wye Valley HPA and Shropshire's Ludlow Brewery Gold grace the hand-pumps at the bar.

CONTACT Old Radnor, Presteigne, Powys LD8 2RH • 01544 350 655 • harpinnradnor.co.uk
HOW MUCH? Double rooms from £120, including breakfast.

Dolaucothi Arms

Tucked into the pleats and folds of the Cambrian Mountains, the remote village of Pumsaint (meaning 'five saints') is named after a nearby standing stone. But the village is better known for its position on the edge of the Dolaucothi Estate, with its Roman gold mines and hill walking. A pub in these parts is gold dust, especially when it has the historic hallmarks of this 16th-century inn, where a convivial warmth greets you like a long-lost friend. A wood-burning stove lights up the interior, with its tiled floors, vintage Chesterfield and armchairs. Add a selection of Welsh real ales, a menu featuring comfort faves and a pretty beer garden overlooking the valley, and you can see why it was voted Countryfile 'Best British Country Pub 2019–20'. In 1854 the novelist George Borrow praised the 'savoury supper' and 'refreshing sleep' he enjoyed here, and it's not changed much since, with 3 Arts & Crafts rooms, decorated in mellow hues, with diamond-paned windows, period furniture and wool-filled mattresses. The complimentary port is a nice touch, and breakfast includes local bacon, sausage, cockles and laverbread.

CONTACT Pumsaint, Llanwrda, Carmarthenshire SA19 8UW • 01558 650 237 • dolaucothiarms.co.uk
HOW MUCH? Double rooms £70–£85 a night, including breakfast.

The Goose & Cuckoo

In the 19th century there was a major pub cull in this part of Wales, brought about by the Temperance Movement and a local teetotal aristocrat by the name of Baroness Llanover. How The Goose & Cuckoo survived is anyone's guess, but it had lots to do with its back-of-beyond location and the fact that at first glance it looks more like a farmhouse than a tavern. We're lucky that it did, because this whitewashed place is one atmospheric boozer, with an inglenook fireplace, a few wooden tables on the flagstones and a bar serving a legendary array of local ales. There's an old piano in one corner, a dartboard in another and an ambience more akin to someone's living room, quirkily bedaubed in yesteryear photographs. There is one double room that can be rented out on a B&B basis and a self-catering annexe with a sitting room and kitchen enjoying glorious views of the valley below. Food is mainly doorstep sandwiches, mighty cheeseboards, and other hunger-busting fare for the hikers who stop by on their way from the gentle slopes of the Usk Valley and the moorland of Blaenavon.

CONTACT Upper Llanover, Monmouthshire NP7 9ER • 01873 880 277 • thegooseandcuckoo.co.uk
HOW MUCH? Double room from £80 a night, including breakfast; self-catering annexe £90–£125 a night.

Black Boy Inn

If this 16th-century tavern's stone walls could speak, they would surely raise an eyebrow or two with their tales of smugglers, shipwrecks and past times when Northgate Street was Caernarfon's red-light district. Within the town's medieval walls, just a cannon-ball throw away from Wales' most extraordinary castle, this inn creaks loudly with the weight of history, with 47 rooms that somehow manage to combine period features with contemporary comfort. Spread across 4 buildings, rooms vary from those in the Edwardian Townhouse to the high-ceilinged Black Jack's courtyard rooms, but best are the rooms in the inn itself, with its low beams, vintage furnishings and thoughtful extras like scallop-shaped Aberffraw biscuits and Duck Island toiletries. For romance, upgrade to a room with a barley-twist 4-poster. The pub itself is as you might expect: oak beams, thick walls, lots of exposed stone, open fires and 20 beers on tap, including a number from this neck of Snowdonia. These go nicely with dishes like Welsh steak-and-ale pie, curries and cask-ale battered haddock, prepared with locally sourced ingredients.

CONTACT Northgate Street, Caernarfon, Gwynedd LL55 1RW • 01286 673 604 • black-boy-inn.com
HOW MUCH? Double rooms from £95 a night, including breakfast.

The Kinmel Arms

Not far from the sea, and only half an hour from Snowdonia, this contemporary village pub makes for the perfect North Wales luxury escape. To be fair, it's less of a pub and more of a hotel these days, but it has all the atmosphere you expect of a busy inn, and it delivers in almost every other respect too. The food is superb: locally sourced and seasonal but also riddled with influences that stretch far beyond North Wales – think satay roasted broccoli followed by pan-fried sea bass with gnocchi and chorizo, or maybe local mussels in ale or a Thai green curry. There's also always a good choice of veggie dishes on the menu, and drinks tend to focus on local favourites, for example good Welsh ales, along with Welsh whisky and craft gins. As for their four guest rooms, they are all enormous – suites really – each with a large en-suite bathroom with bath and shower, high-end toiletries and a little kitchen with a kettle, toaster and other amenities. This is also where your breakfast will be delivered each morning, and each room is large enough to have a dining table and chairs at which to eat it.

CONTACT St George, Abergele, Conwy LL22 9BP • 01745 832207 • thekinmelarms.co.uk
HOW MUCH? Double rooms from £115 a night, including continental breakfast.

Y Talbot

Narrow single-track lanes meander over the moors to Tregaron, a tiny village in the remote Cambrian Mountains, where this 400-year-old inn is always a sight for sore eyes. Inside is snug as can be, with slate floors, grey stone walls, blackened beams and a fire taking the chill off. Given the pub's historic look and feel, the fresh, contemporary design of its 13 rooms is a surprise. Easy-on-the-eye creams and browns dominate, with Welsh wool blankets adding pops of colour. Sash windows allow light to stream in, and views are either over the market square or pub garden. Bathrooms are slick and modern, most with walk-in showers, and tea, coffee and bottled water are provided. The superior and garden suites with sofa beds are big enough for families of 4, and there is one accessible ground-floor room. Meanwhile, in the pub, the menu is equally up to date, swinging from well-executed classics to ingredient-driven dishes along the lines of Mangalitsa pork black pudding Scotch egg with smoked bacon velouté, or confit duck leg with leeks, mash and red wine jus.

CONTACT Tregaron, Ceredigion SY25 6JL • 01974 298208 • ytalbot.com
HOW MUCH? Double rooms £90–£145 a night, including breakfast.

The Boat Inn

Right on the banks of the River Wye, a stone-skim from England, the idiosyncratic stone Boat Inn nestles beside a Victorian former railway bridge, now pedestrian only and coaxing visitors from the car park (in England!) over the Wye to Wales. The interior is small and cosy, with an amazing timber-framed bar, rustic wood tables and chairs and a wood-burning stove. But the appeal lies primarily outside, in the tranquil river-facing terraced garden tumbling down the adjacent hillside: with its waterfalls, wildflowers and surrounding woods. Courtesy of the 2-room apartment above the pub, you can extend your stay at this pocket of bucolic bliss: a fully equipped kitchen gives guests plenty of self-sufficiency and, although stays don't include breakfast, they can be sustained by the hearty pub grub downstairs. The Wye Valley is the domain of pootling country motorists, walkers, cyclists and kayakers, and this is one of a dwindling breed of taverns you can still rock up at on a boat. But perhaps the best thing to do is just to sit on one of the Boat's benches, absorbing the amiable riverside goings-on.

CONTACT Lone Lane, Penallt, Monmouthshire NP25 4AJ • 01600 712 615 • theboatpenallt.co.uk
HOW MUCH? Self-catering apartment £120 a night, not including breakfast.

The Bull

Overlooking the Menai Strait, with its ever-changing light and views of Snowdonia's brooding mountains, this coaching inn has propelled itself into the 21st century with inventive food and chic rooms without losing a jot of its 400-year-old history. The location, in any case, is pretty unbeatable, with the Victorian pier and turreted Beaumaris Castle right on the doorstep, and walkers can strike out on the Anglesey Coastal Path. But old-fashioned the rooms are not: designed with a razor-sharp eye for detail, they weave period features with intricate wallpaper and bursts of colour, Hypnos mattresses draped in Egyptian cotton, Nespresso coffee machines and Welsh Cole & Co toiletries. Deluxe rooms feature roll-top baths; one has an antique 4-poster, another is a romance-ready suite with a scarlet canopy bed. The Coach restaurant pleasingly mixes the old and new, with lots of attention-grabbing art and a flower-rimmed courtyard for outdoor dining. The menu sings of the season and region, with Anglesey honey-glazed chorizo, Welsh crab and crispy pork with mustard piccalilli – all uniformly delicious.

CONTACT Castle St, Beaumaris, Anglesey, LL58 8AP • 01248 810 329 • bullsheadinn.co.uk
HOW MUCH? Doubles £120–£160 a night, including breakfast; suites from £175.

Saracen's Head

Beddgelert is one of Snowdonia's most desirable destinations. Tucked just below the biggest and most famous mountain in Wales, the mesmeric high-altitude scenery will keep your eyes raised for much of your visit, but when they lower to focus on the pressing business of refreshment, they may alight on this impressive recent addition to the village, a Robinson's Brewery pub on the banks of the rushing Afon Colwyn. The 11 rooms in this big, multi-gabled edifice are each individually designed and contemporarily decorated to reflect the local landscape: the greens of the foliage, the steely greys of water and sky and the purplish grey of slate. All rooms have tea- and coffee-making facilities, wifi, flatscreen TVs, hairdryers and irons; and 4 are also dog-friendly. The food takes in dishes like scallops with black pudding and pea puree, beef wellington or Welsh lamb marinated in honey. Wash it down with a beer brewed specially for the pub, the Faithful Gelert. And then get out exploring the surrounding terrain. There is, after all, a certain peak to climb...

CONTACT Caernarfon Rd, Beddgelert, Gwynedd LL55 4UY • 01766 890 329 • saracens-head.co.uk
HOW MUCH? Double rooms from £149 a night.

Lucky Dip

Blue Anchor Inn

If the BBC's 'Escape to the Country' decided to find city dwellers pubs instead of homes, then the Blue Anchor would be the star of the show. But although the 600-year-old stone building is a massive head-turner, the food is actually where the pub really shines. Winner of a plethora of awards, it takes pride in serving hearty portions of great pub food with local ales. No rooms.

CONTACT East Aberthaw, Barry, South Glamorgan CF62 3DD • 01446 750 329 • blueanchoraberthaw.com

The Cricketers

Virtually overlooking the Sophia Gardens cricket ground, this smart-looking pub is adorned with photos and sketches of the great and good of the game, alongside wall-mounted shirts, bats, caps and other memorabilia. The cask-conditioned Evan Evans beers are very moreish and the food is a cut above usual pub fare. There's always a vibrant atmosphere on match days, particularly out on the sunny patio. No rooms.

CONTACT 66 Cathedral Rd, Pontcanna, Cardiff CF11 9LL • 02920 345 102 • cricketerscardiff.co.uk

Hare & Hounds

This old pub just outside Cowbridge in South Wales just happens to serve terrific food from a daily changing menu based on local producers and their own kitchen garden. Refreshingly, though, it retains an essential pubbiness, with a roaring fire, sport on the telly and a warm welcome. No rooms.

CONTACT Aberthin, Cowbridge, Vale of Glamorgan CF71 7LG • 01446 774 892 • hareandhoundsaberthin.com

The Pelican in her Piety

Incredible coastal views with the sands of Merthyr thrown in as well, a fantastic selection of real ales and a menu of pub grub, including good-quality steaks, are the highlights at this Bridgend boozer. It also hosts live music every week and in summer the place is heaving. No rooms.

CONTACT Ogmore Rd, Ogmore, Bridgend, Glamorgan CF32 0QP • 01656 856 464

The Crown at Pantygelli

Nestled in the tiny village of Pantygelli, this whitewashed pub is a perfect place from which to discover not only nearby Abervgavenny but also the castles and mountains of the region. It's a lovely old pub, mainly known for its excellent, locally sourced food. No rooms.

CONTACT Old Hereford Rd, Pantygelli, Monmouthshire NP7 7HR • 01873 853 314 • thecrownatpantygelli.com

The Albion

A beautiful old pub with an almost untouched Art Nouveau interior that was revived by a quartet of local brewers a decade ago, since when it has been named CAMRA 'Wales Pub of the Year' and one of the 'world's best bars' by The Guardian. Settle in for a pint from its owners – Conwy Brewery, Purple Moose, Great Orme Brewery and Bragdy Nant. No rooms.

CONTACT Uppergate St, Conwy LL32 8RF • 01492 582 484 • albionalehouse.weebly.com

The Griffin Inn

This Pembrokeshire seaside local specialises in simple seafood dishes – everything from mackerel and scallops to crab and cod, all fresh off the boat. Lovely views and walks nearby, too. No rooms.

CONTACT Dale, Haverfordwest, Pembrokeshire SA62 3RB • 01646 636 227 • griffininndale.co.uk

The White Horse

Brewery tap of the Evan Evans brewery in Llandeilo, and thus a place to enjoy the best seasonal ales, good food and sometimes live music, especially when they host acts at the annual jazzfest. No rooms.

CONTACT 125 Rhosmaen St, Llandeilo, Carmarthenshire SA19 6EN • 01558 822 424 • evanevansbrewery.com

(Top) Blue Anchor Inn; (middle) The Pelican in her Piety; (bottom) The Albion.

Scotland

Scotland is home to some of the UK's most historic pubs, some of them in truly remote and scenic locations – and as you crest the peak of a mountain or round the end of a loch, some of them can be a very welcome sight indeed! Also, like other parts of the UK, many Scottish pubs have rediscovered the fabulous natural ingredients on their doorstep, which means the food on offer can often be stunning.

The Ship Inn at Elie p.242

OCH
WHEESHT
AND
GET OAN
WAE IT
OCH WHEESHT AND GET OAN WAE IT

The Stables at The Torridon

A dramatically sited inn on Scotland's West Coast that has its own five-star hotel attached.

Situated in a dramatic location on the shores of Loch Torridon on Scotland's west coast, about 40 miles north of Fort William, The Stables is part of the 'Torridon Resort', a turreted baronial castle that makes for a thoroughly indulgent place to stay, with eighteen individually designed contemporary guest rooms, two restaurants and its own farm and kitchen garden. A two-minute walk away across the lawn, The Stables provides a more relaxed alternative – more appropriate for walkers and the muddy boot brigade, and more affordable too, while still giving access to the grander offerings at the hotel if you want them. And the scenery, of course, is the same for everyone!

The Stables is a perfectly self-contained entity, with a selection of double, twin and family options among its twelve guest rooms and suites. Grouped around a courtyard in the former stable block of the main house, the rooms in this old stone bolthole have been given a bright recent makeover; think tartan throws and thoughtfully curated paintings depicting the spectacular local landscapes. They are well equipped, stylish and cosy but they don't have the stunning loch and mountain views of the hotel. What they do have is a variety, with plenty of room for families or groups of friends to muck in together. Bathrooms are recently refurbished and well equipped with bath/showers and Cowshed toiletries, and dogs are welcome in ground-floor bedrooms.

The same building is also home to the hearty Beinn Bar, where you can sup guest Scottish ales and compare walking stories before moving on to posh comfort food at Bo and Muc, a restaurant with such delights as Isle of Harris smoked salmon and 'Hairy Coo burgers'. You can see the local herd of these beautiful horned beasts out the window. Finish off with a decadent Tunnocks Teacake ice cream sundae (yes, seriously!). Herbs and vegetables from The Torridon's kitchen garden find their way into the dishes too.

Finally, there's the location, which is about as good as its gets if you're keen to get outdoors. You can get right in among those hiking - Beinn Damh rises right behind the inn, or tackle the even tougher Munros of the Liathach Ridge across the loch. The hotel can arrange everything from archery lessons to sea kayaking and gorge scrambling, while there are any number of hikes you can undertake from the hotel, perhaps along Loch Torridon or up nearby Beinn Alligin. The only problem you will find is that you can't experience all the area has to offer on a single visit. You will have to come back!

CONTACT By Achnasheen, Wester Ross, Highland IV22 2EY • 01445 791 242 • thetorridon.com/stay/the-stables
HOW MUCH? Double rooms from £155, including breakfast at the Bo and Muc.
ROOMS 12 cosy doubles and family rooms, plus 18 luxury rooms in the main hotel and self-catering accommodation in the Boathouse.

The Sun Inn

If you want easy access into the multiple delights of Edinburgh but are keen to escape the hubbub of the city after a day's sightseeing, the welcoming Sun Inn is for you. It's quite a place, hunkering under a grand old railway viaduct in the Midlothian suburb of Dalkeith. It serves ace Scottish ales but it also has a gin & cocktail bar, a coffee house and a covered courtyard and outside terrace. Upstairs lie half a dozen luxurious bedrooms, provided with Purdeys of Argyll toiletries and Egyptian cotton bedding; one suite comes with a stand-alone bath in the bedroom; Winnie's Suite sports a riverside terrace. The dining is no slouch, either – after all this is a former 'Scottish Gastropub of the Year' winner. There is a nod away from the capital with their Borders burger or you might try their 'Pig on a Plate': crispy pork belly, braised pig cheek, Parma ham wrapped pork loin, black pudding, crackling, creamy mash and savoy cabbage. They serve a barnstorming breakfast until just short of lunchtime too – a feast that will definitely set you up for a day pounding Edinburgh's cobbles.

CONTACT Lothianbridge, Newbattle, Dalkeith EH22 4TR • 0131 663 2456 • thesuninnedinburgh.co.uk
HOW MUCH? Double rooms from £111 a night, including breakfast.

The Peat Inn

There cannot be many inns that lend their name to the surrounding village; Fife's Peat Inn is one. Calling it a mere inn even seems like doing it something of a disservice: The Peat Inn sports a Michelin star and its chef and owner Geoffrey Smeddle is one of Scotland's most celebrated culinary figures. Let's face it, most guests these days are here to eat, indeed many are not even aware you can stay over, in a selection of bedrooms to the rear – plush suites that are the ideal setting for a romantic getaway and come with beautiful en-suite bathrooms, robes and toiletries and just about everything else you could need, including breakfast delivered to your door each morning. As for dining, you are treated to immaculately presented local produce infused with a dash of eye-catching creativity (wild halibut with steamed mussels, loin of wild roe deer…) while the setting retains the stone solidity of an inn, evoking a simpler time with a drink around the fire to welcome you. The various charms of St Andrews beckon nearby, as do the wee fishing villages of Scotland's Cornwall, the East Neuk.

CONTACT Peat Inn, Near St Andrews, Fife KY15 5LH • 01334 840 206 • thepeatinn.co.uk
HOW MUCH? Doubles from £240 a night, including breakfast.

Hawes Inn

Okay, so cards on the table, the Hawes Inn is part of a nationwide chain. But there are lots of good reasons to come here. It's one of Scotland's most historic inns, an oasis where you can sleep in the room in which Robert Louis Stevenson was inspired to write a chapter of his novel 'Kidnapped'. The pub also comes with views that are more dramatic than even Stevenson could conjure up, in the shadow of the iron-red Forth Bridge. It's also tucked away in South Queensferry, one of Scotland's most charming towns, on the banks of the Firth of Forth. The long-distance John Muir Way runs right by; and 'Maid of the Forth' tour boats await right outside for trips to the Isle of Inchcolm, with its abbey and views of Edinburgh; and the capital is only 15 minutes away by train. And the pub? It stocks an ever-changing selection of Scottish ales, and is similarly strong on single malts; and the food is hearty and good after a day's sightseeing. The 14 rooms are cosy too, with Hypnos beds and some with original fireplaces. If you can, book an estuary view.

CONTACT 7 Newhalls Rd, South Queensferry EH30 9TA • 0131 331 1990 • vintageinn.co.uk
HOW MUCH? Double rooms from £72 a night, including breakfast.

Polochar Inn

This is the sort of whitewashed, historic inn, set in an impossibly pretty spot, that bewitches people who've never left Kansas into booking a flight across the ocean. It is every bit as dramatic as the Scotland portrayed in Mel Gibson movies and on shortbread tins. Not that the locals even raise a glance driving past. On the southern fringes of remote South Uist, the Polochar Inn has gazed out over the Atlantic since the mid-18th century, as have many of its 11 comfortable bedrooms. Once a 'change-house' (where people waited for the ferry between South Uist and Barra), its rooms have been updated in contemporary style and come with en-suite bathrooms, flatscreen TVs, wifi and tea and coffee. Take a dram – these, after all, are the waters where the SS Politician (of 'Whisky Galore' fame) went down. In the lounge bar, with its views of the Sound of Barra, you can enjoy great fish and chips served with a smouldering Hebridean sunset for company. Cosy up afterwards for a few tall tales by the fire in the public bar alongside your spellbound friends from Kansas.

CONTACT Polochar, Isle of South Uist HS8 5TT • 01878 700 215 • polocharinn.com
HOW MUCH? Double rooms from £109 a night, including breakfast.

The Ship Inn at Elie

Shhh - don't tell anyone about this East Neuk beachside gem with rooms!

The East Neuk of Fife is that travel rarity – a favourite of 'the locals' that people beyond have never heard of. The Ship Inn has dared, in recent years, to put both the former fishing village of Elie and the East Neuk on the map, with a set of six swish, New England-style refurbished rooms and some lovingly fashioned drinking and dining spaces.

One of the best things about The Ship is that it's almost literally on the beach. Four of the rooms have sea views and the pick is probably the Admiral on the top floor, with sweeping views over the bay, roll-top bath and walk-in shower. The trio of Captains rooms also faces the sea, and all rooms feature handmade Siabann toiletries, Nespresso machines, Egyptian cotton bed linen, flatscreen TVs and wifi; one – on the ground floor – also welcomes dogs. It's a family friendly sort of place, too, with a kids menu in the restaurant and bedrooms that can accommodate additional beds for little ones.

The menu, meanwhile, stays solidly local – 100% of their fish and meat is Scottish, and East Neuk lobster and langoustines frequently play a starring role alongside mighty fish and chips. You can enjoy all this in the main bar of the pub, which is bright and light in summer and in winter impressively cosy, with a log fire and wood-burning stove – and there is a great beer garden, too. They've also recently added the 'Ship's Cabin', whose floor-to-ceiling windows give great views of the beach and beyond, and which serves as a function venue or private dining room – plus, on match days, it's the pavilion of The Ship's cricket team!

Finally, there's the delightful village of Elie, which is at your disposal, with its golden sands, bracing strolls, year-round seabirds and special draw of whale-watching activities – indeed this stretch of the Fife coast is full of desirable and pretty shoreline villages, and the university town (and golfing Mecca) of St Andrews is only a short drive away, with its various gastronomic, seaside and historic charms. We strongly encourage you to discover this gem in the East Neuk; just please don't tell anyone else!

CONTACT The Toft, Elie, Fife KY9 1DT • 01333 330 246 • shipinn.scot

HOW MUCH? Double rooms from £100 a night, including breakfast.

ROOMS 6 double or twin rooms, 4 with views over Elie Bay.

The Horseshoe Inn

This multi award-winning hideaway is tucked within a half hour's drive of Edinburgh, in Tweeddale, the heart of Sir Walter Scott country. Scott famously eulogised the rolling hills and gushing rivers around here, and you can explore them from this bolthole on a web of lazy drives, or even on the top-notch mountain bike trails at nearby Glentress. Kids and dogs are very much welcome at this family-run, community-spirited inn. The rooms are housed in a lovingly re-imagined Victorian schoolhouse adjacent to the Inn and are individually designed and very comfortable, bedecked in calming creams with plush fabrics, with Tunnocks teacakes biscuits adding a welcome local touch. Don't snack too much, though – you will want to leave room for a satisfying creamy, salty Cullen Skink haddock and potato chowder, or maybe local Stewarts IPA-battered haddock, served, of course, with proper chips. The Borders is also renowned for its world-class venison and lamb, which often feature, as do superb local steaks, best savoured with a haggis sauce and a wee dram. Slainte!

CONTACT Eddleston, Peebles EH45 8QP • 01721 730 225 • horseshoeinn.co.uk
HOW MUCH? Double rooms £80–£100 a night, including breakfast.

The Drovers Inn

This old-world inn on the fringes of Loch Lomond stakes a fair claim to being the most haunted in Scotland. We're talking classic spooks, like drowned young girls and waylaid walkers along with more contemporary ghouls (room 6 is said to be the most haunted, if you're feeling brave). Haunted or not, The Drovers is certainly one of the most characterful and unique inns in Caledonia, with all sorts of weapons, taxidermy and weird and wonderful artefacts – not so much a feast for the senses as a full-on tartan assault; like being in an old movie version of a Scotland that probably never really existed. In short, staying at The Drover's is immense fun, and what the inn lacks in luxury it makes up for with its beguiling atmosphere. Patrons include everyone from walkers on the West Highland Way to day-trippers from Glasgow. You can stay in the newer lodge across the road, but it's not the same. Food is almost an afterthought, with a wide-ranging comfort menu featuring such delights as a 'Loch Lomond Monster Burger'. They just cannot help themselves.

CONTACT 7 North Loch Lomond, Inverarnan. Argyll & Bute G83 7DX • 01301 704 234 • droversinn.co.uk
HOW MUCH? Double rooms from £90 a night, including breakfast.

Oak Tree Inn

There are any number of characterless places to stay on and around Loch Lomond. Mercifully the Oak Tree Inn isn't one of them. It reclines in the relaxed village of Balmaha, on the quieter eastern shores of the loch, and is quite some operation: they roast their own coffee here and also make their own ice-cream in the St Mocha Coffee Shop & Ice Cream Parlour, as well as running the village shop. Above all, though, it's a great place to sit outside on a glorious day, admiring the views, sipping a local ale and tucking into their signature steak and ale pie. Bedrooms are sprinkled above the inn and in cottages a few minutes' walk away and have flatscreen TVs, wifi and tea and coffee. The inn also has a selection of glamping pods, tucked away at the rear of the inn, each with double beds and private outdoor seating areas. Snare a deluxe room for a view of the Loch, Scotland's largest, with its necklace of forested islands and its grandstand setting, flanked by Munro mountains, including the eponymous Ben Lomond – for which the inn proves a handy base.

CONTACT Balmaha, by Loch Lomond G63 0JQ • 01360 870 357 • theoaktreeinn.co.uk
HOW MUCH? Double rooms from £140 a night, including breakfast. Pods from £150 a night.

Applecross Inn

Were the Applecross Inn just a langoustine-serving bus stop it would be worth visiting – both for the world-class crustaceans you can enjoy and the spirit-soaring sunsets they tend to get over the jagged Cuillin mountains of Skye. Fortunately, it is much more than that: a trimly run whitewashed bolthole with a lively pub and dining room and 7 tempting bedrooms upstairs. You will want a sea view for those sunsets, and for dolphin-spotting and whale-watching too. Then it's time to settle into the dining room for those plump langoustines and superb lobster, followed by a dram of the local Talisker before the mountain-rippled sky erupts in a wonderland of fiery orange, blue and smouldering ochre. By the way, getting here is part of the show too – making your way up a serpentine road and over the Bealach na Ba ('Pass of the Castle'). Be sure to make a stop at the summit to take in views that are normally only afforded to knackered Munro-baggers, and also to allow your car a fighting chance of making it all the way back down again.

CONTACT Shore St, Applecross, Wester Ross IV54 8LR • 01520 744 262 • applecrossinn.co.uk
HOW MUCH? Double rooms from £150 a night, including breakfast.

The Old Inn

Situated on the increasingly popular 'North Coast 500' long-distance driving route, Highland coaching inns don't come much more traditional – nor more welcoming – than this one, nesting in a wee glade just back from the Atlantic in wild – and wildly scenic – Wester Ross, on Scotland's northwest fringes. It's a whitewashed stunner, and it's well worth lingering for a longer pit stop if you can. Ably steered by Alastair and Ute Pearson since 1999, the pub's bedrooms are cosy and well kept, with en-suite bathooms, flatscreen TVs, wifi and tea- and coffee-making facilities, and there are family rooms available too. Then there is the food, with lots of Atlantic seafood and game culled from the mountainous hinterland. A night is best finished off with one of the regular music slots but if there are no tunes on, just head outside and check out the big night skies. The next day, there's a range of sandy beaches to tempt you and the wee village of Gairloch awaits, with its popular whale-watching cruises, plus there's a mass of hills and mountains that are just begging to be tackled by well-prepared walkers.

CONTACT Flowerdale Glen, Gairloch, Wester Ross IV21 2BD • 01445 712 006 • theoldinn.net
HOW MUCH? Double rooms from £99 a night, including breakfast.

The Mishnish

You can tell anyone who has spent a night in The Mishnish, not just because they will invariably call this legendary Mull oasis 'The Mish' but also because a part of them won't quite have recovered. Yes, The Mish is very special indeed, for its live music, good whisky and, above all, for its life-affirming Hebridean craic; if you're seriously lucky you may just be in when the legendary Vatersay Boys are breezing through en-route from the Outer Hebrides. The pub has been one of the pastel-hued delights of the Tobermory waterfront since 1869. Porpoises splash in the aquarium-clear waters as sea eagles soar in the thermals, while inside distillery drams star alongside a treasure chest of Scottish ales. Their next-door dining room excels with a boat-fresh seafood platter that money just cannot buy in London. The chances are you will scarcely remember your night in one of the dozen simple bedrooms above, but do make sure to snare a sea view to wake with the sea soothing your senses as the memory of frantically played fiddles fills your heart.

CONTACT Main St, Tobermory, Isle of Mull PA75 6NT • 01688 302 500 • themishnish.co.uk
HOW MUCH? Double rooms from £115 a night, including breakfast.

Champany Inn

Not many families stick around running an inn for 4 decades, but then again there are not many families like the Davidsons. Anne and Clive have a legendary status on the Scottish hospitality scene, and, with son Jason and his wife Bridget, have reinvented this low-slung, whitewashed old inn half an hour outside Edinburgh, elevating it briefly to the heights of a Michelin star, with home-smoked Scottish salmon, world-class Scotch beef butchered and hung on site, live lobster from their tank and one (superb) Stilton as a 'cheeseboard'. It is easy to rack up a T-bone-sized bill in their charmingly dated main dining room, but savvy visitors also consider the more informal Chop House, where steaks still sizzle alongside some of the best burgers you'll ever taste. With triple-cooked animal fat chips? You bet! You can stay in the plush tartan-clad bedrooms, enjoying walks to nearby Blackness Castle or a jaunt around the shops of historic Linlithgow, and you'll leave waxing lyrical about the homemade Lorne sausage that you devoured at breakfast.

CONTACT Linlithgow, West Lothian EH49 7LU • 01506 834 532 • champany.com
HOW MUCH? Double rooms from £124 a night, including breakfast.

Loch Lomond Arms

You could just rattle up the busy road on the western flanks of Loch Lomond, bashing from Glasgow to the Highlands without stopping. Don't. Not while this remarkable old coaching inn is still around, anyway. Located in Luss, a village so picturesque that it starred in the long-running Scottish TV series 'Take the High Road', the Loch Lomond Arms boasts a heritage dating back to the 17th century, when Jacobite clans and cattle raiders roamed these wild environs. A sleek 2012 makeover has brought in more home comforts and made it a great place to stay, with smoothly luxurious bedrooms and a trio of suites (some with 4-poster beds), plus 5 spacious cottages close to the Loch. The décor throughout is muted Scottish, with tartan throws and mood lighting, and you can dine in the Bar, Library or Dining Room on such delights as venison culled from the inn's estate, Loch Etive sea trout or Ayrshire pork chop. They make their own haggis too. By day, staff can arrange myriad activities, from watersports on the Loch through to 4x4 nature safaris in the glens.

CONTACT Old Luss Rd, Luss, Argyll & Bute G83 8NY • 01436 860 420 • lochlomondarmshotel.com
HOW MUCH? Double rooms from £165 a night, including breakfast.

The Bonnie Badger

Uber Scottish chef Tom Kitchin knows what he is doing both on and off the plate. Not content with running his eponymous Michelin-starred restaurant in Edinburgh, he has also expanded into running a sprinkling of gastropubs in the city, and now beyond, with this new inn in deepest East Lothian. One of Scotland's sunniest escapes, Lothian – and specifically the trim, well-to-do beachfront village of Gullane – makes an ideal setting, with its big skies, excellent local produce and escape-the-city vibe. There is golf, walks on the John Muir Way and a slew of coastal villages to explore. The Deluxe, Superior and Loft bedrooms have each been individually designed by Mairi Helena, and your sleep will be cosy, with Egyptian cotton linen and Hypnos mattresses. There is good wifi, coffee and tea, and bathrooms are stylish and contemporary, with handmade Scottish toiletries; and for more space you can huddle away in one of 2 cottages, Hazel and Honeysuckle. And the food? Orkney scallop, Jerusalem artichoke and kale sets the tone, before roasted loin of Borders venison, braised shoulder and celeriac fondant.

CONTACT Main St, Gullane, East Lothian EH31 2AB • 01620 621 111 • bonniebadger.com
HOW MUCH? Double rooms from £195 a night, including breakfast.]

Creggans Inn

Who could resist a night or two at James Bond's favourite inn? The man thought to have been an inspiration for the world's most famous spy was Scot Sir Fitzroy Maclean, a daring soldier who was Churchill's main man in Yugoslavia in WWII. You can imagine Bond caressing his Aston Martin around the languorous corners of Loch Fyne, Scotland's longest sea loch, which this historic whitewashed inn overlooks. The current incumbents, Archie and Gill MacLellan, have held the reins since 2008 and have won a string of awards, including 'Scottish Inn of the Year' – plaudits that are richly deserved. The vibe is a seriously relaxed escape-the-modern-world one, with bright en-suite bedrooms, some with superb loch views. Food and drink highlights include hand-dived Loch Fyne scallops and oysters, local estate venison and ales courtesy of Fyne Ales at the head of the loch. After dinner, a wee dram of Maclean's MacPhunn whisky by the fire awaits, or a stroll along the rocky shores where once Viking longships roamed, long before super spies cruised by.

CONTACT Strachur, Loch Fyne, Argyll PA27 8BX • 01369 860 279 • creggans-inn.co.uk
HOW MUCH? Double rooms from £120 a night, including breakfast.

Cluanie Inn

One of the most remote inns in Scotland, the Cluanie sits proudly defiant beneath a mountainous backdrop of soaring peaks, vaulting ridges and plunging glens. If you love walking, or just being in the mountains, then you'll instantly feel at home here, even more so thanks to the creative Indian team who have rejuvenated this whitewashed historic inn, which had become a little faded. They have refurbished the bar and restaurant without losing the traditional mountain inn feel, and created an eclectic menu that sways from pizzas and burgers through to local seafood and Indian, with a superb dal makhani. Look out also for their new stand-alone bakery. As for the rooms, they've been done up in a bold, rustic style that complements the mountain setting; the 'Glen' rooms are their standard doubles, they have 'Quad' rooms for hikers, as well as the more upscale 'Highland Suites', one of which has an in-room sauna – the ideal tonic after a Munro mountain bash. Follow that with a dram in the bar and a meal planning more adventures. As John Muir famously said, 'The mountains are calling and I must go.'

CONTACT Glenmoriston, Inverness-Shire IV63 7YW • 01320 340 238 • blacksheephotels.com
HOW MUCH? Double rooms from £153 a night, including breakfast.

The Harbour Inn

The Harbour Inn on the Isle of Islay is as close to paradise as any devotee of Scottish whisky could ever wish for. And if you love being by the sea and savouring boat-fresh seafood, the whitewashed Harbour Inn will work perfectly for you too. A relaxed bolthole on fertile, bare Islay, the Harbour Inn is ideally located, not just on scenic Loch Indaal but also opposite the Bowmore Distillery (the inn's owners), right in the heart of the unofficial capital. The 7 bedrooms are quite simple: comfortable, trim and well finished, although you will want a sea loch view room to watch for seals, otters and dolphins. They also have self-catering options in the distillery cottages just across the road, where you will wake up reeking of the good stuff. For drinks – whisky, of course! – there is the Schooner Bar, which is just a warm-up for dinner, and locally landed scallops, Islay oysters and renowned local beef enjoyed with views over the water. The next day, all 9 distilleries await, starting with Bowmore, a sherry-tinged, not-too-peaty wonder.

CONTACT Bowmore, Isle of Islay PA43 7JR • 01496 810 330 • bowmore.com
HOW MUCH? Double rooms from £174 a night, including breakfast. .

The Bridge Inn

A delightful waterside inn that's handy for Edinburgh, the Union Canal and the John Muir Way.

If, like us, you tend to associate canalside inns with narrowboats neatly moored outside with England, prepare to be surprised by this Central Scotland hideaway. Just seven miles from Edinburgh – and even closer to its airport – sits a heritage inn in the conservation village of Ratho, overlooking a stone bridge and reclining right on the Union Canal, which runs from the remarkable Falkirk Wheel to Edinburgh city centre. Based here, you can take boat trips out towards Linlithgow, cycle along the canal into Edinburgh, or even hike east to pick up the John Muir Way long-distance walking trail.

You don't even have to fight with your fellow guests for a waterfront view, as each of inn's 4 individually designed guest rooms gazes out towards the canal and its aquatic wildlife. They all have flatscreen TVs with Freeview, wifi and tea- and coffee-making facilities, but each one is different: one – the smallest – has an elegant 4-poster bed, another a brass bedstead, while another is simple and predominantly white. The largest room has a free-standing bath. Breakfast is superb, with a generous Full Scottish with black pudding and potato scones and American-style pancakes as an alternative.

Downstairs there is proper local pub life, as the inn is at the heart of the local community, with a terrace overlooking the canal for dreamy summer evenings and cosy fires inside for the depths of winter. The menu is well above standard pub grub, with homegrown vegetables and pork that they rear themselves setting the tone. It's beautifully presented too, and the service is spot-on. You could kick off with some Hopetoun Estate pheasant (it's close enough for the bird to have flown in awkwardly on its own) and Ayrshire bacon terrine, before tucking into a perfectly cooked Borders beef ribeye with handcut chips and a spicy peppercorn sauce. There are Scottish ales on tap, but there is cider and bitter too if you're missing the quintessential English canal experience, and families might like to know that there is a large wooden playboat in the lovely beer garden. No surprise, then, that the pub has won an award for something or other virtually every year for the last seven years, and was AA 'Scottish Pub of the Year' a few years back.

CONTACT 27 Baird Rd, Ratho, Newbridge, Midlothian EH28 8RA • 0131 333 1320 • bridgeinn.com

HOW MUCH? Double rooms from £80 a night, including breakfast.

ROOMS 4 en-suite double bedrooms.

Clachaig Inn

Scotland's most historic inn - going strong since the 17th century in spite of the Campbells!

In some countries, history is trapped safely behind museum glass. Not in Scotland. Here history is very much of the living variety. Take the Clachaig Inn. When they warn you, above the entrance, that Campbells are not welcome, they are not kidding. It's understandable, when you delve into the story of a spectacular, remote glen haunted by the baleful Massacre of Glencoe in 1692. After the Campbell-led British Government soldiers took advantage of the traditional clan hospitality of the local Macdonalds, the order came to slay them in their beds – men, women and children. Many of the survivors didn't last long as they staggered, partly clothed, into the biting winter's night. History in Glencoe is not a distant ghost, but an in-your-face-don't-ignore-me kilted clansman.

The nearby visitor centre adds depth to the story, as does walking the rugged, unforgiving mountains that surround the Inn. Glencoe offers some of Scotland's finest mountaineering, and the Clachaig is the ideal base, cowering beneath hulking Highland massifs; a welcome redoubt against hurricane-force winds. The main building sports 23 bedrooms, divided between 'Classic' rooms and 'Glencoe View' rooms, which look out directly over the moutains of Glencoe. All the rooms are decorated in a modern style, with wifi and flatscreen TVs, tea- and coffee-making facilities, and five of the rooms are dog-friendly. There are self-catering options, too, with a dozen self-catering chalets, cottages and lodges at the Inn and in and around Glencoe itself. Other facilities include a large room for drying your stuff after a wet and windy walk, and the chance to order a packed lunch the night before to take with you on your walk. Breakfast is a terrific send-off too – with Lorne sausage and bacon, black pudding, haggis and tattie scones among the highlights.

Like Scotland in the 17th century, the Inn is largely split into two halves: the Bidean Lounge is relaxed and calm, with windows gazing out at the mountains; an ideal retreat for officers to feast on Macsween of Edinburgh Haggis. The clansmen are in charge at the Boots Bar, where it can get riotous, with live music and over 400 whiskies (over 130 Scottish gins too) to sample. The Inn has its own whisky and gin, and even runs its own whisky-tasting masterclasses from time to time. As for food, you never know what the landscape is going to throw at you so the pub serves food all day – everything from cheeseburgers to fish and chips and haggis, neeps and tatties.

CONTACT Glencoe, Argyll PH49 4HX • 01855 811 252 • clachaig.com

HOW MUCH? Doubles from £137 a night, including breakfast.

ROOMS 23 en-suite double bedrooms. and 12 self-catering options.

DECEMBER

Lucky Dip

The Bow Bar

An evocative, if not entirely original, representation of a venerable Edinburgh 'howf', or drinking house, this is a place to seek out real ales, good whisky and the hubbub of conversation. Its wood-panelled walls are lined by old mirrors advertising whiskies and beer, while blackboards list cask and guest ales, and patrons settle on to leather benches around small fixed wooden tables. No rooms.

CONTACT 80 West Bow, Edinburgh EH1 2HH • 0131 226 7667 • thebowbar.co.uk

The Oxford Bar

Edinburgh's literary connections can get quite high-falutin at times, yet the truth is that these days more people read Irvine Welsh and Ian Rankin than Sir Walter Scott. The Oxford is one of Rankin's favourite pubs, and anyone acquainted with his Inspector Rebus series will feel they know it well. It's an honest, no-nonsense and typical old-school Edinburgh drinking den, resolutely unmodernised, with little time for fancy lagers, fancy food or the trappings of fame, for that matter. No rooms.

CONTACT 8 Young St, Edinburgh EH2 4JB • 0131 539 7119

The King's Wark

This historic waterfront pub on Leith's trendy Shore was once perfect for salty auld seadogs and has been done up recently as a full-on gastropub, serving excellent fish and seafood. No rooms.

CONTACT 36 Shore, Leith, Edinburgh EH6 6QU • 0131 554 9260 • kingswark.co.uk

Prestoungrange Gothenburg

This century old pub-cum-community centre brings life to the otherwise quiet coastal resort of Prestonpans, with its own CAMRA-endorsed microbrewery, along with an arts festival, music nights and lots of cultural events. There's also a Sunday afternoon carvery and Real Ale Jug Bar for those sweet carry-outs. No rooms.

CONTACT 227–229 High St, Prestonpans EH32 9BE • 01875 898 200 • prestoungrange.org/gothenburg

The Horseshoe Bar

This is one of Glasgow city centre's most characterful old pubs, with a history dating back as far as 1864 and actually rather grand inside, with a sweeping horseshoe-shaped bar. Cold and creamy Scottish 'heavy' ales are the stars, alongside well priced whiskies. The talk is often of football and the craic hearty. Just don't ask for a Pimms. No rooms.

CONTACT 17–19 Drury St, Glasgow G2 5AE • 0141 248 6368 • thehorseshoebarglasgow.co.uk

Variety Bar

This deceptively simple-looking art deco bar on Sauchiehall Street has been a meeting-place for creative types and pop stars since the 1980s, when the likes of Hue & Cry practically used to live here. No one seems to know how and why the fish tank got here, but somehow it works. Today, live DJs, a good selection of beers and a quietly cool vibe mean that the Variety is as aptly named as ever. No rooms.

CONTACT 401 Sauchiehall St, Glasgow G2 3LG • 0141 332 4449 • variety-bar.com

The Meikleour Arms

This iconic Estate pub is a proper country inn for modern times, with a restaurant serving great food based on meat, game and produce from the Estate and a baker's dozen of boutique rooms. But it also retains some things that only an old-fashioned pub can properly deliver: darts and some terrific local ales.

CONTACT Meikleour, Perthshire PH2 6EB • 01250 883 206 • meikleourarms.co.uk

The Allanton Inn

This lovely Berwickshire coaching inn is just a hop, skip and a jump from the English border and makes a terrific place to stop if you're making your way north, with 7 contemporarily styled bedrooms and a restaurant that is known for its excellent food, including legendary seafood platters and beef from the family farm.

CONTACT Main St, Allanton, Borders TD11 3JZ • 01890 818 260 • allantoninn.co.uk

Kilchrenan Inn

A few miles east of Oban, close to the banks of Loch Awe, this revamped coaching inn is more a place to stay and eat than to pop by for a drink. But it does the job well, with good food and slick, comfortable guest rooms.

CONTACT Taynuilt, Kilchrenan PA35 1HD • 01866 833 000 • kilchrenaninn.co.uk

(Top) The Horseshoe Bar; (middle) The Oxford Bar; (bottom) The Bow Bar.

INDEX: Pubs by Location

INDEX: Pubs by Location (cont.)

INDEX: Pubs by Location (cont.)

INDEX: Pubs by Name

INDEX: Cool Pubs & Inns (cont.)

INDEX: Cool Pubs & Inns (cont.)

S

T

U

V

W

Y

Dog Friendly Britain

Cool Places to Stay with Your Dog

Dog Friendly Britain showcases the very best places to stay in the UK with your four-legged friend – everything from boutique hotels and cosy gastropubs to seaside B&Bs, country cottages and the latest glamping sites.

Based on recommendations from the popular UK website coolplaces.co.uk, it includes places that really go the extra mile for dogs and their owners – often with beds, bowls, treats and toys and suggestions for nearby walks – and it also has extra features on the UK's best dog walks.

Illustrated with hundreds of colour photos, it not only highlights Britain's best dog-friendly accommodation, but the best of Britain's dogs too!

So whether you're after a country cottage, a luxury hotel or just a cosy pub with rooms, put yourself in the hands of Cool Places and find your perfect UK dog-friendly place to stay.

Price £18.99

The Crown at Stoke by Nayland p.131

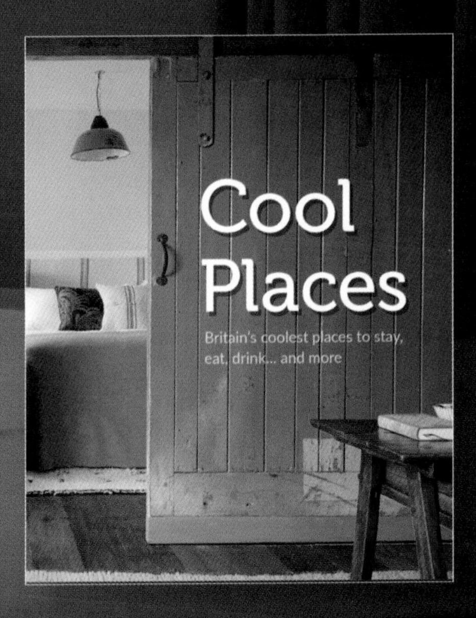
Cool Places
Britain's coolest places to stay, eat, drink... and more

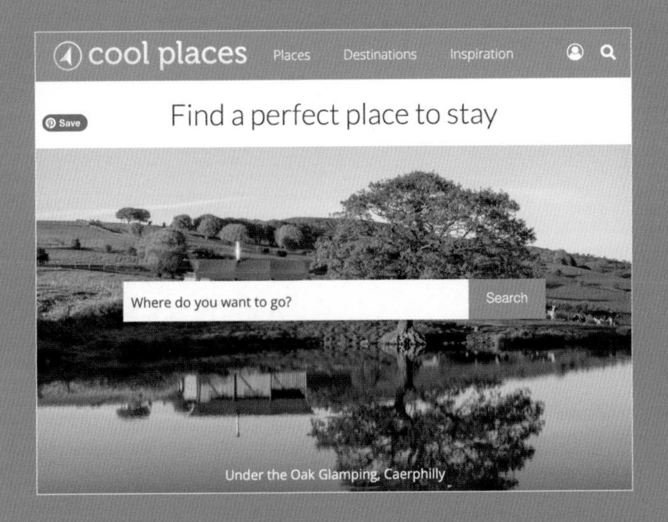

Cool Places is the only website of its kind to focus purely on all kinds of UK accommodation, recommending great places to stay all over the country from cosy B&Bs and idyllic cottages to country pubs and the most stylish boutique hotels.

Uniquely each entry also includes links to all the best stuff to do nearby – local pubs, great walks, the best places to shop, eat and more – making it easy to plan your trip in advance.

Browse by location, type of accommodation or by theme – and book on the Cool Places site or with the property direct.

Acknowledgements and credits

COOL PUBS AND INNS: BRITAIN'S BEST PUBS WITH ROOMS

Published in the UK by Cool Places & Punk Publishing, 81 Rivington Street, London EC2A 3AY

www.coolplaces.co.uk
A catalogue record of this book is available from the British Library
ISBN 978-1-906889-43-2

CREDITS

Editor: Martin Dunford.
Contributors: Jules Brown, Kerry Christiani, Martin Dunford, Stuart Forster, Wendy Gommersall, Phil Lee, Norm Longley, Robin McKelvie, Harriet O'Brien, Beth Pipe, Sandra Shields, Victoria Trott and Luke Waterson. Thanks also to the many other UK writers who have contributed to Cool Places over the years, and thus to this book.
Design & layout: Diana Jarvis and Kenny Grant.
Proofreading: Leanne Bryan.

THANKS & ACKNOWLEDGEMENTS

The biggest thanks are due to Lauren and Patrick, who were with this project every step of the way, and of course Diana for her usual unflappability. Also to Fiona Reece for all sorts of things but especially great pub finds; Caroline for proofreading and her usual wisdom (and with whom in a pub I am at my happiest); and to Daisy and Lucy for many and varied pub lunches and dinners, but whose favourite pub is sadly not in this book. Big thanks also to pubnames.co.uk for the Top 20 Pub Names on p.11, and to all of the lovely pub owners, workers, dogs and other customers featured in this book.

PICTURE CREDITS

Images are used with permission from the property owners or the establishments themselves, except for those listed below: p.163 The Crown at Woolhope © Russell Lewis Photography; p.177 The Lion Inn © George Tod; p.180 The Black Swan © Andrew Hayes-Watkins; p.180 The George & Dragon © Andrew Bowden; p.227 Brigands Inn © Peter Broster.
Cover photographs: The Bull Inn, Oxfordshire (front); The Bell at Skenfrith (back); The Richard Onslow, Surrey; The White Hart, Devon; The Crown and Anchor, Wiltshire (front flap) The Swan, Oxfordshire (back flap).
Front page: The Duke William, Kent.
Front spread: The Swan at Wedmore.
Contents page: The Saracen's Head, Herefordshire.
p.7 Lord Poulett Arms, Somerset; The Lion Inn, Gloucestershire; The Gin Trap, Norfolk.
p.8 The Sheppey, Somerset; The Talbot, Herefordshire.
p. 9 The Rose & Crown, Durham.
pp.10–11 The Swan at Ascott-under-Wychwood, Oxfordshire.

SALES

UK Sales: Compass IPS Limited; sales@compassips.co.uk; www.compassips.london
Printed by Bell & Bain Ltd, Glasgow, Scotland.
This book has been printed on paper made from renewable sources.